Montessori Reading Games Workbook

a beginning phonics program

Level 1

by Katie Key
montessoriforhomeschoolers.com

Policy Page

Copyright © 2022. Katie Key.
 All rights reserved.

No part of this publication may be reproduced, stored in a retrieval system or transmitted in any form or by any means – electronic, mechanical, photocopying, and recording or otherwise – without prior written permission from the author. To perform any of the above is an infringement of copyright law.

Handwriting Font Credit: KG Neatly Printed

ISBN: 978-1-7353980-4-4

Montessori Reading Games, Level 1, A Beginning Phonics Program
montessoriforhomeschoolers.com

Disclaimers

Reading success varies by family and individual. No success is guaranteed.

While this Workbook is heavily based in the Montessori approach, there are differences in the way I have presented the material than how Dr. Maria Montessori originally presented her reading material, mostly because I have adapted it for ease of use and for a homeschool setting and incorporated extra games. If you would like more information on the Montessori Method, please see Dr. Montessori's *The Absorbent Mind* or *The Montessori Method*.

Companion Webpage

On the companion webpage for the *Montessori Reading Games Workbook*, you will find helpful hints, links to related blog posts, and have an opportunity to receive emails for tips and tricks as you work through this curriculum with your child!

Go to
http://montessoriforhomeschoolers.com/pages/montessori-reading-games-workbook.

Make sure to sign up to receive emails, and even get a coupon for 10% off your next purchase!

Additional Products

Are you looking for more open-and-go Montessori solutions? Or even a full, scripted curriculum for your homeschool? Check out our other products!

Descriptions and videos for each product can be found at **montessoriforhomeschoolers.com**.

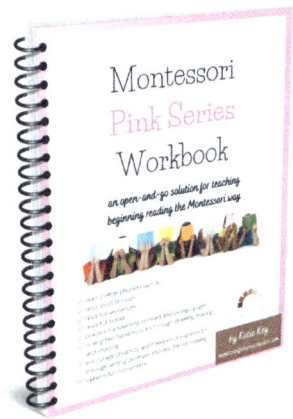

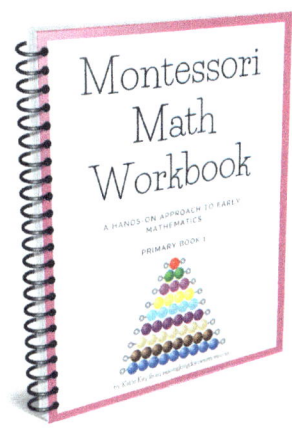

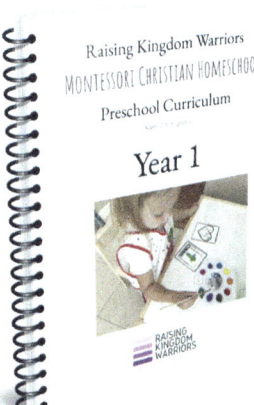

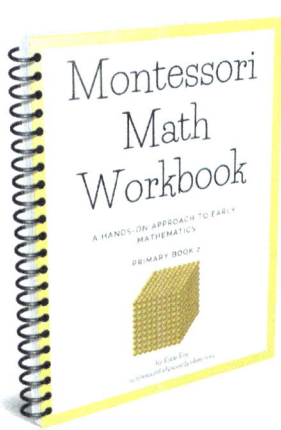

Table of Contents

Introduction...1
The Hybrid Workbook and Hands-On Method..........1
The Montessori Way of Learning to Read...............2
Supplemental Materials..2
Storage..2
Schedule...3

Unit 1 (s m a t)..5
- [ ] Pronunciation and Handwriting Guide.............5
- [ ] Lesson 1.1..6
- [ ] Lesson 1.2..7
- [ ] Lesson 1.3..8
- [ ] Lesson 1.4..9
- [ ] Lesson 1.5..11
- [ ] Lesson 1.6..12
- [ ] Lesson 1.7..13
- [ ] Lesson 1.8..15
- [ ] Lesson 1.9..17
- [ ] Lesson 1.10..21
- [ ] Lesson 1.11..27
- [ ] Lesson 1.12..29
- [ ] Lesson 1.13..31
- [ ] Lesson 1.14..33
- [ ] Unit 1 Assessment...36

Unit 2 (c d o h)..39
- [ ] Pronunciation and Handwriting Guide...........39
- [ ] Lesson 2.1..40
- [ ] Lesson 2.2..41
- [ ] Lesson 2.3..42
- [ ] Lesson 2.4..43
- [ ] Lesson 2.5..45
- [ ] Lesson 2.6..46
- [ ] Lesson 2.7..47
- [ ] Lesson 2.8..49
- [ ] Lesson 2.9..51
- [ ] Lesson 2.10..55
- [ ] Lesson 2.11..61
- [ ] Lesson 2.12..63
- [ ] Lesson 2.13..65
- [ ] Lesson 2.14..67
- [ ] Unit 2 Assessment...72

Unit 3 (b r i g)..75
- [ ] Pronunciation and Handwriting Guide...........75
- [ ] Lesson 3.1..76
- [ ] Lesson 3.2..77
- [ ] Lesson 3.3..78
- [ ] Lesson 3.4..79
- [ ] Lesson 3.5..81
- [ ] Lesson 3.6..82
- [ ] Lesson 3.7..83
- [ ] Lesson 3.8..85
- [ ] Lesson 3.9..87
- [ ] Lesson 3.10..91
- [ ] Lesson 3.11..97
- [ ] Lesson 3.12..99
- [ ] Lesson 3.13..101
- [ ] Lesson 3.14..103
- [ ] Unit 3 Assessment...110

Unit 4 (p n u w)..113
- [ ] Pronunciation and Handwriting Guide.........113
- [ ] Lesson 4.1..114
- [ ] Lesson 4.2..115
- [ ] Lesson 4.3..116
- [ ] Lesson 4.4..117
- [ ] Lesson 4.5..119
- [ ] Lesson 4.6..120
- [ ] Lesson 4.7..121
- [ ] Lesson 4.8..123
- [ ] Lesson 4.9..125
- [ ] Lesson 4.10..129
- [ ] Lesson 4.11..135
- [ ] Lesson 4.12..137
- [ ] Lesson 4.13..139
- [ ] Lesson 4.14..141
- [ ] Unit 4 Assessment...150

Unit 5 (j f e l)..153
- [ ] Pronunciation and Handwriting Guide.........153
- [ ] Lesson 5.1..154
- [ ] Lesson 5.2..155
- [ ] Lesson 5.3..156
- [ ] Lesson 5.4..157
- [ ] Lesson 5.5..159
- [ ] Lesson 5.6..160
- [ ] Lesson 5.7..161
- [ ] Lesson 5.8..163
- [ ] Lesson 5.9..165
- [ ] Lesson 5.10..169
- [ ] Lesson 5.11..175
- [ ] Lesson 5.12..177
- [ ] Lesson 5.13..179
- [ ] Lesson 5.14..181
- [ ] Unit 5 Assessment...189

Unit 6 (k q v x y z) 191
- ☐ Pronunciation and Handwriting Guide 191
- ☐ Lesson 6.1 192
- ☐ Lesson 6.2 193
- ☐ Lesson 6.3 194
- ☐ Lesson 6.4 195
- ☐ Lesson 6.5 197
- ☐ Lesson 6.6 198
- ☐ Lesson 6.7 199
- ☐ Lesson 6.8 201
- ☐ Lesson 6.9 203
- ☐ Lesson 6.10 204
- ☐ Lesson 6.11 205
- ☐ Lesson 6.12 207
- ☐ Lesson 6.13 209
- ☐ Lesson 6.14 215
- ☐ Lesson 6.15 225
- ☐ Lesson 6.16 229
- ☐ Lesson 6.17 233
- ☐ Lesson 6.18 237
- ☐ Unit 6 Assessment 245

Next Steps 247

Appendix A 248
- Letter-Picture Card Sorting Directions 248
- Letter-Picture Card Game Options 248
- Simple Scavenger Hunt 249
- Advanced Scavenger Hunt 251
- Sound Scavenger Hunt Checklists 253
- Treasure Hunt 257
- Roll, Spot, and Cover 258
- Dice for Roll Spot, and Cover 259
- Swat the Sound 265
- Four Corners 265
- Hopscotch 266

Appendix B 267
- My Letter Sound Adventure Directions 267
- My Letter Sound Adventure Game board 269
- My Letter Sound Adventure Spinners 271

Appendix C 274
- Movable Alphabet Organizer 274
- Pink Word Building Cards Directions 277

Appendix D 279
- Household Items for Sound Games 279

Appendix E 280
- How to Play BINGO 281
- How to Play Go-Fish 281

Appendix F 281
- Sound Sorting Cards: Sound Group 1 281
- Sound Sorting Cards: Sound Group 2 283
- Sound Sorting Cards: Sound Group 3 285
- Sound Sorting Cards: Sound Group 4 287
- Sound Sorting Cards: Sound Group 5 289
- Sound Sorting Cards: Sound Group 6 291

Appendix G: Handwriting Guide 295

Introduction

Teaching your child to read can be intimidating. Following through with a "reading program" is hard. I've been there. Your child is squirmy, reluctant, angry, *not cooperative*, and getting through a lesson is next to impossible. You might or might not have literally thrown the reading curriculum in the trash (or was that me? I can't remember.)

Teaching your child to read **does not have to be that way**! Teaching your child to read can be as natural as how you taught her to walk or talk. You really didn't actually *teach* her those things; she miraculously reached the point where she was able to do those things by merely living, observing, and existing in her environment. God made children perfectly capable of learning. We just tend to make a mess of things sometimes when we feel we should step in and take the authoritative position as the "giver of knowledge."

Children aren't wired like university level students or adults. Children are their own entities, their own separate beings on the spectrum of humanity, uniquely designed to learn vast amounts of information with little "help" that we, adults, usually think we need to be giving.

I challenge you to stop thinking about teaching your child to read as *teaching your child to read*, and, instead, look at it as a time of **connecting** with your child through purposeful play.

If you play these games with your child, she is going to learn how to read. She won't even know that you taught her. She will not really know how she knows how to read, and that, my friends, is your measure of success.

The Hybrid Workbook and Hands-On Method

Workbooks have a bad reputation in Montessori circles - and for a good reason. Children remember best when working with their *hands* and *bodies* at the same time. When a child is playing, there is little need for reinforcement or drudgery for the child to remember. Play allows learning to happen naturally and without *tears* or frustration.

So why a workbook?

As I've progressed along my homeschooling journey, I have seen over and over again the need for a kitchen table-top solution for the Montessori lessons my children and I love so much. Prepping a Montessori learning environment is a full time job in itself - just ask any Montessori teacher or homeschooler! The cutting, laminating, storing, displaying, and presenting of materials is a large task. Many times, homeschoolers are preparing these materials for *one* child at a time, too. If a family has more than one child, this work is multiplied. On top of the prep work, we wonder if we are doing it "right" and at the "right time." Consequently, we feel behind, we feel we are failing our children, and we are likely to give up on the beauty of Montessori for our sanity. And that's okay! BUT I am offering another solution.

In an open-and-go workbook (as far as possible) that includes crayon and paper exercises *in addition to* the wonderful hands-on components inspired by the Montessori Method, I hope to empower more homeschoolers (and classroom teachers) to "stick with it" and embrace Montessori learning as something that is *attainable* for everyone!

The open-and-go workbook format is combined with printable manipulatives.

Inside this workbook, you will find 6 units. Units 1-5 each cover a group of 4 letter sounds. Unit 6 covers a group of 6 letter sounds. Units 1 through 5 each have 14 lessons. Unit 6 has 18 lessons. There is an optional assessment at the end of each unit. The lessons repeat in each unit for consistency and an aid to independence for the beginning reader (and busy teacher!) By varying the way the child interacts with the letter sounds in each mastery-building lesson within each unit, we cover the full spectrum of kinesthetic, tactile, visual, and auditory learning. There are materials *inside* this workbook and prompts to bring in household items in certain lessons. You will be making your own sandpaper letters and movable alphabet, as well as a variety of games, using the provided printables within these workbook pages!

Instead of prepping and storing hundreds of manipulatives at the start of the program, as you progress through the pages of the Workbook, you will be prompted to **cut out and prepare the materials as you go along.** Your collection of manipulatives will grow throughout the course, with each sound group containing its own set of materials.

The Montessori Way of Learning to Read

While the literature on Montessori reading and writing education is vast, the method is quite simple.

Here are the basics:
1. Introduce your young children to rich language by speaking, singing, and reading often to your baby and toddler.
2. **Play sound games to help your child isolate the different sounds of our language.**
3. **Introduce the sandpaper letters in groups.**
4. **Combine work with the sandpaper letters and miniature objects.**
5. **Introduce the movable alphabet and allow your child to "write" words.**
6. Introduce short phonetic words in a variety of ways for a child to read and work with independently.
7. Introduce longer phonetic words and sound blends for a child to read and work with independently.
8. Introduce homophones, changing rules, and trickier words for a child to read and work with independently.

In this workbook, we will cover Steps 2-5! Children often need a long time with this stage before moving onto reading words in Steps 6-8.

Supplemental Materials

Wherever possible, I have included printable materials for anything you may need for this curriculum!

In addition to the printables, you may want to purchase:
- cardstock weight paper (if you are printing this workbook yourself)
- laminating sheets
- laminator
- paper cutter

For the hands-on components of the workbook, you will need:
- glitter glue (or regular liquid school glue and sand or glitter)
- household items for beginning sounds (see list in Appendix D). [NOTE: In Appendix F, there is a printable version to replace the real household objects that you can use if that makes completing these lessons easier for you!]

Optional:
If you have the desire to purchase a real movable alphabet, sandpaper letters, or miniature objects, I have included links in my Amazon store (amazon.com/shop/raisingkingdomwarriors) for your convenience. I have also included links of other items I suggest for storage, game-playing accessories, and more! If you purchase through my links, I receive a small commission to help fund future curriculum endeavors. Thank you for checking it out!

Amazon shopping list: amazon.com/shop/raisingkingdomwarriors

Storage

As you progress through the *Montessori Reading Games Workbook,* you will accumulate printables for each of the sound groups. You can store these in labeled envelopes, plastic zip-top bags, plastic sleeve protectors in a 3-ring notebook, or, if you are interested in keeping work out for your student to revisit, you can display them on open shelving.

I have found the easiest method for our family depends on our season of life. With toddlers, we use bags and binders out of reach. With slightly older toddlers, we use a box for each sound group and fill them as we go. With no babies or toddlers in the mix, you can try your hand at setting up a Montessori-style learning shelf with the materials displayed on trays or in baskets.

Further Reading

If you are interested in reading Maria Montessori's own writings related to child development, the Montessori methodology, and specifically how to teach a child to read the Montessori way, check out this book:
- *The Discovery of the Child* (formerly entitled *The Montessori Method*) by Maria Montessori

I also love the following books written *about* the Montessori method:
- *Montessori: A Modern Approach* by Paula Polk Lillard (This is an excellent overview of Maria Montessori and her work, and there are specific chapters for reading and writing instruction.)
- *Teaching Montessori in the Home: The Pre-School Years* by Elizabeth Hainstock (She gives an overview of Montessori education and provides lists of activities you can do with your child in each subject area and even DIY instructions!)

Schedule

How many days per week should we play the reading games?
Try to play reading games three days per week consistently so your child will not forget information and will be able to easily build upon prior knowledge. There are 88 lessons in this Workbook plus 6 optional assessments. By completing 3 lessons (which are mostly games) per week, the entire workbook will be completed in 29-31 weeks, depending on if you choose to include the assessments.

Note: Some children may choose to repeat games on non-lesson days, which is highly encouraged.

What if I am starting with an older (or overly eager) child?
A child that is really ready to read may progress through this workbook very quickly. You can do multiple lessons a day if your child shows interest! I don't recommend *pushing* a child through this program, though, no matter his age. Follow your child's pace. If your child does progress quickly, reviewing past letter sounds becomes even more important. Make sure to include past sound groups when playing games. You can even just pull a couple past sandpaper letters out to review each time you introduce a new one.

How long is each session?
The lessons in this Workbook were intentionally created to be *short* lessons: 15 minutes maximum. Due to the game nature of many of the lessons, though, you will want to spend as much time on these games as your child shows interest. This can be five minutes or an hour, and each session will likely not be the same length of time.

There are also *more* materials than you may use in each unit. For example. you may use only one BINGO board instead of all four. You also may use only a handful of the cards each time you play "My Letter Sound Adventure." For CVC word building, you may choose to give your student three word building cards instead of the ten or more available in the workbook.

Let your student lead the way as far as her understanding, interest, and attention, instead of the materials within the lessons dictating your pace.

If you find that your student is taking *more* time to do each lesson than is ideal, (and is perhaps getting frustrated), you may want to do lessons 5 days per week to be able to keep the lessons short or plan to take longer than 29 weeks to cover all of the material at your child's pace.

What time of day is best?
Before you start the games with your child, take a couple days and *observe* your child. Pick a time of the day that your child seems interested in interacting with you. Although the games incorporate movement (and you can always add more movement), your child might be particularly rambunctious at specific times throughout the day. Don't try to sit and play games during that time! Instead, that time should be spent outside, if possible, or at least running, jumping, and playing.

- **Look out for these signs that might indicate a proper time for playing reading games:**
    - Your child follows you around the house.
    - Your child sits and colors or paints.
    - Your child is rested but not overly active.
    - Your child is moving from one activity to the next, not really finding something satisfying.

- **Look out for these signs that your child is probably *not* going to react well to playing reading games:**
    - Overly energetic.
    - Absorbed in an independent activity (don't interrupt!)
    - Whiny, tired, hungry, grumpy.

Sticking to a Strict Schedule...
Please do what works for your family! Whether you employ a strict schedule or an interest-led schedule, the Montessori approach would have you follow your child's interests and abilities, not force learning. My hope is that your child will have so much fun playing with you that this will never feel like a chore and will be a magical time of connection.

The Lesson Checklist: Presented-Attempted-Mastered (How to keep a record of lessons and mastery using the Table of Contents.)
If you present a lesson, mark it like this: [/]
If your child attempts the lesson, add another slash to make an X, like this: [X]
If your child masters the lesson, meaning you don't feel like you need to review it again, add a vertical line through the X, like this: [⧈]

Correlation to Reading Material

If you have an older child who is ready to learn sounds, write words, and *read* at the same time, you can introduce beginning reading work to your child. To make it easy, I created the **Montessori Pink Series Reading Workbook** to follow the same progression of sounds as the **Montessori Reading Games Workbook - Level 1.**

So you will be able to jump right into reading even before you cover all of the sounds if you have a child who is ready! The **Montessori Pink Series Reading Workbook** teaches reading progressively - from single CVC words to phrases to full sentences and even beginning readers.

Montessori Pink Series Reading Workbook by Katie Key

- Unit 1: Do after completing Sound Group #1 and #2.
- Unit 2: Do after completing Sound Group #3.
- Unit 3: Do after completing Sound Group #4.
- Unit 4: Do after completing Sound Group #5.
- Unit 5: Do after completing Sound Group #6.
- Unit 6: Do after completing Sound Group #6.

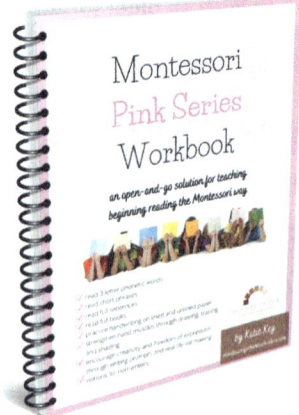

Get the *Montessori Pink Series Reading Workbook* Here on Amazon:
https://amzn.to/3aA14Je

For even more reading practice, the *Reading Games* are correlated to the **Bob Books, Set 1: Beginning Readers** by Bobby Lynn Maslen. These are delightful, inexpensive early readers. My children have found them particularly humorous!

Bob Books, Set 1: Beginning Readers by Bobby Lynn Maslen

- **Sound Group #1 (s, m, a, t):**
  - Book 1: s, m, a, t

- **Sound Group #2 (c, d, o, h):**
  - Book 2: c, d

- **Sound Group #3 (g, r, i, b):**
  - Book 3: o, h, g, r
  - Book 4: b

- **Sound Group #4 (p, n, u, w):**
  - Book 5: n, p, i
  - Book 6: none

- **Sound Group #5 (j, f, e, l):**
  - Book 7: j, w
  - Book 8: u, f
  - Book 9: no new sounds
  - Book 10: e

- **Sound Group #6 (k, q, v, x, y, z):**
  - Book 11: k, l
  - Book 12: v, y, z

Get *BOB Books* Here on Amazon:
https://amzn.to/3z4XtMM

Unit 1

Pronunciation Guide

In traditional Montessori education settings, only **one sound** is used when introducing each letter. We all know there is more than one sound for the letter "a," but we only use the short sound /a/ like in alligator in this Reading Games curriculum. Later on, in the Green Reading material, a child is learned multiple pronunciations for letters. For example, a child will learn that when adding a silent e, the letter a makes the long /a/ sound.

For now, stick with the sounds represented in each pronunciation guide. Do not use the names of the letters, just use the sounds

Note: All vowels will be pronounced with their short sounds in this curriculum.

> **⚠ IMPORTANT:**
>
> During all of these games, we *never, ever* say the **name** of the letter. We only say the letter's sound. This takes away a huge stumbling block when it comes to early reading and writing. When your child sees the letter "c,"Instead of hearing "see," she will hear /k/ ("kuh") in her head! This cuts down on so much unnecessary confusion and frustration!
>
> Your child will later learn the names of the letters, after she is already reading, and this comes easily.

Handwriting Guide

We won't be doing too much handwriting on paper, but every time you show your child how to write a letter by tracing a sandpaper letter, you need to be sure to use the proper handwriting strokes.

Most of the time, you will not pick up your pencil from the paper (or fingers from the sandpaper letter). The only time you will pick up your hand is when you see a **red number 2**.

Important: If your child is left-handed, show her the strokes using your left hand. If your child is right-handed, show her the strokes with your right hand.

| Start at the dot and curve up to the midline, then around the other way to the baseline, using one stroke. | Start at the midline and go straight down to the baseline. Follow that line back up to make two humps that touch the midline, never picking up your pencil. | Start at the midline and make a straight line down to the baseline. Retrace that line and then curve to the left, up to the baseline and in a circle. | Start near (or at) the top line and draw a straight line down to the baseline. Pick up your pencil and cross the line at the midline. |

5

Lesson 1.1

Directions:
1. Say, "We are going to play *I Spy*. Listen carefully and follow my directions."
2. "I spy something that starts with /s/ and slithers on the ground. Can you put your finger on it? What is it?" [Snake.] "What sound do you hear at the beginning of *snake*?" [/s/] "Color the snake green."
3. "I spy something that starts with /s/ and shines in the night sky. Can you put your finger on it? What is it?" [Star.] "What sound do you hear at the beginning of *star*?" [/s/] "Color the star yellow."
4. "I spy something that starts with /s/. When you do this with your mouth, it shows that you are happy! Can you put your finger on it? What is it?" [Smile.] "What sound do you hear at the beginning of *smile*?" [/s/] "Circle the smile."
5. "I spy something that starts with /s/ and sometimes stinks when it is dirty. Put your finger on it. What is it?" [Sock.] "What sound do you hear at the beginning of *sock*?" [/s/] "Draw stripes on the sock."
6. "I spy something that starts with /s/ and you can use it to build castles at the beach. Put your finger on it. What is it?" [Sand.] "What sound do you hear at the beginning of *sand*?" [/s/] "Draw a box around the sand."

Directions:
1. Say, "We are going to play *I Spy*. Listen carefully and follow my directions."
2. "I spy something that starts with /m/ and makes your voice louder when you speak into it. Can you put your finger on it? What is it?" [Microphone.] "What sound do you hear at the beginning of *microphone*?" [/m/] "Color the microphone pink."
3. "I spy something that starts with /m/ and helps clean the floor. Can you put your finger on it? What is it?" [Mop.] "What sound do you hear at the beginning of *mop*?" [/m/] "Draw a pile of mud by the mop."
4. "I spy something that starts with /m/. It can come in many different flavors like chocolate chip or blueberry! Can you put your finger on it? What is it?" [Muffin.] "What sound do you hear at the beginning of *muffin*?" [/m/] "Color the muffin."
5. "I spy something that starts with /m/, swings from trees, and eats bananas. Put your finger on it. What is it?" [Monkey.] "What sound do you hear in the beginning of *monkey*?" [/m/] "Draw a banana in the monkey's hand."
6. "I spy something that starts with /m/ and shines in the sky at night by reflecting light from the sun. Put your finger on it. What is it?" [Moon.] "What sound do you hear at the beginning of *moon*?" [/m/] "Color the moon yellow."

s m a t

☐ green and yellow crayons

Lesson 1.2

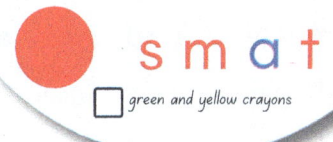

Directions: Color the objects that begin with **/s/ green** and **/m/ yellow**.

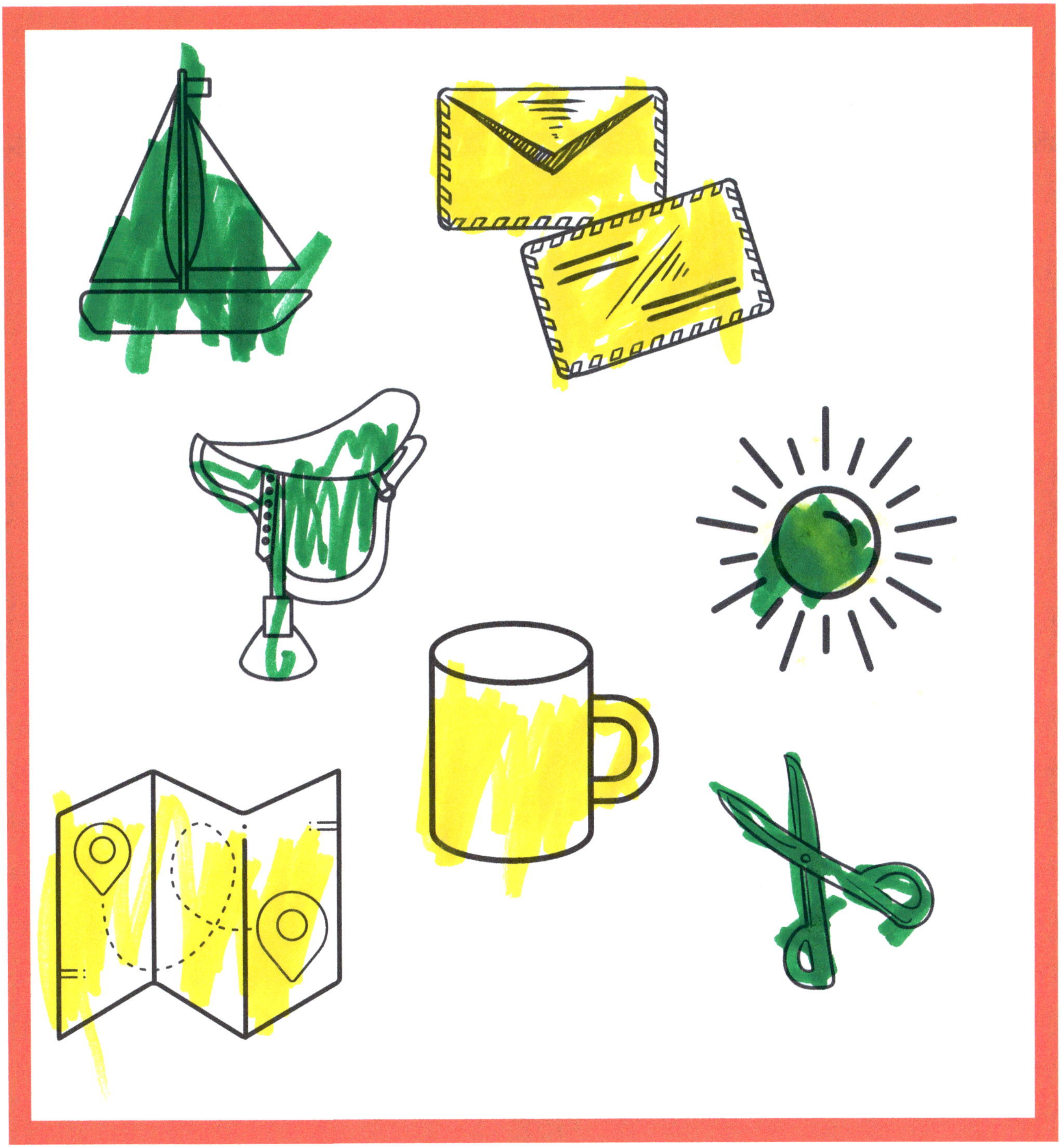

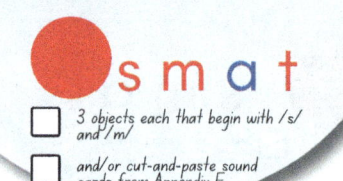

- ☐ 3 objects each that begin with /s/ and /m/
- ☐ and/or cut-and-paste sound cards from Appendix F

Lesson 1.3

Head's up!:
Prep sandpaper letters for tomorrow's lesson.

Directions - Option #1:
1. Gather 3 objects for each sound that are small enough to fit (or roughly fit) onto this page. (Salt, mail, sock, mitt, stapler, map, or see Appendix D for more ideas.)
2. Place objects in a basket or on the table in mixed order.
3. Name each picture ("slide" and "muffin.")
4. Invite your child to sort the objects into the boxes with the same beginning sound.

Directions - Option #2:
1. Locate the proper sound group sorting cards in Appendix F. Cut apart (or invite your child to cut apart) the sound cards.
2. Sort then save for the upcoming sandpaper letter sorting lesson.

Lesson 1.4

- laminating sheet (optional)
- glitter glue
- objects from previous lesson

☐ **Part 1 Directions:**
1. Make the sandpaper letters. See Appendix E.
2. Introduce the sandpaper letters. Show one at a time and follow the script below.

   Sandpaper Letter Script:
   1. Pick up the s in the opposite of your child's dominant hand. (If your child is right-handed, pick up the letter with your left hand. If your child is left-handed, pick up the letter with your right hand.)
   2. Say, "This says /s/."
   3. With the pointer and middle fingers of your other hand (matching child's dominant hand), trace the letter the same way you would write it as you say the sound /s/. Do this 3 times.
   4. Invite your child to say the sound while tracing the letter three times.
   5. Repeat for the next sound.

☐ **Part 2 Directions:**
Sort the household objects used in the previous lesson underneath each sandpaper letter.

Lesson 1.5

Directions:
1. Say, "We are going to play *I Spy*. Listen carefully and follow my directions."
2. "I spy something that starts with /a/, has big teeth, and scales. Can you put your finger on it? What is it?" [Alligator.] "What sound do you hear at the beginning of *alligator*?" [/a/] "Color the alligator green."
3. "I spy something that starts with /a/, grows on a tree, and is delicious to eat. Can you put your finger on it? What is it?" [Apple.] "What sound do you hear at the beginning of *apple*?" [/a/] "Circle the apple."
4. "I spy something that starts with /a/. It has fur and eats ants. Can you put your finger on it? What is it?" [Anteater.] "What sound do you hear at the beginning of *anteater*?" [/a/] "Color the tail of the anteater."
5. "I spy something that starts with /a/, is very small, and lives in colonies underground. Put your finger on it. What is it?" [Ant.] "What sound do you hear at the beginning of *ant*?" [/a/] "Trace the antennae on the ant."
6. "I spy something that starts with /a/ and you can use it to chop down trees. Put your finger on it. What is it?" [Ax.] "What sound do you hear at the beginning of *ax*?" [/a/] "Draw a box around the ax."

Directions:
1. Say, "We are going to play *I Spy*. Listen carefully and follow my directions."
2. "I spy something that starts with /t/ and grows from the ground. Can you put your finger on it? What is it?" [Tree.] "What sound do you hear at the beginning of *tree*?" [/t/] "Color the tree."
3. "I spy something that starts with /t/ and swims in the ocean. Can you put your finger on it? What is it?" [Turtle.] "What sound do you hear at the beginning of *turtle*?" [/t/] "Draw water surrounding the turtle."
4. "I spy something that starts with /t/. It has wheels and drives on highways. Can you put your finger on it? What is it?" [Truck.] "What sound do you hear at the beginning of *truck*?" [/t/] "Draw a box around the truck."
5. "I spy something that starts with /t/ and is used to talk across long distances. Put your finger on it. What is it?" [Telephone.] "What sound do you hear in the beginning of *telephone*?" [/t/] "Draw a circle around the telephone."
6. "I spy something that starts with /t/, uses coal for fuel, and drives along a track. Put your finger on it. What is it?" [Train.] "What sound do you hear at the beginning of *train*?" [/t/] "Color the train red."

s m a t

☐ orange and purple crayons

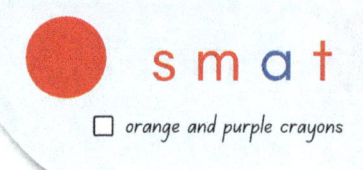

Lesson 1.6

Directions: Color the objects that begin with **/a/ orange** and **/t/ purple**.

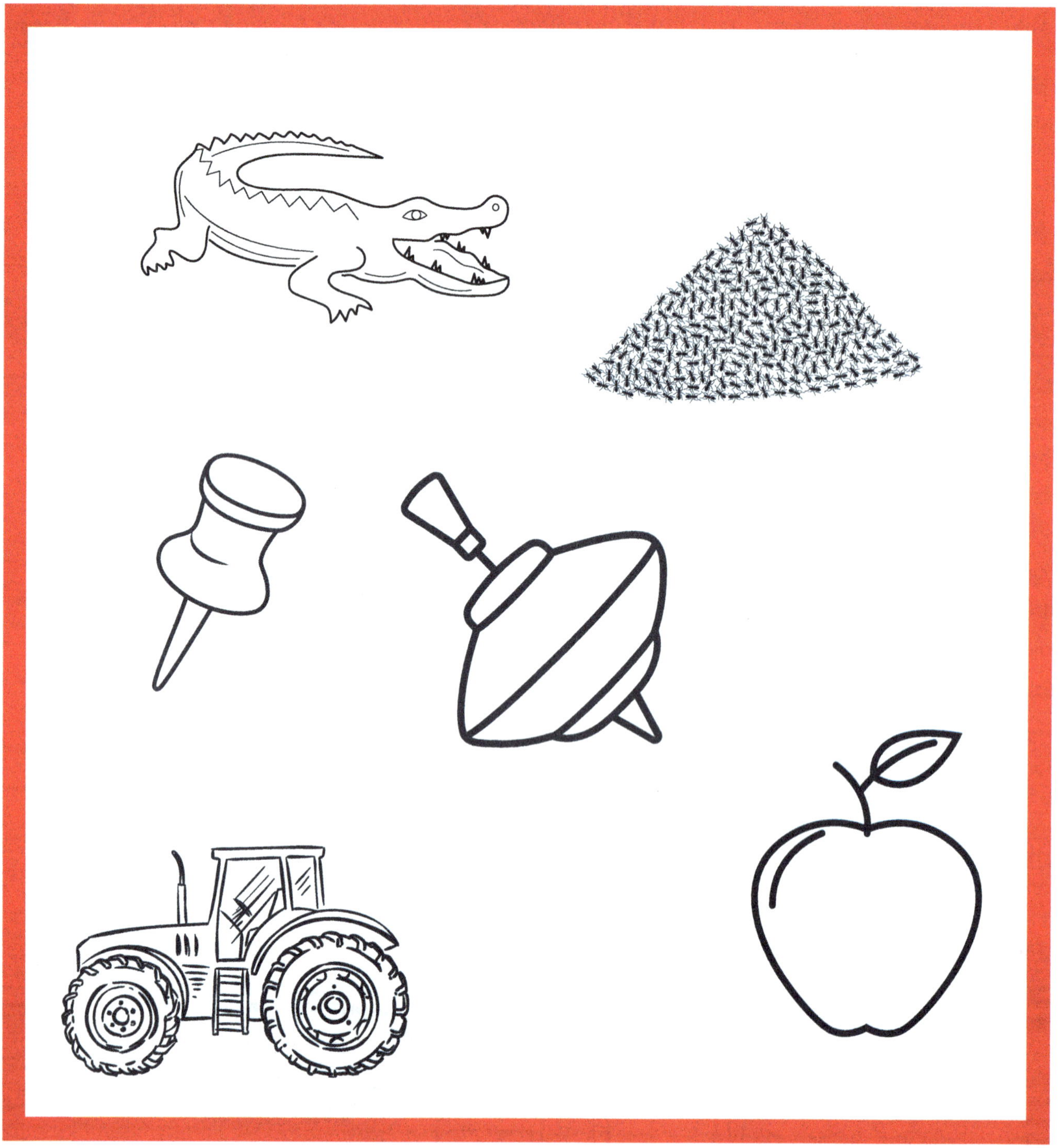

KEY: alligator, ants, tack, top, tractor, apple

Head's up!: Prep sandpaper letters for tomorrow's lesson.

Lesson 1.7

☐ 3 objects each that begin with /a/ and /t/
☐ and/or cut-and-paste sound cards from Appendix F

Directions - Option #1:
1. Gather 3 objects for each sound that are small enough to fit (or roughly fit) onto this page. (apple, apricot, ax toy, ant trap, top, tack, tie, or see Appendix D for more ideas.)
2. Place objects in a basket or on the table in mixed order.
3. Name each picture ("alligator" and "tiger.")
4. Invite your child to sort the objects into the boxes with the same beginning sound.

Directions - Option #2:
1. Locate the proper sound group sorting cards in Appendix F. Cut apart (or invite your child to cut apart) the sound cards.
2. Sort then save for the upcoming sandpaper letter sorting lesson.

Lesson 1.8

s m a t

- ☐ laminating sheet (optional)
- ☐ glitter glue
- ☐ objects from previous lesson

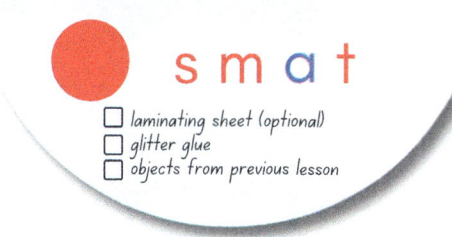

☐ **Part 1 Directions:**

1. Make the sandpaper letters. See Appendix E.
2. Introduce the sandpaper letters. Show one at a time and follow the script below.

Sandpaper Letter Script:

1. Pick up the *a* in the opposite of your child's dominant hand. (If your child is right-handed, pick up the letter with your left hand. If your child is left-handed, pick up the letter with your right hand.)
2. Say, "This says /*a*/."
3. With the pointer and middle fingers of your other hand (matching child's dominant hand), trace the letter the same way you would write it as you say the sound /*a*/. Do this 3 times.
4. Invite your child to say the sound while tracing the letter three times.
5. Repeat for the next sound.

☐ **Part 2 Directions:**

Sort the household objects used in the previous lesson underneath each sandpaper letter.

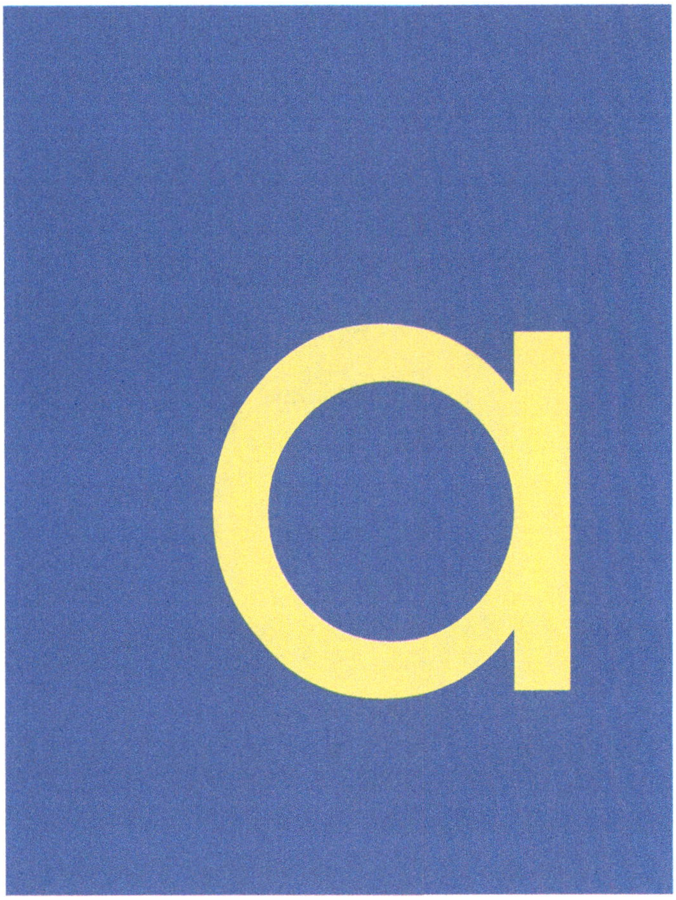

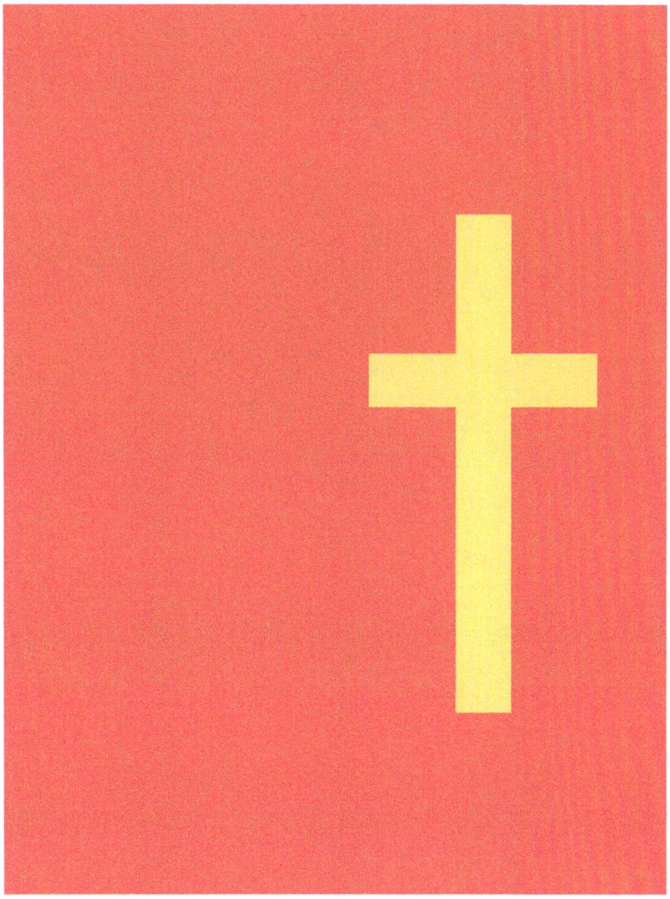

Lesson 1.9

s m a t

☐ counters/chips

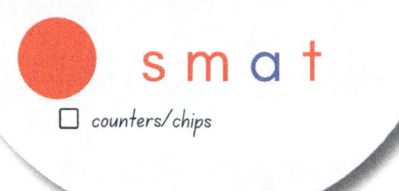

Directions:

1. Cut out the BINGO cards.
2. Choose a game board and play with your student(s). Cut them from the workbook or leave them attached.
3. Shuffle and place cards face down in a single pile.
4. Take turns drawing one card at a time. Each player places a chip (any counter will work) on top of the matching letter on his/her BINGO game board.
5. Each player should cover his/her entire board.

Optional Extra Game: Go Fish

See Appendix E for directions.

KEY:
a: apple, alligator, ant
t: tap, tickets, table
s: snake, sandwich, soap
m: map, mop, mug

a

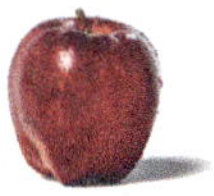

a

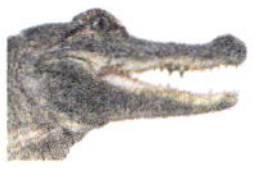

a

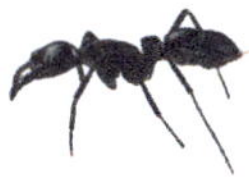

m

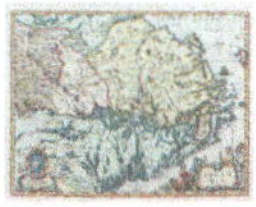

t

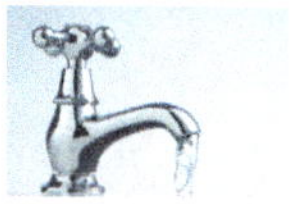

t

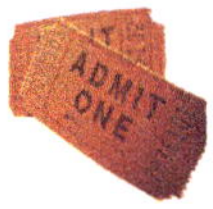

t

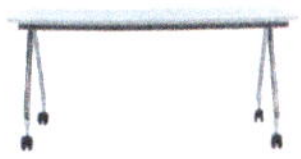

m

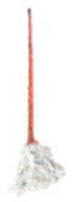

s

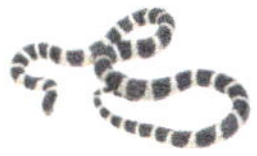

s

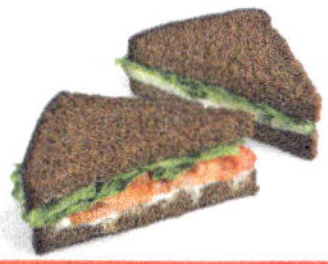

s

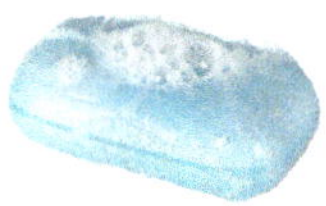

m

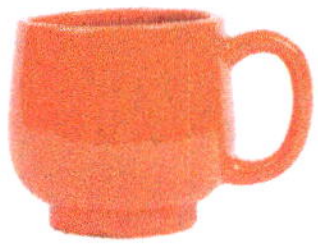

s	m	a
t	a	m
s	t	t

m	a	t
s	a	s
m	t	a

a	s	t
t	s	a
m	m	a

s	m	m
t	a	s
a	m	t

Directions: Play one round of the **"My Letter Sound Adventure Game."** Here are the new cards for your **My Letter Sound Adventure Game.** See Appendix B for directions on *how* to play the game and the removable game board.

Lesson 1.10

☐ My Letter Sound Adventure Game (Appendix B)

1

2

3

4

5

6

7

8

9

21

Key 1-24

1. cat
2. apple
3. llama
4. bat
5. ax
6. soda/cola
7. bus
8. snail
9. snake
10. ask
11. salt
12. gas
13. mop
14. ram
15. emu
16. mail
17. amp
18. jam
19. hat
20. bat
21. tie
22. rat
23. turtle
24. tiger

Lesson 1.11

s m a t
☐ My Letter Sound Adventure Game (Appendix B)
☐ Scavenger hunt cards (Appendix A)

Part 1 Directions:
1. Laminate page (optional) then cut apart individual cards.
2. Invite your student to spread the letter cards out across the top of his/her work space horizontally.
3. Shuffle the picture cards and invite your child to look at the picture, say the name of the object, and identify the beginning sound. Then place the picture card underneath the proper letter, making a column. There is a control of error on the back of each card so your child can learn to do this activity independently. See Appendix A for a visual.

Part 2 Directions:
Make this into a game! Play "Scavenger Hunt." **See game instructions in Appendix A.**

s: snake, soap, sandwich   a: apple, ant, alligator
m: mop, mug, map   t: table, tap, tickets

ant	apple	soap	snake
table	alligator	mop	sandwich
tickets	tap	map	mug

Lesson 1.12

s m a t
- ☐ sensory tray - salt, sand, or cornmeal
- ☐ sandpaper letters
- ☐ scissors

☐ **Part 1 Directions:**
1. Prepare a shallow tray and fill it with salt, sand, or cornmeal.
2. Review the sandpaper letter /s/. Trace three times while saying the sound, then invite your child to do the same.
3. Show your child how to write the letter in the sensory tray with your finger after tracing the sandpaper letter. Show your child how to gently shake the tray to redistribute the material to give a clean writing surface. Invite your child to write the letter with her finger.
4. Repeat with the other three letters in this sound group.

☐ **Part 2 Directions:**
1. Invite your child to make a book out of the letters by cutting apart the strips on this page, stacking them, and stapling the booklet on the left-hand side.
2. Your child should be able to identify the letter sound and connect the letter sound to the beginning sound in each picture.
3. On the back of each strip, your child can practice writing with a pencil.
4. NOTE: To make these re-usable, laminate then cut, and use a dry-erase marker for tracing and writing.

a: apple, alligator, ax   t: tree, tack, tape   m: mop, monkey, mitten.   s: sandwich, snake, socks a

t

m

s

Lesson 1.13

smat

☐ pencil or counters
OR
☐ laminating sheets + 4 clothes pins

Directions:
Invite your child to circle or place a counter on top of the correct picture to match each beginning letter sound.

Re-Usable Shelf Work:
Laminate sheet. Cut individual cards. Place clothespins in a basket next to the cards and invite your child to clip the clothespin on the correct picture to match each beginning sound.
Show your child how to turn the card over to check his own work.

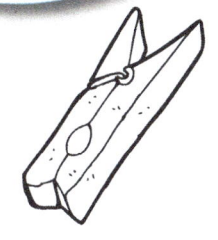

KEY: tree, apple, sandwich, mop

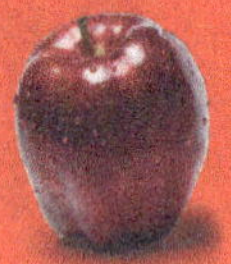
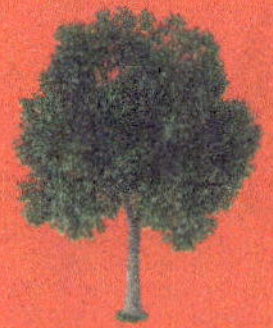
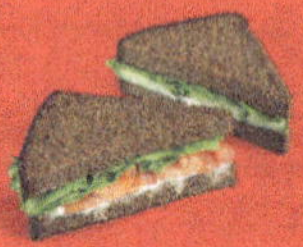
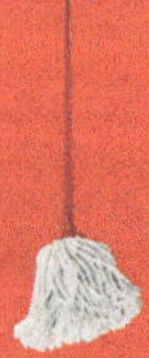

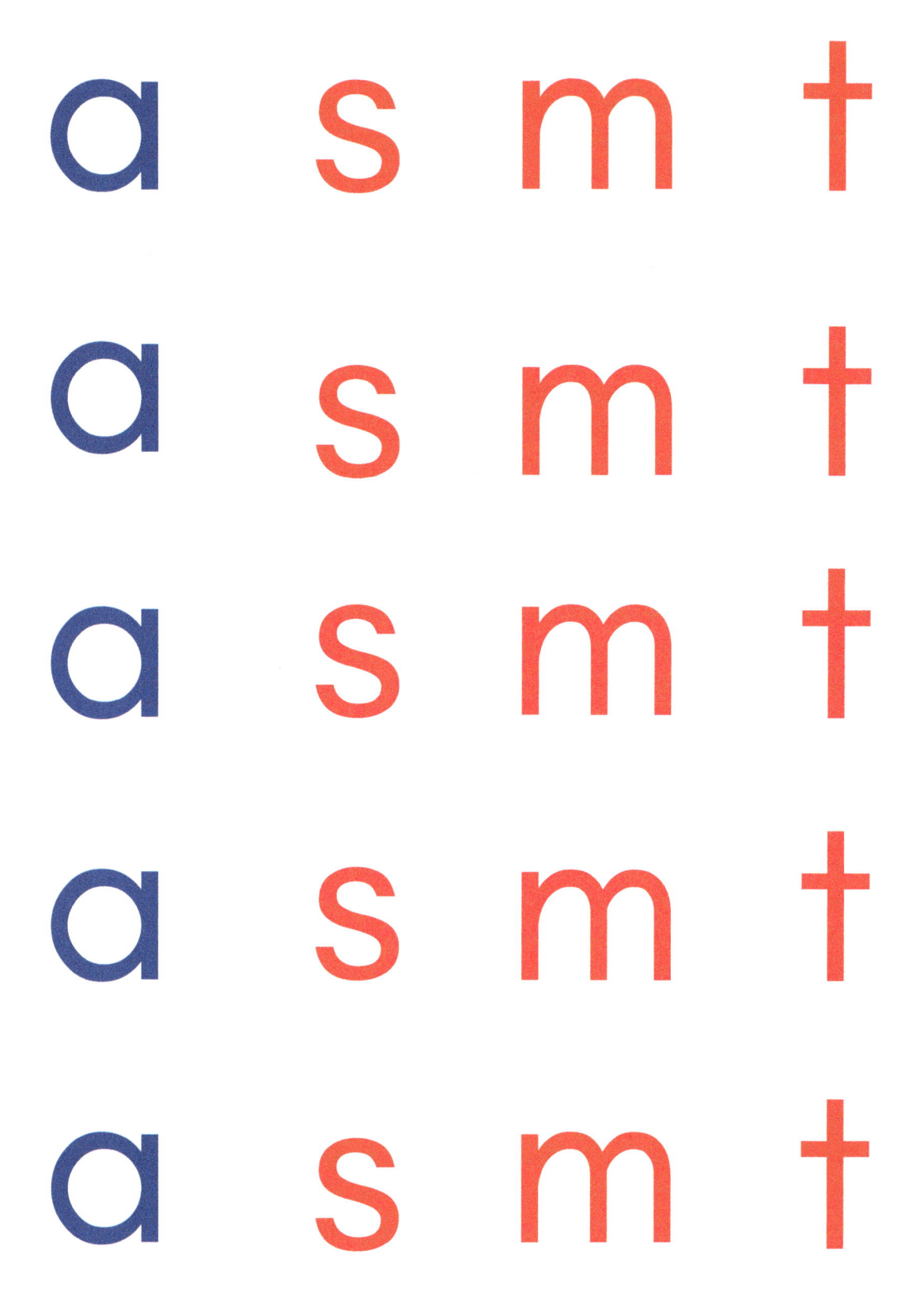

Lesson 1.14

s m a t

☐ laminating sheet
☐ movable alphabet organizer

Directions:
1. Assemble the Movable Alphabet Organizer found in Appendix C for your growing movable alphabet. See **Appendix C.**
2. Cut apart the tiles and store in their appropriate compartments of the Organizer.
3. Introduce the movable alphabet by reading each sound. Say, "When we put sounds together, we can make words." Show your child how to make the word "mat."
4. Move onto the next part of the lesson where you will use the Pink Series Word Building Cards.

Note: You may want to laminate the letter cards for durability.

a s m t

a s m t

a s m t

a s m t

a s m t

33

Lesson 1.14
continued

movable alphabet: s m a t

Directions:
1. Use these Pink Series Word Building Cards to build words alongside your child, slowly creating independence. Say the name of the image, then sound out each letter clearly.
2. Sample script for Card 1: "This is a picture of the word, "sat." What sound do you hear in the beginning of the word *sat*? /s/. Can you find the letter that says /s/?" [Child retrieves *s*.] "What sound do you hear next in the word *sat*?" (Say the word slowly, enunciating each sound by segmenting the word into its sounds /s/ /a/ /t/.) [Child says /a/ and retrieves *a*.] "What sound do you hear at the end of the word *sat*?" (Again, segment the word *sat* into its individual sounds.) [Child says /t/ and retrieves *t* to finish building the word *sat* in the pink box.]
3. See **Appendix C** for visual step-by-step instructions.

KEY (see full KEY in Appendix C.)

□ sand tray (optional)
□ movable alphabet

Unit 1 Assessment

Directions:
1. Using the sandpaper letters you made for this unit (s, m, a, and t), invite your child to identify each sound as you hold up one letter at a time.

□ s   □ m   □ a   □ t

2. Using your sensory tray OR the writing lines below, invite your child to write one of each letter.

s   m   a   t

3. Match the letter to the object by its beginning sound.

s

m

a

t

36

Unit 1 Assessment

s m a t
☐ *movable alphabet*

4. Build the following words with the movable alphabet by segmenting the words into their individual sounds.

Assessment Results and Next Steps:

Depending on how your child performed on this assessment, you may want to review letter sounds and letter formation before moving on to Unit 2. If your child made minor errors, feel free to move on, as there is review built into the entire program!

For further review if needed, see **Appendix A** for a list of games you can play with your child using the materials in the workbook!

If handwriting is a concern, consider incorporating more fine motor work into your child's day, such as: cutting, sewing, using puzzles with knobs, coloring, tracing, shading, helping in the kitchen, sorting, buttoning, zipping etc. In a Montessori environment, these kinds of activities are usually referred to as "Practical Life" activities and the uses are twofold: teaching practical skills that the child can use each day to help himself, and strengthening the muscles of the hand, wrist, and fingers to prepare for writing. Do not let handwriting prevent you from moving forward. Children can "write" with the movable alphabet for the duration of this program.

Unit 2

c d o h

Pronunciation Guide

In traditional Montessori education settings, only **one sound** is used when introducing each letter. We all know there is more than one sound for the letter "a," but we only use the short sound /ă/ like in alligator in this Reading Games curriculum. Later on, in the Green Reading material, a child is learned multiple pronunciations for letters. For example, a child will learn that when adding a silent e, the letter a makes the long /ā/ sound.

For now, stick with the sounds represented in each pronunciation guide.

Note: All vowels will be pronounced with their short sounds in this curriculum.

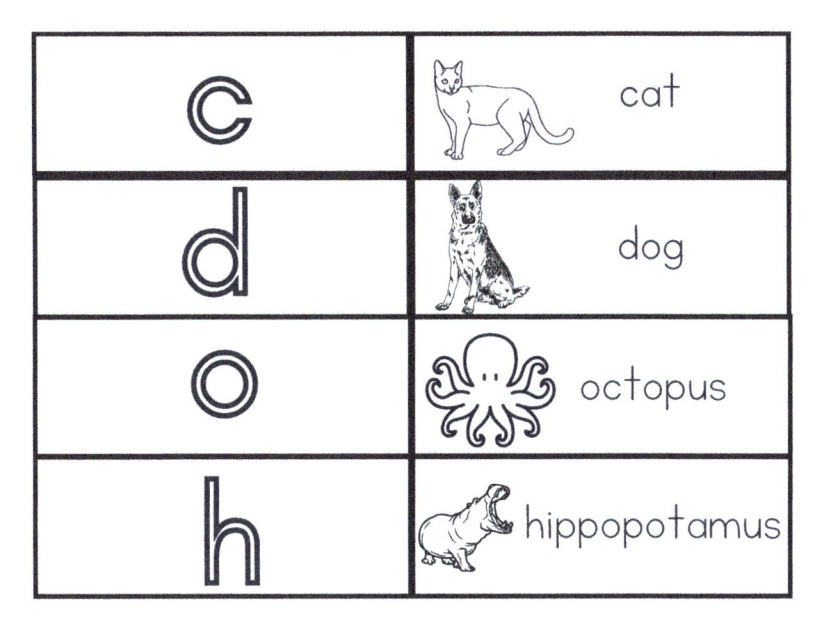

c		cat
d		dog
o		octopus
h		hippopotamus

Handwriting Guide

We won't be doing too much handwriting on paper, but every time you show your child how to write a letter by tracing a sandpaper letter, you need to be sure to use the proper handwriting strokes.

Most of the time, you will not pick up your pencil from the paper (or fingers from the sandpaper letter). The only time you will pick up your hand is when you see a **red number 2**.

Important: If your child is left-handed, show her the strokes using your left hand. If your child is right-handed, show her the strokes with your right hand.

top line

midline

baseline

| Start at the dot and curve up to the midline, then around to the baseline, using one stroke. | Start near (or at) the top line and draw a straight line down to the baseline. Retrace your line up almost to the midline, then curve around in a circle to the left, curving up to touch the midline and circling down to the baseline and back to your vertical line in one stroke. | Start at the dot and curve up to the left to touch the midline. Circle down to the baseline and back to your starting point. | Start near (or at) the top line and draw a straight line down to the baseline. Without picking up your pencil, retrace your line almost to the midline and curve up to the right to touch the midline, then down to the baseline.. |

39

c d o h
☐ crayons

Lesson 2.1

Directions:
1. Say, "We are going to play *I Spy*. Listen carefully and follow my directions."
2. "I spy something that starts with /c/ and has an engine to make it go. Can you put your finger on it? What is it?" [Car.] "What sound do you hear at the beginning of *car*?" [/c/] "Color the car your favorite color."
3. "I spy something that starts with /c/ and says "meow." Can you put your finger on it? What is it?" [Cat.] "What sound do you hear at the beginning of *cat*?" [/c/] "Draw a ball of yarn by the cat's front paws."
4. "I spy something that starts with /c/ and makes a yummy snack. You can put cheese on them, too. Can you put your finger on them? What are they?" [Crackers.] "What sound do you hear at the beginning of *crackers*?" [/c/] "Draw a box around the crackers."
5. "I spy something that starts with /c/, tastes sweet, has frosting, and is beautiful. Put your finger on it. What is it?" [Cake.] "What sound do you hear at the beginning of *cake*?" [/c/] "Draw decorations on the cake."
6. "I spy something that starts with /c/. You can use it to take pictures. Put your finger on it. What is it?" [Camera.] "What sound do you hear at the beginning of *camera*?" [/c/] "Color the camera black."

Directions:
1. Say, "We are going to play *I Spy*. Listen carefully and follow my directions."
2. "I spy something that starts with /d/. You can throw at a target to try to hit the bullseye in the middle. Can you put your finger on it? What is it?" [Dart.] "What sound do you hear at the beginning of *dart*?" [/d/] "Draw a bullseye at the tip of the dart."
3. "I spy something that starts with /d/, waddles, and quacks. It has feathers and a beak. Can you put your finger on it? What is it?" [Duck.] "What sound do you hear at the beginning of *duck*?" [/d/] "Color the duck's beak and feet orange."
4. "I spy something that starts with /d/, and you have to open it to walk through it. Can you put your finger on it? What is it?" [Door.] "What sound do you hear at the beginning of *door*?" [/d/] "Draw a wreath on the door."
5. "I spy something that starts with /d/. It barks and wags its tail. It makes a great pet. Put your finger on it. What is it?" [Dog.] "What sound do you hear in the beginning of *dog*?" [/d/] "Draw a collar and leash on the dog."
6. "I spy a person whose title starts with /d/. He helps sick people get better. He has a stethoscope around his neck. Put your finger on the person. What is he?" [A doctor.] "What sound do you hear at the beginning of *doctor*?" [/d/] "Color the doctor."

Lesson 2.2

c d o h
☐ blue and gray crayons

Directions: Color the objects that begin with **/c/ blue** and **/d/ gray**.

41

c d o h

☐ 3 small objects for each sound
☐ and/or cut-and-paste sound cards from Appendix F

Lesson 2.3

Directions - Option #1:
1. Gather 3 objects for each sound that are small enough to fit (or roughly fit) onto this page. (Toy cat, car, cap, clock, dog, dish, dinosaur, dessert, dragon or see Appendix D for more ideas.)
2. Place objects in a basket or on the table in mixed order.
3. Name each picture ("cake" and "dog.")
4. Invite your child to sort the objects into the boxes with the same beginning sound.

Directions - Option #2:
1. Locate the proper sound group sorting cards in Appendix F. Cut apart (or invite your child to cut apart) the sound cards.
2. Sort then save for the upcoming sandpaper letter sorting lesson.

Lesson 2.4

c d o h
☐ glitter glue
☐ 3+ objects for each sound

☐ **Part 1 Directions:**
1. Make the sandpaper letters. See Appendix E.
2. Introduce the sandpaper letters. Show one at a time and follow the script below.

Sandpaper Letter Script:
1. Pick up the c in the opposite of your child's dominant hand. (If your child is right-handed, pick up the letter with your left hand. If your child is left-handed, pick up the letter with your right hand.)
2. Say, "This says /c/." (As in "cat.")
3. With the pointer and middle fingers of your other hand (matching child's dominant hand), trace the letter the same way you would write it as you say the sound /c/. Do this 3 times.
4. Invite your child to say the sound while tracing the letter three times.
5. Repeat for the next sound.

☐ **Part 2 Directions:**
Sort the household objects used in the previous lesson underneath each sandpaper letter.

Lesson 2.5

c d o h
☐ crayons

Directions:
1. Say, "We are going to play *I Spy*. Listen carefully and follow my directions."
2. "I spy something that starts with /o/ and is a mammal that loves the water. It has fur and likes to swim on its back eat sea urchins. Can you put your finger on it? What is it?" [Otter.] "What sound do you hear at the beginning of *otter*?" [/o/] "Color the otter gray."
3. "I spy something that starts with /o/, lives underwater, and has eight tentacles. Can you put your finger on it? What is it?" [Octopus.] "What sound do you hear at the beginning of *octopus*?" [/o/] "Color the tentacles on the octopus."
4. "I spy some things that start with /o/ and grow on trees. They make a healthy snack on their own, or they can be pressed to make oil. Can you put your finger on them? What are they?" [Olives.] "What sound do you hear at the beginning of *olives*?" [/o/] "Draw a circle around the olives."
5. "I spy an animal that starts with /o/ and runs fast. It has feathers but cannot fly. Put your finger on it. What is it?" [Ostrich.] "What sound do you hear at the beginning of *ostrich*?" [/o/] "Color the ostrich's feathers."
6. "I spy an action that starts with /o/. You do this when you want the room to be dark. Put your finger on the action. What is it?" [Turning the lights *off*.] "What sound do you hear at the beginning of *off*?" [/o/] "Draw a box around the on/off switch"

Directions:
1. Say, "We are going to play *I Spy*. Listen carefully and follow my directions."
2. "I spy something that starts with /h/ and is a shape. Sometimes it means love. Can you put your finger on it? What is it?" [Heart.] "What sound do you hear at the beginning of *heart*?" [/h/] "Color the heart pink."
3. "I spy something that starts with /h/ and is attached to the end of an arm. Can you put your finger on it? What is it?" [Hand.] "What sound do you hear at the beginning of *hand*?" [/h/] "Color and count the fingers on the *hand*."
4. "I spy something that starts with /h/ and can be worn on your head to keep sun out of your eyes. It is soft, not hard. Can you put your finger on it? What is it?" [Hat.] "What sound do you hear at the beginning of *hat*?" [/h/] "Color the hat your favorite color."
5. "I spy a large mammal that starts with /h/. It loves the water. Its name actually means "water horse." Put your finger on it. What is it?" [Hippopotamus.] "What sound do you hear in the beginning of *hippopotamus*?" [/h/] "Draw water around the hippopotamus."
6. "I spy something that starts with /h/. It protects a person's head from injuries, especially when playing sports. Put your finger on it. What is it?" [Helmet.] "What sound do you hear at the beginning of *helmet*?" [/h/] "Circle the helmet."

c d o h
☐ red and black crayons

Lesson 2.6

Directions: Color the objects that begin with **/o/ red** and **/h/ black**.

KEY: olives, otter, hopscotch, office building, hog, hairbrush

46

Lesson 2.7

c d o h

☐ 3 small objects for each sound
☐ and/or cut-and-paste sound cards from Appendix F

Directions - Option #1:
1. Gather 3 objects for each sound that are small enough to fit (or roughly fit) onto this page. (Toy animals: ostrich, otter, octopus, hippopotamus, hedgehog, horse ; olives, optical lens, "on" switch, hat, hairbrush, hairspray, or see Appendix D for more ideas.)
2. Place objects in a basket or on the table in mixed order.
3. Name each picture ("octopus" and "horse.")
4. Invite your child to sort the objects into the boxes with the same beginning sound.

Directions - Option #2:
1. Locate the proper sound group sorting cards in Appendix F. Cut apart (or invite your child to cut apart) the sound cards.
2. Sort then save for the upcoming sandpaper letter sorting lesson.

Lesson 2.8

c d o h
☐ glitter glue
☐ 3+ objects for each sound

☐ **Part 1 Directions:**
1. Make the sandpaper letters. See Appendix E.
2. Introduce the sandpaper letters. Show one at a time and follow the script below.

   Sandpaper Letter Script:
   1. Pick up the o in the opposite of your child's dominant hand. (If your child is right-handed, pick up the letter with your left hand. If your child is left-handed, pick up the letter with your right hand.)
   2. Say, "This says /o/." (As in "off.")
   3. With the pointer and middle fingers of your other hand (matching child's dominant hand), trace the letter the same way you would write it as you say the sound /o/. Do this 3 times.
   4. Invite your child to say the sound while tracing the letter three times.
   5. Repeat for the next sound.

☐ **Part 2 Directions:**
Sort the household objects used in the previous lesson underneath each sandpaper letter.

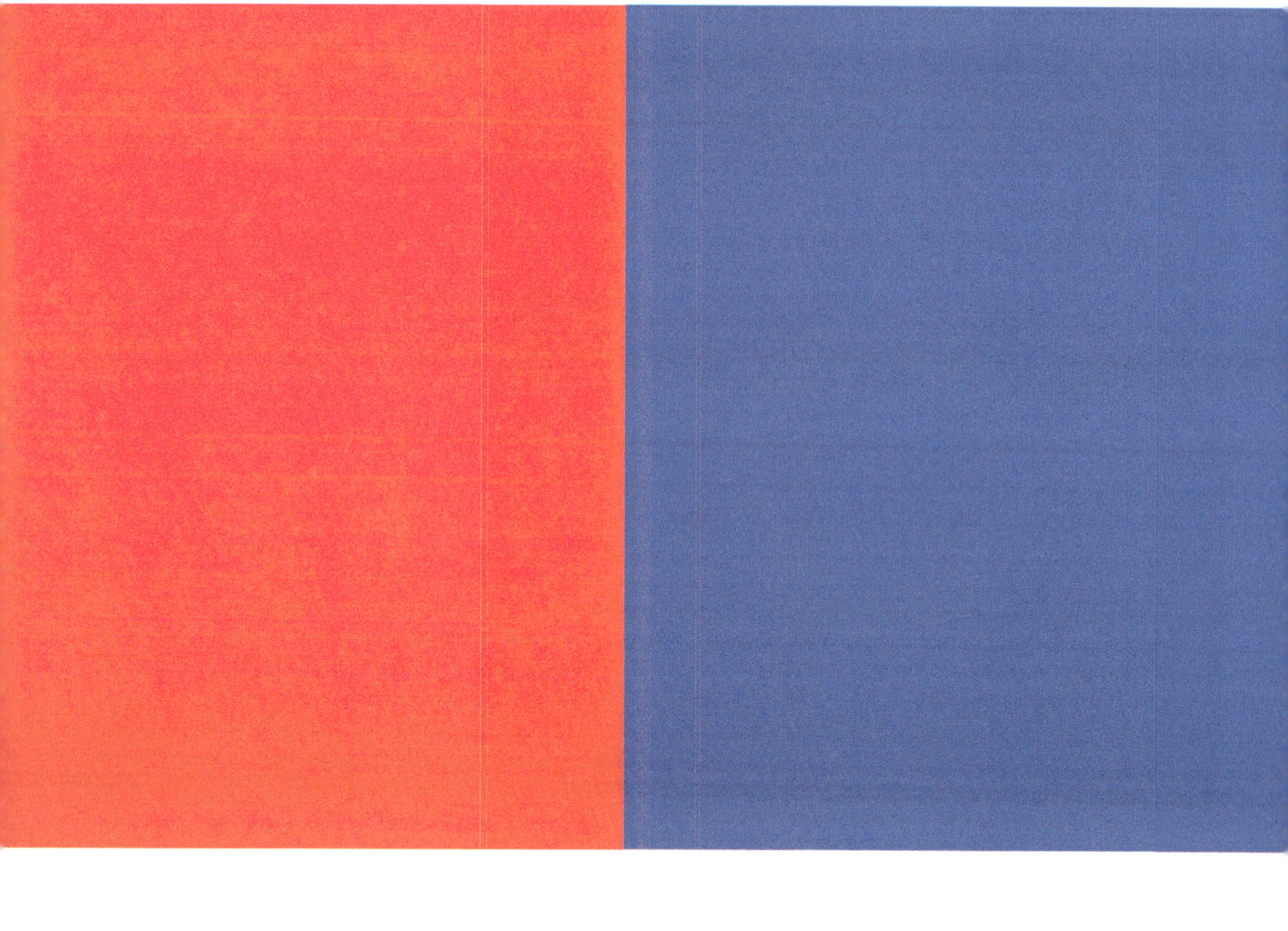

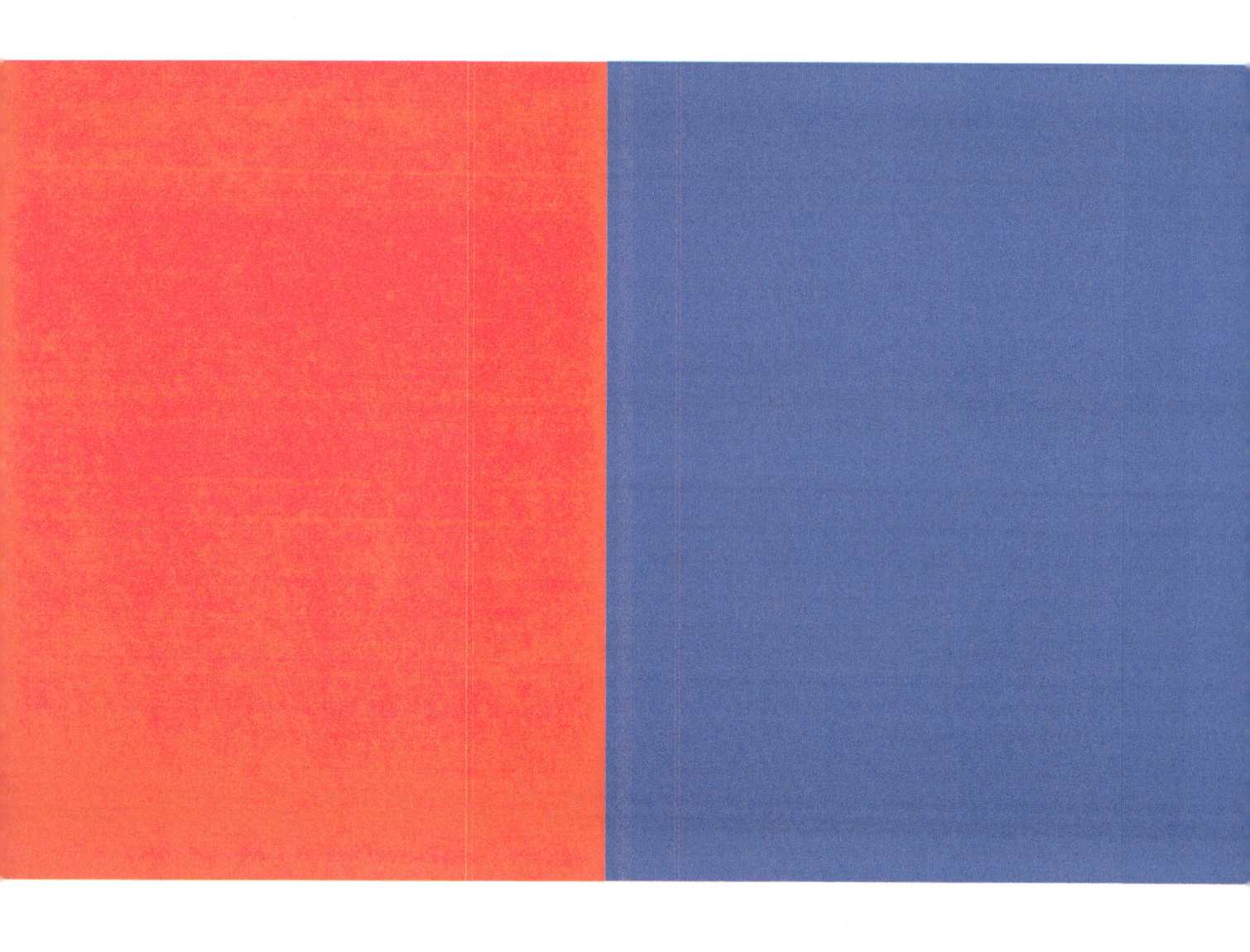

Lesson 2.9

c d o h
☐ counters/chips

Directions:
1. Cut out the BINGO cards.
2. Choose a game board and play with your student(s). Cut them from the workbook or leave them attached.
3. Shuffle and place cards face down in a single pile.
4. Take turns drawing one card at a time. Each player places a chip (any counter will work) on top of the matching letter on his/her BINGO game board.
5. Each player should cover his/her entire board.

Optional Extra Game: Go Fish
See Appendix E for directions.

KEY:
c: can, cube, camera
d: duck, dancer, donut
o: on, olives, octopus
h: hammer, hamburger, helmet

51

c	d	o
h	o	d
c	h	h

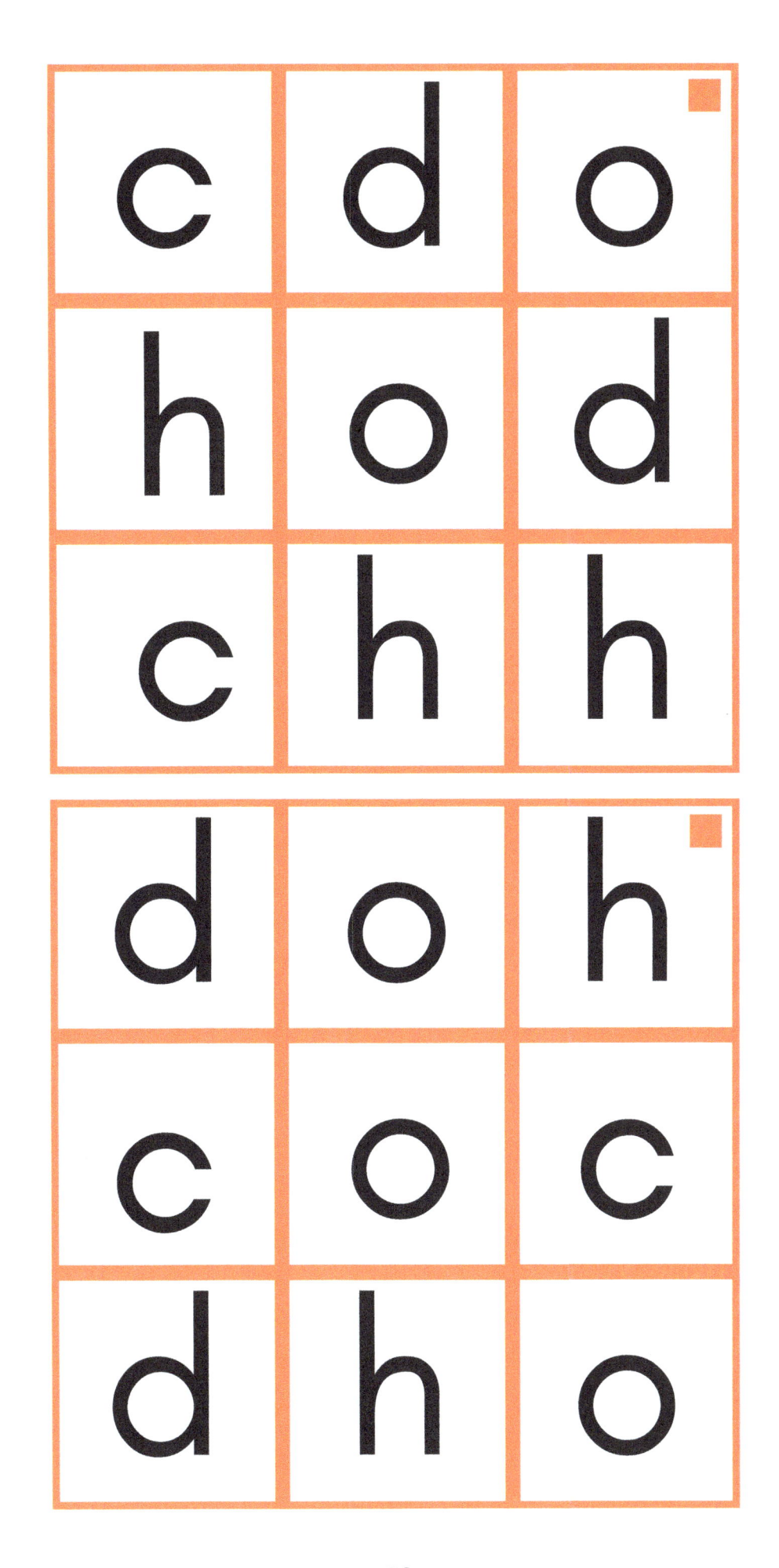

d	o	h
c	o	c
d	h	o

c	d	d
h	o	c
o	d	h

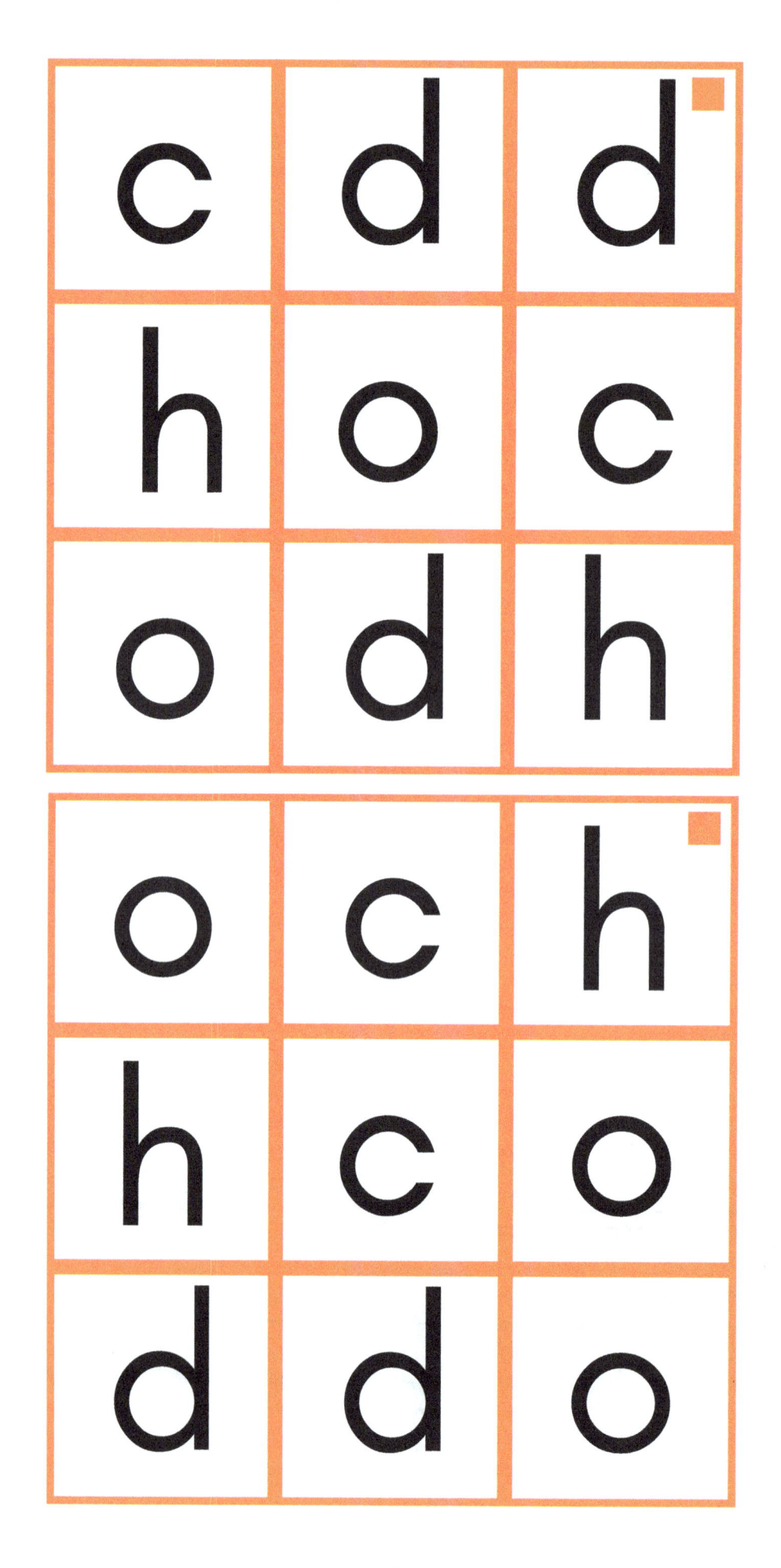

o	c	h
h	c	o
d	d	o

Directions: Play one round of the **"My Letter Sound Adventure Game."** Here are the new cards for your **My Letter Sound Adventure Game.** See Appendix B for directions on *how* to play the game and the removable game board.

Lesson 2.10

cdoh
My Letter Sound Adventure Game (Appendix B)

25
26
27
28
29
30
31
32
33

55

57

43	44	45
46	47	48

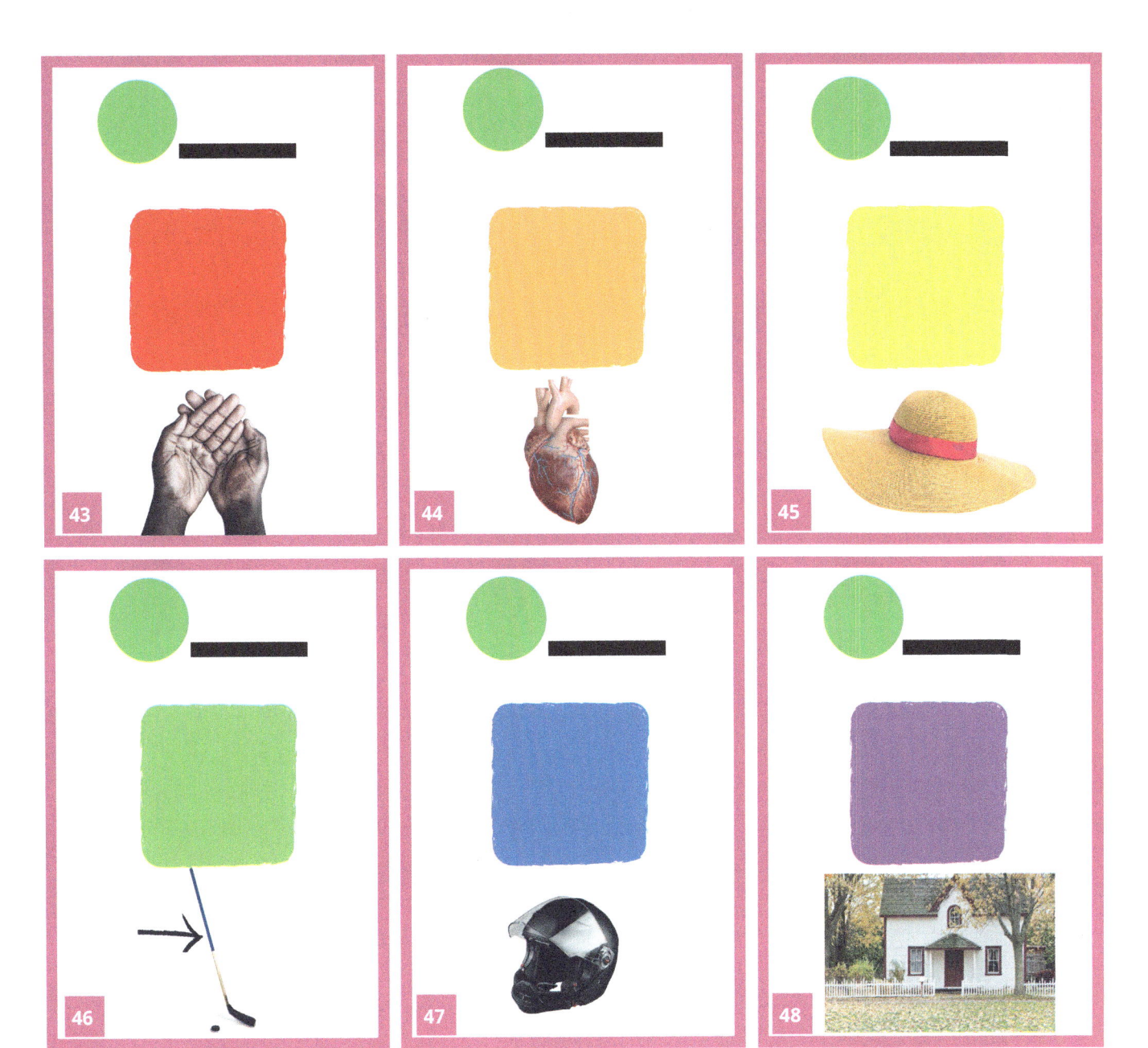

Key 25-48

25. act
26. candy
27. music
28. car
29. camera
30. arc
31. dog
32. bed
33. ads
34. door
35. sad
36. dolphin
37. mop
38. octopus
39. olive
40. off
41. ostrich
42. fog
43. hands
44. heart
45. hat
46. hockey stick
47. helmet
48. house

Lesson 2.11

c d o h
- [ ] laminating sheet
- [ ] sensory bin
- [ ] contact paper
- [ ] tape

Part 1 Directions:
1. Laminate page (optional) then cut apart individual cards.
2. Invite your student to spread the letter cards out across the top of his/her work space horizontally.
3. Shuffle the picture cards and invite your child to look at the picture, say the name of the object, and identify the beginning sound. Then place the picture card underneath the proper letter, making a column. There is a control of error on the back of each card so your child can learn to do this activity independently. See **Appendix A** for a visual.

Part 2 Directions:
Make this into a game! Play "Treasure Hunt." See game instructions in **Appendix A.**

c: car, cat, candy
d: dog, diamond, dice
o: octopus, olives, ostrich
h: hat, hanger, house

diamond	cat	dog	car
hat	octopus	dice	candy
house	ostrich	hanger	olives

Lesson 2.12

c d o h
☐ sandpaper letters
☐ sensory tray
☐ stapler

Part 1 Directions:
1. Prepare a shallow tray and fill it with salt, sand, or cornmeal.
2. Review the sandpaper letter /c/. Trace three times while saying the sound, then invite your child to do the same.
3. Show your child how to write the letter in the sensory tray with your finger after tracing the sandpaper letter. Show your child how to gently shake the tray to redistribute the material to give a clean writing surface. Invite your child to write the letter with her finger.
4. Repeat with the other three letters in this sound group.

Part 2 Directions:
1. Invite your child to make a book out of the letters by cutting apart the strips on this page, stacking them, and stapling the booklet on the left-hand side.
2. Your child should be able to identify the letter sound and connect the letter sound to the beginning sound in each picture.
3. On the back of each strip, your child can practice writing with a pencil.
4. NOTE: To make these re-usable, laminate then cut, and use a dry-erase marker for tracing and writing.

c

d

o

h

Lesson 2.13

c d o h

☐ pencil OR counters
OR
☐ laminating sheet + 4 clothes pins

Directions:
Invite your child to circle or place a counter on top of the correct picture to match each beginning letter sound.

Re-Usable Shelf Work:
Laminate sheet. Cut individual cards. Place clothespins in a basket next to the cards and invite your child to clip the clothespin on the correct picture to match each beginning sound.
Show your child how to check his work by flipping over the card.

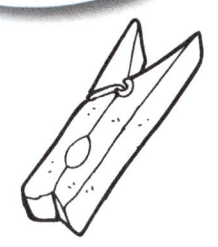

c

d

o

h

KEY: cat, dog, hat, otter

65

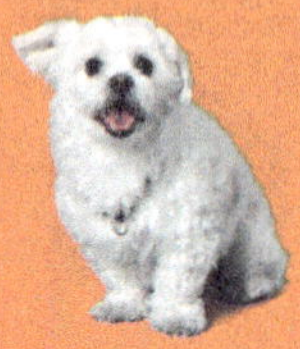

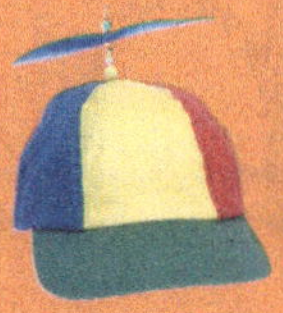

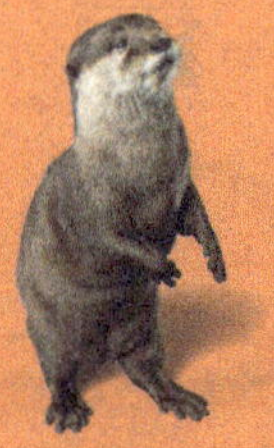

Lesson 2.14

Directions:
1. Laminate (optional, but recommended), cut, and add the alphabet tiles to your organizer.
2. Read each new letter sound.
3. Build the word, "cat" together on the first Pink Series Word Building Card for this unit.
4. Invite your child to build as many of the words as he shows interest on the Pink Series Word Cards pages.

c d o h
- [ ] laminating sheet (optional)
- [ ] movable alphabet organizer

o c d h
o c d h
o c d h
o c d h
o c d h

Lesson 2.14
continued

cdoh movable alphabet

Directions:
1. Build the first card together, segmenting each sound slowly.
2. Invite your child to build as many words as he shows interest and/or as time permits.
3. See **Appendix C** for visual step-by-step instructions.

3

4

5

69

6

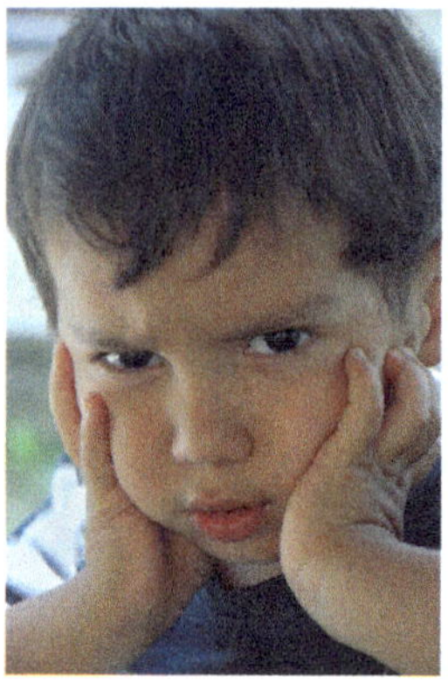

7

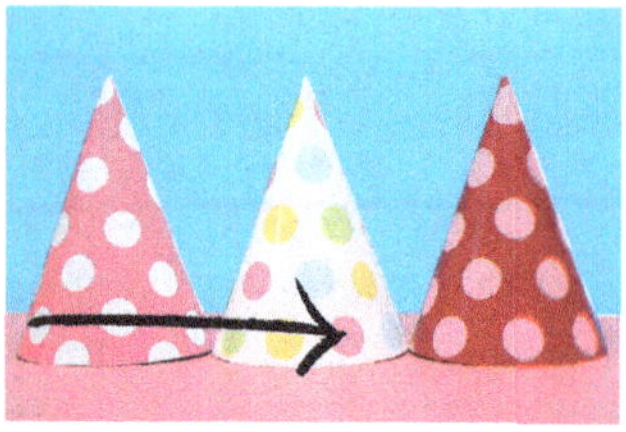

8

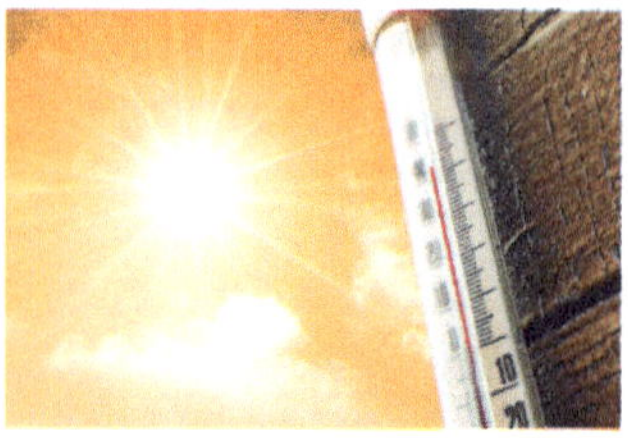

9

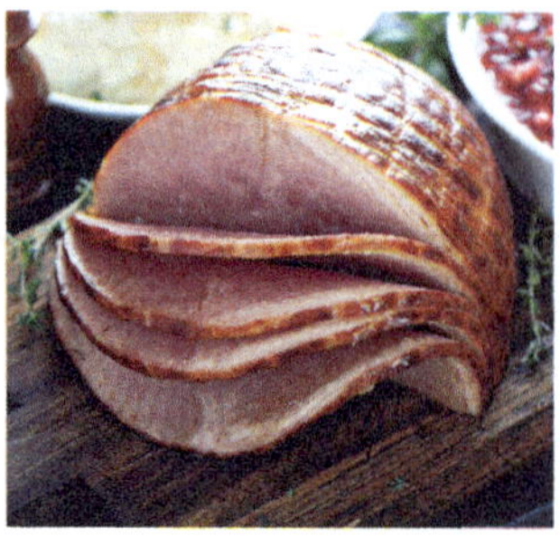

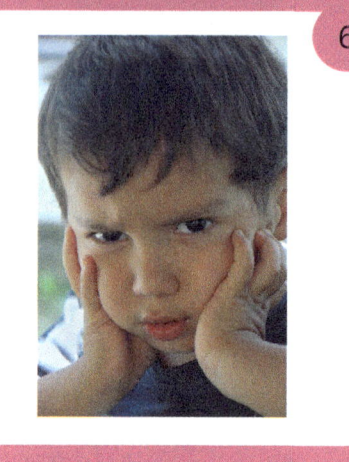

10

11

12

71

13

c d o h
☐ sandpaper letters
☐ sensory tray (optional)
☐ movable alphabet

Unit 2 Assessment

Directions:
1. Using the sandpaper letters you made for this unit (c, d, o, and h), invite your child to identify each sound as you hold up one letter at a time.

☐ c   ☐ d   ☐ o   ☐ h

2. Using your sensory tray or the writing lines below, invite your child to write one of each letter.

c   d   o   h

3. Match the letter to the object by its beginning sound.

o

c

d

h

72

Unit 2 Assessment

4. Build the following words with the movable alphabet by segmenting the words into their individual sounds.

Assessment Results and Next Steps:

Depending on how your child performed on this assessment, you may want to review letter sounds and letter formation before moving on to Unit 3. If your child made minor errors, feel free to move on, as there is review built into the entire program!

For further review if needed, see **Appendix A** for a list of games you can play with your child using the materials in the workbook!

If handwriting is a concern, consider incorporating more fine motor work into your child's day, such as: cutting, sewing, using puzzles with knobs, coloring, tracing, shading, helping in the kitchen, sorting, buttoning, zipping etc. In a Montessori environment, these kinds of activities are usually referred to as "Practical Life" activities and the uses are twofold: teaching practical skills that the child can use each day to help himself, and strengthening the muscles of the hand, wrist, and fingers to prepare for writing. Do not let handwriting prevent you from moving forward. Children can "write" with the movable alphabet for the duration of this program.

Unit 3

Pronunciation Guide

In traditional Montessori education settings, only **one sound** is used when introducing each letter. We all know there is more than one sound for the letter "a," but we only use the short sound /ă/ like in alligator in this Reading Games curriculum. Later on, in the Green Reading material, a child is learned multiple pronunciations for letters. For example, a child will learn that when adding a silent e, the letter a makes the long /a/ sound.

For now, stick with the sounds represented in each pronunciation guide.

Note: All vowels will be pronounced with their short sounds in this curriculum.

b	🐻	bear
r	🐀	rat
i	🐛	inchworm
g	🐐	goat

Handwriting Guide

We won't be doing too much handwriting on paper, but every time you show your child how to write a letter by tracing a sandpaper letter, you need to be sure to use the proper handwriting strokes.

Most of the time, you will not pick up your pencil from the paper (or fingers from the sandpaper letter). The only time you will pick up your hand is when you see a **red number 2**.

Important: If your child is left-handed, show her the strokes using your left hand. If your child is right-handed, show her the strokes with your right hand.

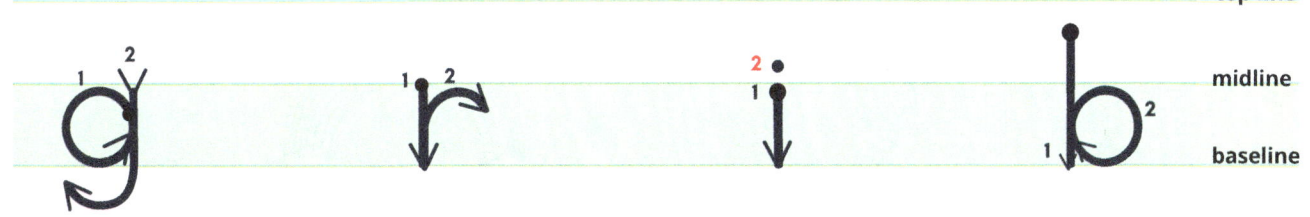

g	r	i	b
Start at the dot and curve to the left up to the midline, then curve down to the baseline, back through the dot and straight up to the midline. Then retrace the line straight down through the baseline, making a hook to the left under the baseline all in a single stroke.	Start at the midline and draw a straight line down to the baseline. Retrace your line, curving away to the right and up to the midline, ending slightly below the midline.	Start at the midline and draw a straight line down to the baseline. Pick up your pencil and draw a dot above the midline.	Start near (or at) the top line and draw a straight line down to the baseline. Without picking up your pencil, retrace your line almost to the midline and curve up to the right to touch the midline, then down to the baseline and curve back to your vertical line.

75

b r i g
☐ crayons

Lesson 3.1

Directions:
1. Say, "We are going to play *I Spy*. Listen carefully and follow my directions."
2. "I spy something that starts with /b/ and can hold many different things. It is often made of cardboard. Can you put your finger on it? What is it?" [Box.] "What sound do you hear at the beginning of *box*?" [/b/] "Color the box brown."
3. "I spy something that starts with /b/ that children like to snuggle and hug. Can you put your finger on it? What is it?" [Bear.] "What sound do you hear at the beginning of *bear*?" [/b/] "Draw a circle around the bear."
4. "I spy something that starts with /b/. You can put it on a present or in a little girl's hair. Can you put your finger on it? What is it?" [Bow.] "What sound do you hear at the beginning of *bow*?" [/b/] "Draw polka-dots on the bow."
5. "I spy something that starts with /b/ and has a cover and pages. Put your finger on it. What is it?" [Book.] "What sound do you hear at the beginning of *book*?" [/b/] "Draw a square around the book."
6. "I spy something that starts with /b/ and you can use it to play with your friends at the beach. Put your finger on it. What is it?" [Ball.] "What sound do you hear at the beginning of *ball*?" [/b/] "Color the ball however you want."

Directions:
1. Say, "We are going to play *I Spy*. Listen carefully and follow my directions."
2. "I spy something that starts with /r/, shines in the sky after rain, and has many colors. Can you put your finger on it? What is it?" [Rainbow.] "What sound do you hear at the beginning of *rainbow*?" [/r/] "Color the rainbow."
3. "I spy something that starts with /r/ and is useful when gardening or clearing the yard of fallen leaves. Can you put your finger on it? What is it?" [Rake.] "What sound do you hear at the beginning of *rake*?" [/r/] "Circle the rake."
4. "I spy something that starts with /r/. When you see this falling from the sky, you may choose to use an umbrella. Can you put your finger on it? What is it?" [Rain.] "What sound do you hear at the beginning of *rain*?" [/r/] "Color the rain drops."
5. "I spy something that starts with /r/ and is a path for cars. Put your finger on it. What is it?" [Road.] "What sound do you hear in the beginning of *road*?" [/r/] "Color the road black."
6. "I spy something that starts with /r/ and is used to tie things together. Put your finger on it. What is it?" [Rope.] "What sound do you hear at the beginning of *rope*?" [/r/] "Put an X through the rope."

Lesson 3.2

brig
☐ pink and brown crayons

Directions: Color the objects that begin with **/b/ brown** and **/r/ pink.**

77

brig

☐ 3 small objects each that begin with /b/ and /r/
☐ and/or cut-and-paste sound cards from Appendix F

Lesson 3.3

Head's up!: Prep sandpaper letters for tomorrow's lesson.

Directions - Option #1:
1. Gather 3 objects for each sound that are small enough to fit (or roughly fit) onto this page. (block, bug, bun, buckle, bear, rice, rope, raspberry, remote, race car, or see Appendix D for more ideas.)
2. Place objects in a basket or on the table in mixed order.
3. Name each picture ("bike" and "rat.")
4. Invite your child to sort the objects into the boxes with the same beginning sound.

Directions - Option #2:
1. Locate the proper sound group sorting cards in Appendix F. Cut apart (or invite your child to cut apart) the sound cards.
2. Sort then save for the upcoming sandpaper letter sorting lesson.

Lesson 3.4

b r i g
☐ glitter glue
☐ 3+ small objects for each sound /b/, /r/

☐ **Part 1 Directions:**
1. Make the sandpaper letters. See Appendix E.
2. Introduce the sandpaper letters. Show one at a time and follow the script below.

   Sandpaper Letter Script:
   1. Pick up the *b* in the opposite of your child's dominant hand. (If your child is right-handed, pick up the letter with your left hand. If your child is left-handed, pick up the letter with your right hand.)
   2. Say, "This says /b/."
   3. With the pointer and middle fingers of your other hand (matching child's dominant hand), trace the letter the same way you would write it as you say the sound /b/. Do this 3 times.
   4. Invite your child to say the sound while tracing the letter three times.
   5. Repeat for the next sound.

☐ **Part 2 Directions:**
Sort the household objects used in the previous lesson underneath each sandpaper letter.

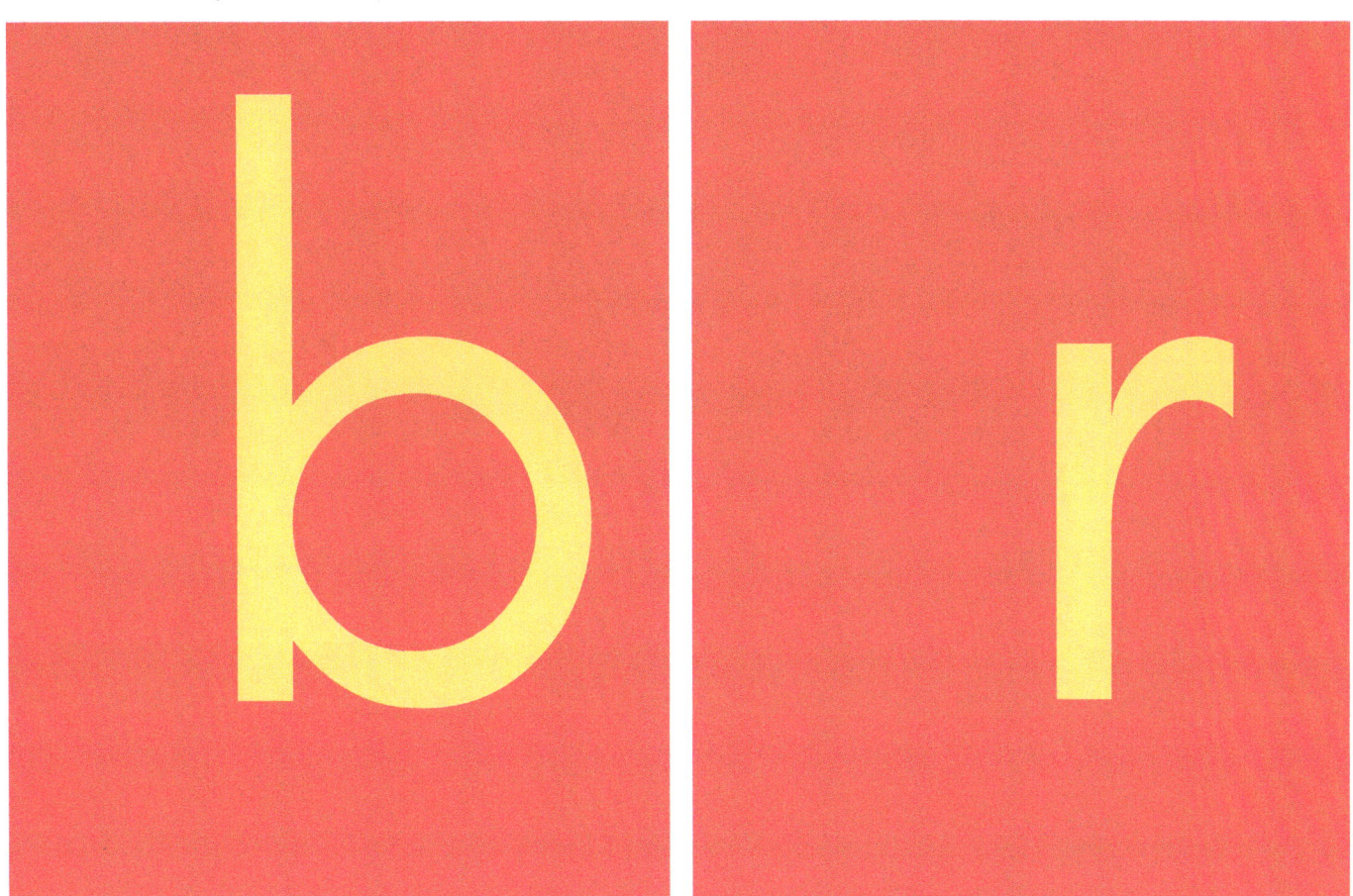

79

Lesson 3.5

Directions:
1. Say, "We are going to play *I Spy*. Listen carefully and follow my directions."
2. "I spy something that starts with /i/ and is the opposite of out. Can you put your finger on it? What is it?" [In.] "What sound do you hear at the beginning of *in*?" [/i/] "Trace the "in" arrow with any color."
3. "I spy something that starts with /i/, and can be measured with a ruler. There are 12 of these in 1 foot. Can you put your finger on it? What is it?" [Inch.] "What sound do you hear at the beginning of *inch*?" [/i/] "Shade the ruler between the numbers 1 and 2, to represent 1 inch."
4. "I spy something that starts with /i/. It is a group of bugs. What is another name for bugs? Can you put your finger on them? What are they called?" [Insects.] "What sound do you hear at the beginning of *insects*?" [/i/] "Circle the group of insects."
5. "I spy something that starts with /i/ and is a lizard with a long tail. Put your finger on it. What is it?" [Iguana.] "What sound do you hear at the beginning of *iguana*?" [/i/] "Color the iguana green."
6. "I spy something that starts with /i/ and is a home that can be found in very cold regions of the world. It is made out of ice. Put your finger on it. What is it?" [Igloo.] "What sound do you hear at the beginning of *igloo*?" [/i/] "Draw a box around the igloo."

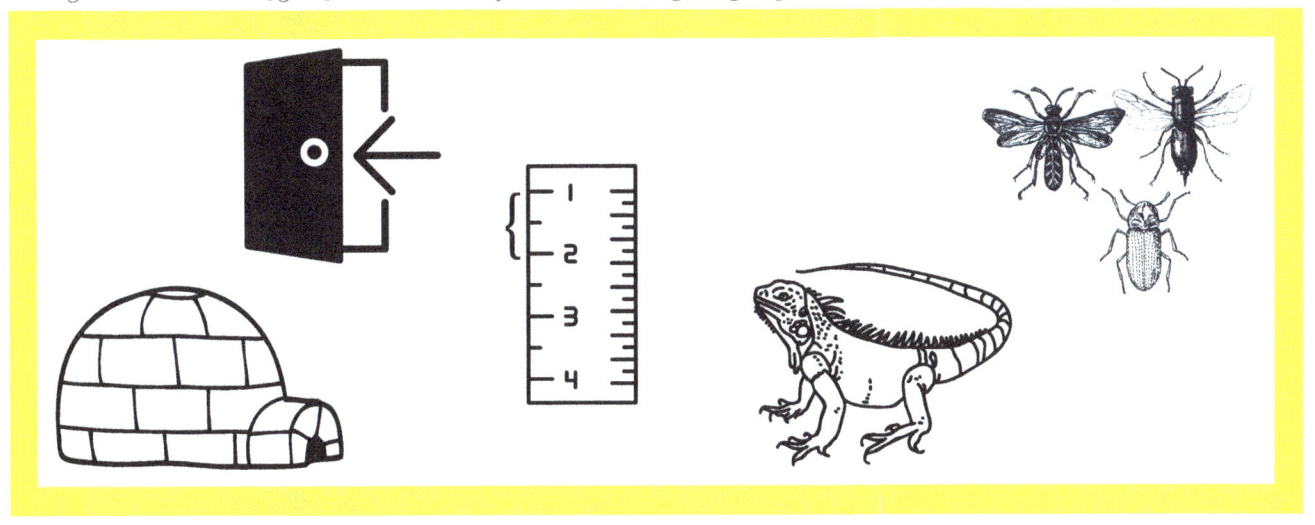

Directions:
1. Say, "We are going to play *I Spy*. Listen carefully and follow my directions."
2. "I spy something that starts with /g/ and lives on a farm. Its milk can be made into a soft cheese. Can you put your finger on it? What is it?" [Goat.] "What sound do you hear at the beginning of *goat*?" [/g/] "Draw a circle around the goat."
3. "I spy something that starts with /g/ and is used to block a path. It opens and closes. Can you put your finger on it? What is it?" [Gate.] "What sound do you hear at the beginning of *gate*?" [/g/] "Draw an X through the gate."
4. "I spy something that starts with /g/. It is small, white, round, and sinks in water. It is hit with a club. Can you put your finger on it? What is it?" [Golfball.] "What sound do you hear at the beginning of *golfball*?" [/g/] "Draw a smiley face on the golf ball."
5. "I spy something that starts with /g/ and is inside a machine. You can chew this, but you shouldn't swallow it. Put your finger on it. What is it?" [Gum.] "What sound do you hear in the beginning of *gum*?" [/g/] "Color the balls of gum inside the machine."
6. "I spy something that starts with /g/ and contains fuel for vehicles. Put your finger on it. What is it?" [Gas pump.] "What sound do you hear at the beginning of *gas*?" [/g/] "Color the gas pump red."

brig
☐ red and green crayons

Lesson 3.6

Directions: Color the objects that begin with **/i/ red** and **/g/ green**.

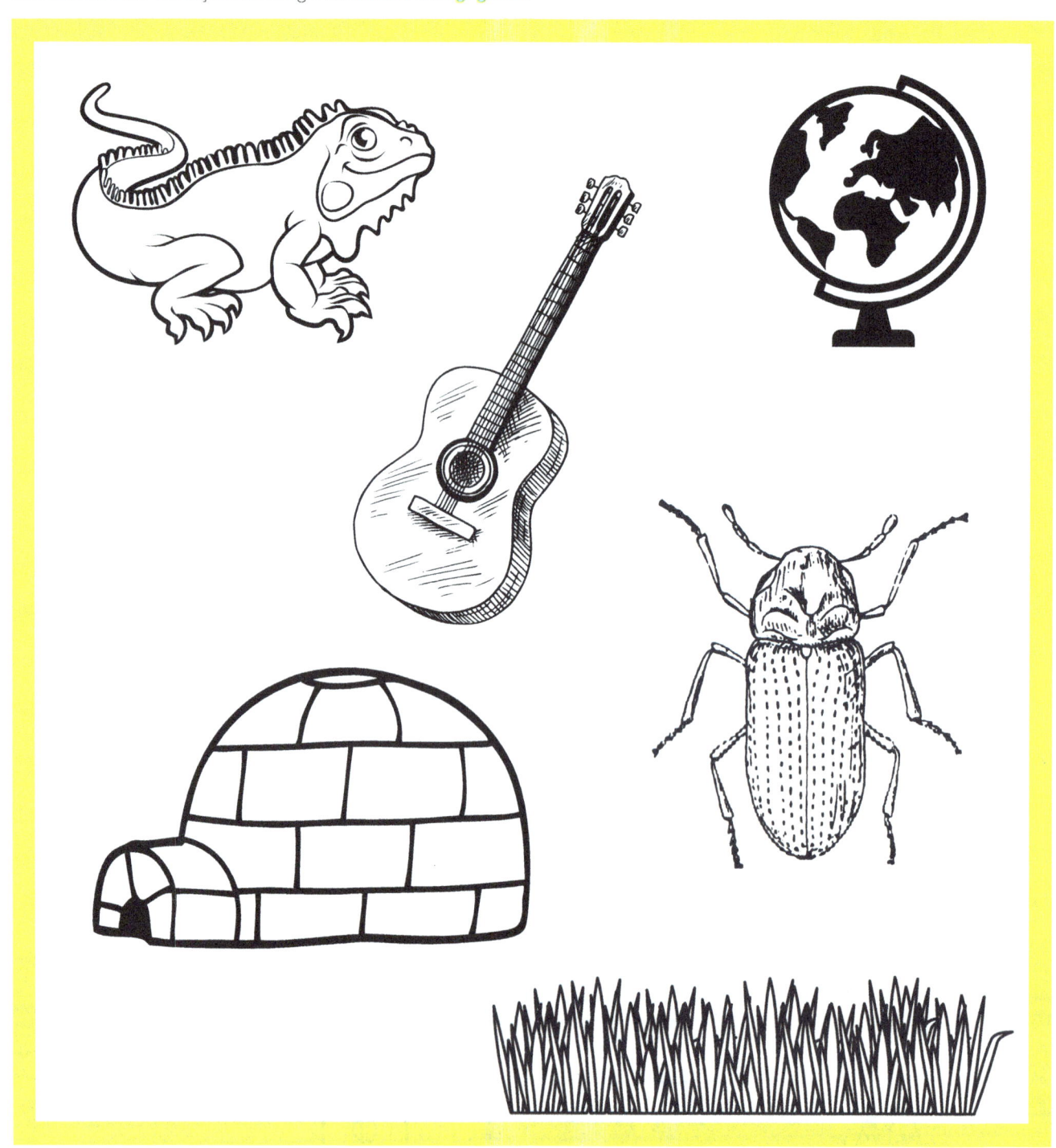

key: iguana, slope, guitar, insect, igloo, grass

82

Head's up!:
Prep sandpaper letters for tomorrow's lesson.

Lesson 3.7

b r i g

☐ 3 objects each that begin with /i/ and /g/
☐ and/or cut-and-paste sound cards from Appendix F

Directions - Option #1:
1. Gather 3 objects for each sound that are small enough to fit (or roughly fit) onto this page. (Inch marked on ruler, ink, iguana toy, itch cream, goat toy, game, green crayon or color tablet, glue, grass or see Appendix D for more ideas.)
2. Place objects in a basket or on the table in mixed order.
3. Name each picture ("igloo" and "glue.")
4. Invite your child to sort the objects into the boxes with the same beginning sound.

Directions - Option #2:
1. Locate the proper sound group sorting cards in Appendix F. Cut apart (or invite your child to cut apart) the sound cards.
2. Sort then save for the upcoming sandpaper letter sorting lesson.

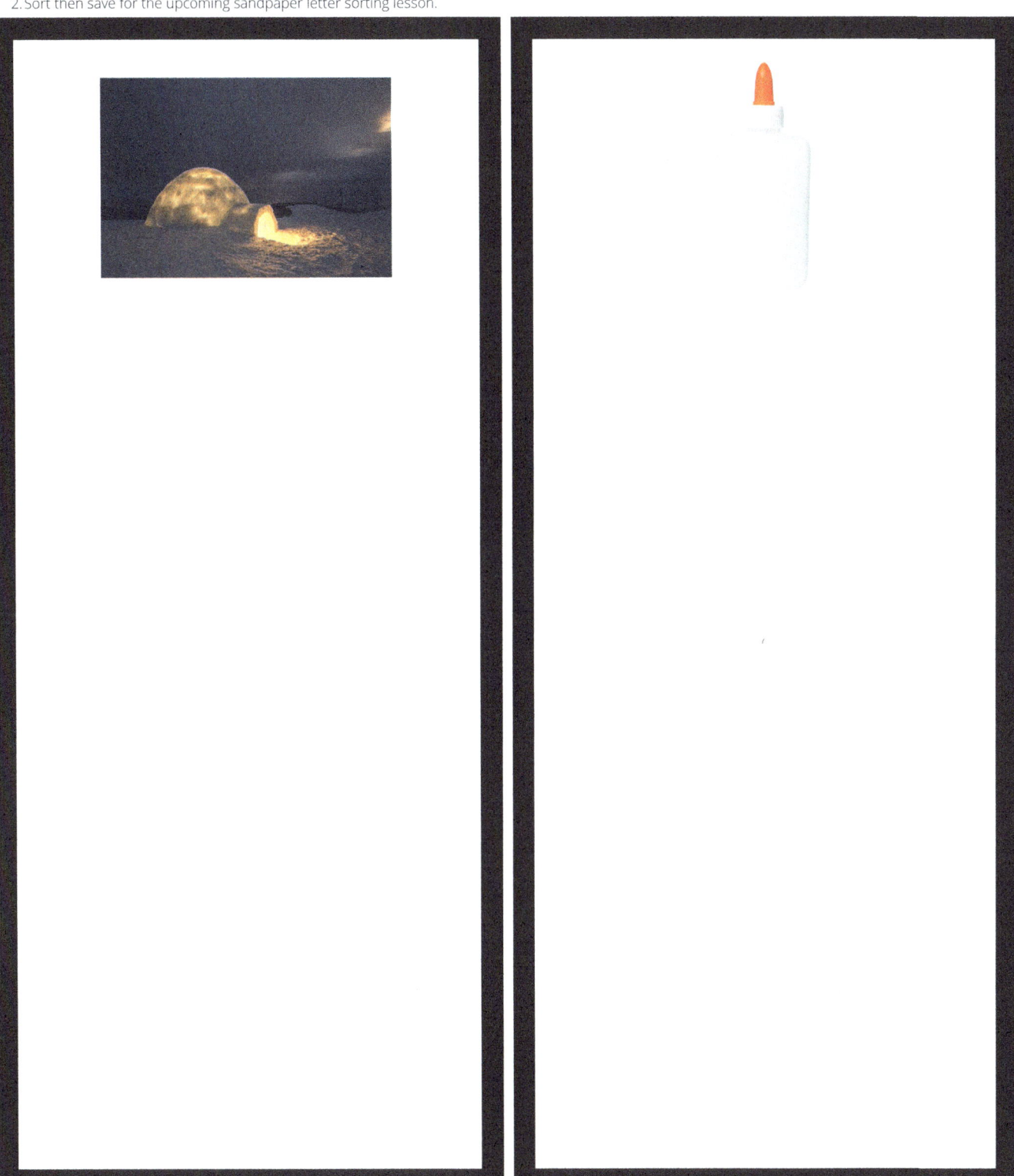

83

Lesson 3.8

b r i g
☐ glitter glue
☐ 3+ small objects for /i/ and /g/

☐ **Part 1 Directions:**
1. Make the sandpaper letters. See Appendix E.
2. Introduce the sandpaper letters. Show one at a time and follow the script below.

   Sandpaper Letter Script:
   1. Pick up the *i* in the opposite of your child's dominant hand. (If your child is right-handed, pick up the letter with your left hand. If your child is left-handed, pick up the letter with your right hand.)
   2. Say, "This says /i/."
   3. With the pointer and middle fingers of your other hand (matching child's dominant hand), trace the letter the same way you would write it as you say the sound /i/. Do this 3 times.
   4. Invite your child to say the sound while tracing the letter three times.
   5. Repeat for the next sound.

☐ **Part 2 Directions:**
Sort the household objects used in the previous lesson underneath each sandpaper letter.

85

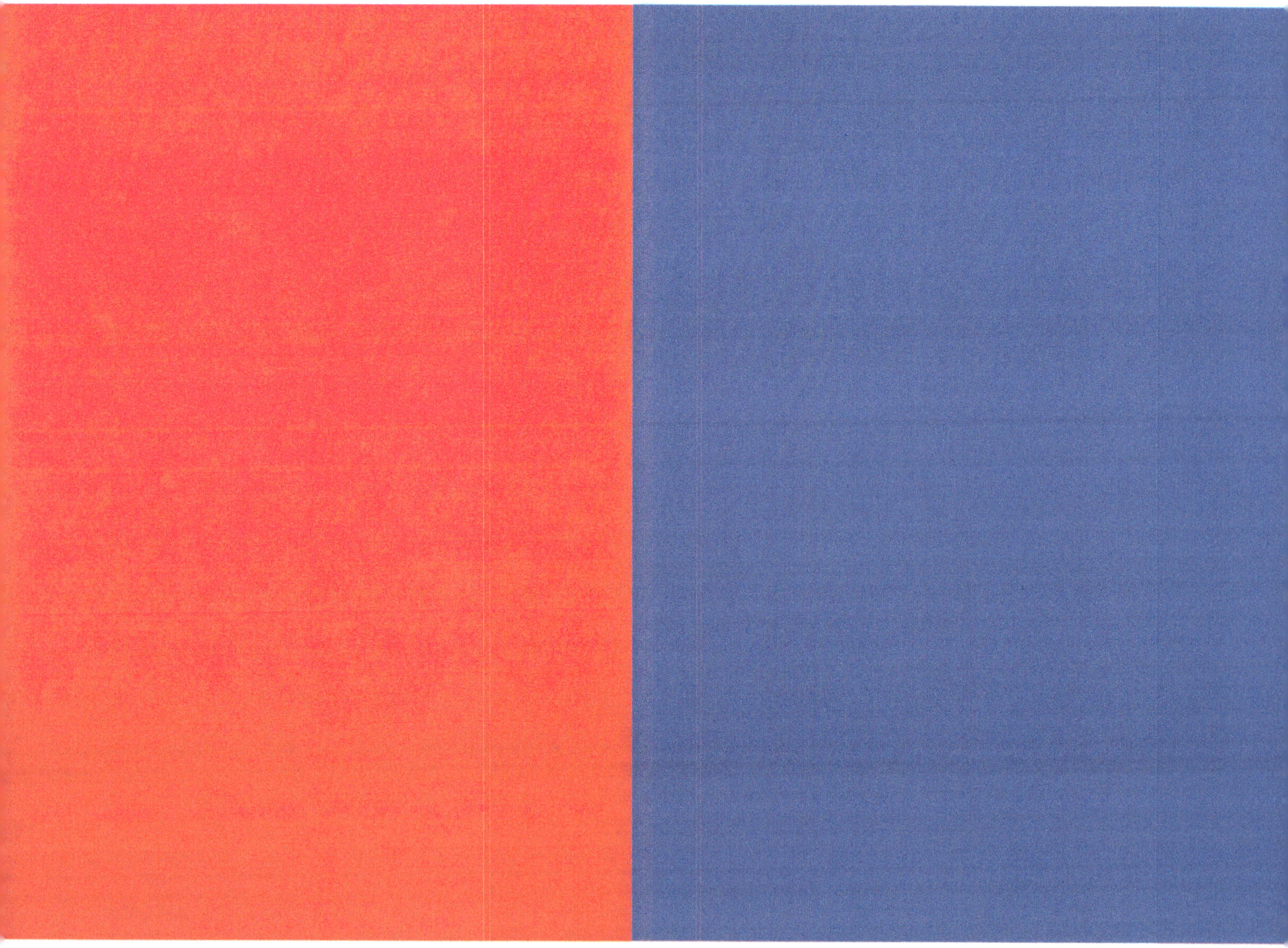

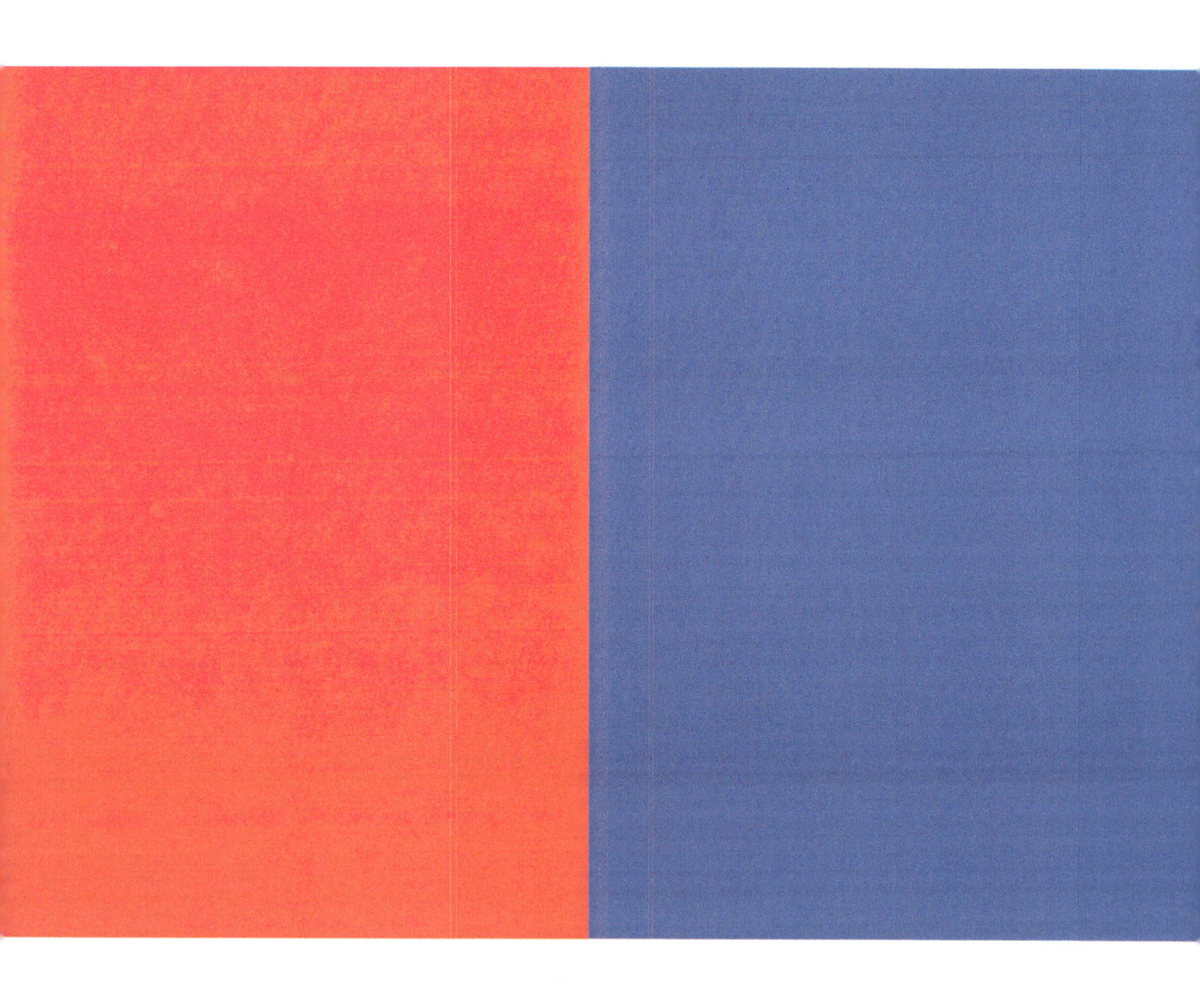

Lesson 3.9

brig
☐ counters/chips

Directions:
1. Cut out the BINGO cards.
2. Choose a game board and play with your student(s). Cut them from the workbook or leave them attached.
3. Shuffle and place cards face down in a single pile.
4. Take turns drawing one card at a time. Each player places a chip (any counter will work) on top of the matching letter on his/her BINGO game board.
5. Each player should cover his/her entire board.

Optional Extra Game: Go Fish
See Appendix E for directions.

KEY:
g: gold, green, grass
r: rose, rocks, rain
i: iguana, inchworm, itch
b: bed, beans, belt

g	g	g	b
r	r	r	b
i	i	i	b

87

g	r	i
b	i	r
g	b	b

r	i	b
g	i	g
r	b	i

g	r	r
b	i	g
i	r	b

i	g	b
b	g	i
r	r	i

Directions: Play one round of the **"My Letter Sound Adventure Game."** Here are the new cards for your **My Letter Sound Adventure Game.** See Appendix B for directions on *how* to play the game and the removable game board.

Lesson 3.10

brig
☐ My Letter Sound Adventure Game (Appendix B)

49
50
51
52
53
54
55
56
57

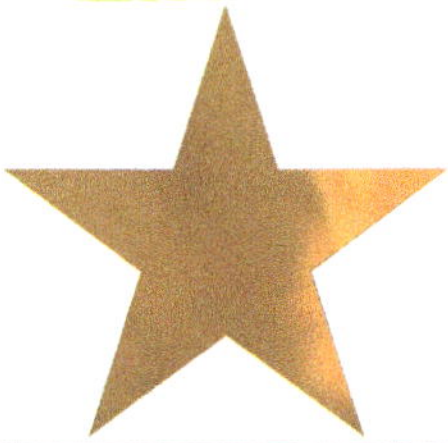

58

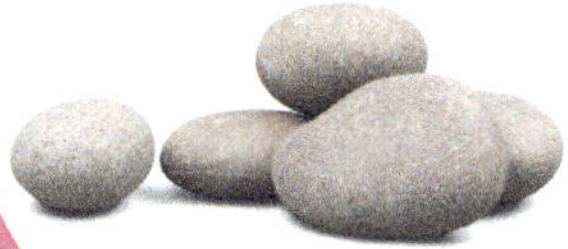

59

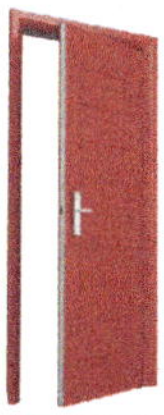

60

61

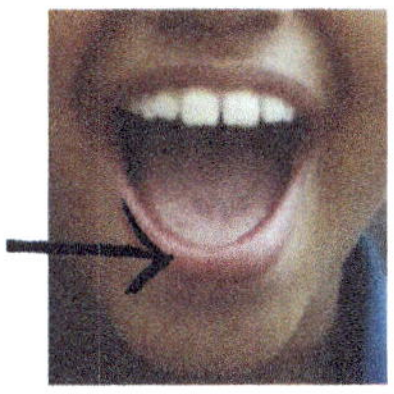

62

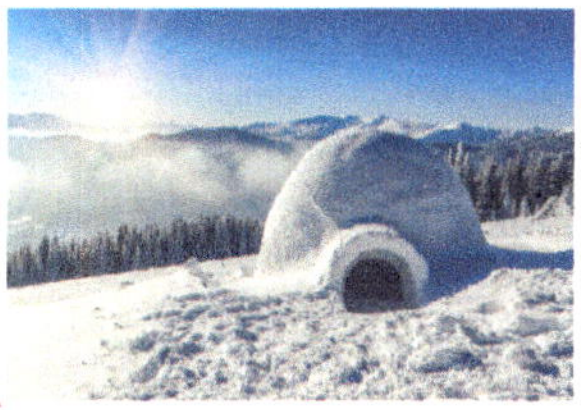

63

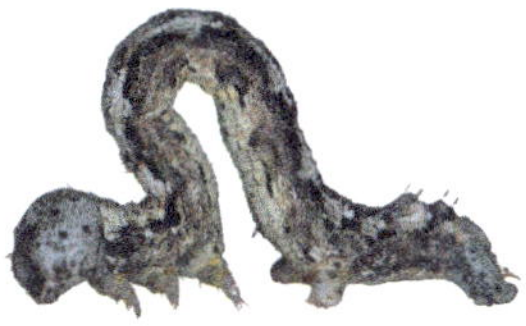

64

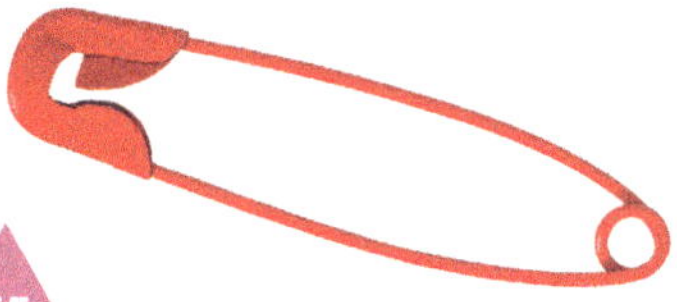

65

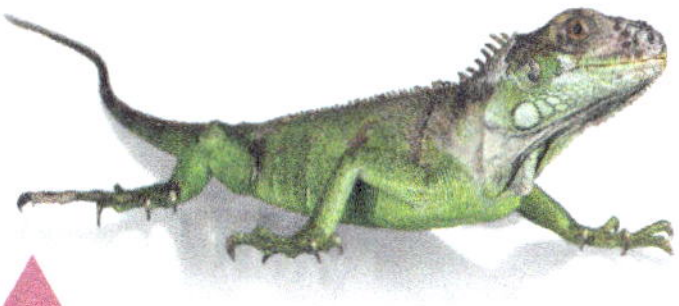

66

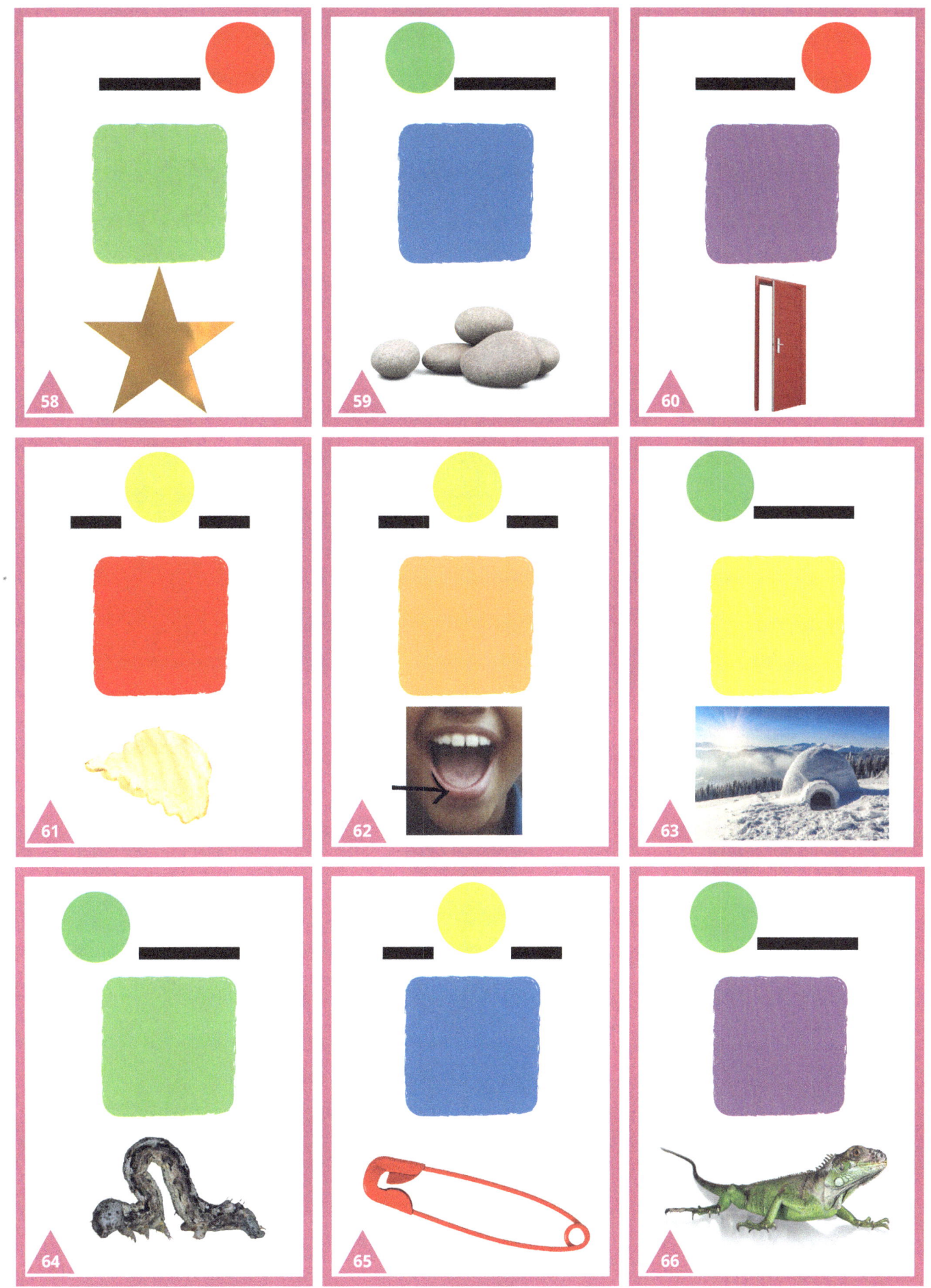

Key 49-72

49. gold
50. hog
51. bag
52. grass
53. log
54. gate
55. rake
56. rabbit
57. car
58. star
59. rocks
60. door

85. umbrella
86. cup
87. umpire
88. up
89. mug
90. hug
91. water
92. whale
93. cow
94. bow
95. worm
96. mow

Lesson 3.11

b r i g
- dice printable (Appendix A)
- chips/counters

☐ **Part 1 Directions:**
1. Laminate page (optional) then cut apart individual cards.
2. Invite your student to spread the letter cards out across the top of his/her work space horizontally.
3. Shuffle the picture cards and invite your child to look at the picture, say the name of the object, and identify the beginning sound. Then place the picture card underneath the proper letter, making a column. There is a control of error on the back of each card so your child can learn to do this activity independently. See Appendix A for a visual.

☐ **Part 2 Directions:**
Make this into a game! Play "Roll, Spot, and Cover." See game instructions and printable dice in Appendix A.

| g | r | i | b |

g: goat, gas, gate.   r: rice, raspberries, rake   i: igloo, iguana, inch.   b: boat, baseball, bat

97

raspberries	gate	rice	goat
boat	igloo	rake	gas
bat	inch	baseball	iguana

Lesson 3.12

brig
☐ sensory tray
☐ stapler

☐ **Part 1 Directions:**
1. Prepare a shallow tray and fill it with salt, sand, or cornmeal.
2. Review the sandpaper letter /s/. Trace three times while saying the sound, then invite your child to do the same.
3. Show your child how to write the letter in the sensory tray with your finger after tracing the sandpaper letter. Show your child how to gently shake the tray to redistribute the material to give a clean writing surface. Invite your child to write the letter with her finger.
4. Repeat with the other three letters in this sound group.

☐ **Part 2 Directions:**
1. Invite your child to make a book out of the letters by cutting apart the strips on this page, stacking them, and stapling the booklet on the left-hand side.
2. Your child should be able to identify the letter sound and connect the letter sound to the beginning sound in each picture.
3. On the back of each strip, your child can practice writing with a pencil.
4. NOTE: To make these re-usable, laminate then cut, and use a dry-erase marker for tracing and writing.

g: galaxy, garage, gate   r: rattle, rocks, rain   i: itch, inchworm, igloo.   b: bacon, bell, bike g

r

i

b

Lesson 3.13

brig

☐ pencil or counters
OR
☐ laminating sheet + 4 clothes pins

Directions:
Invite your child to circle or place a counter on top of the correct picture to match each beginning letter sound.

Re-Usable Shelf Work:
Laminate sheet. Cut individual cards. Place clothespins in a basket next to the cards and invite your child to clip the clothespin on the correct picture to match each beginning sound.
Show your child how to check the back of each card as a control of error.

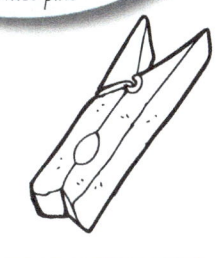

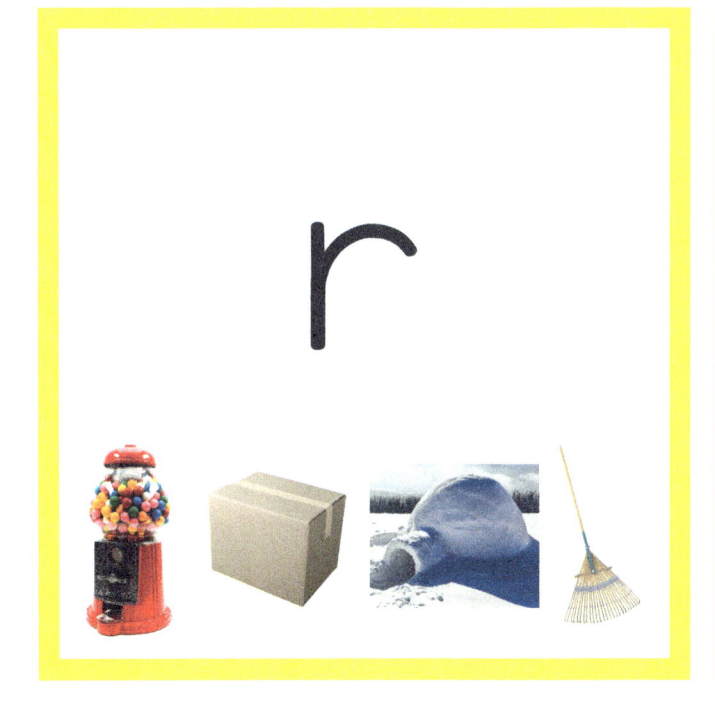

KEY: gum, rake, igloo, box

101

Lesson 3.14

Directions:
1. Laminate (optional, but recommended), cut, and add the alphabet tiles to your organizer.
2. Read each new letter sound.
3. Build the word, "rat" together on the first Pink Series Word Building Card for this unit.
4. Invite your child to build as many of the words as he shows interest on the Pink Series Word Cards pages.

brig
movable alphabet organizer

i b r g
i b r g
i b r g
i b r g
i b r g

Lesson 3.14
continued

▲ b r i g
☐ movable alphabet organizer

Directions:
1. Build the first card together, segmenting each sound slowly.
2. Invite your child to build as many words as he shows interest and/or as time permits.
3. See **Appendix C** for visual step-by-step instructions.

14

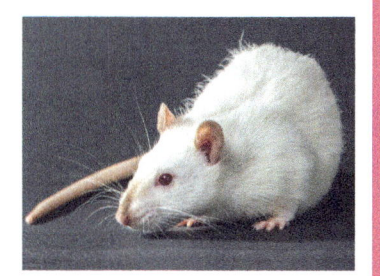

15

16

105

17

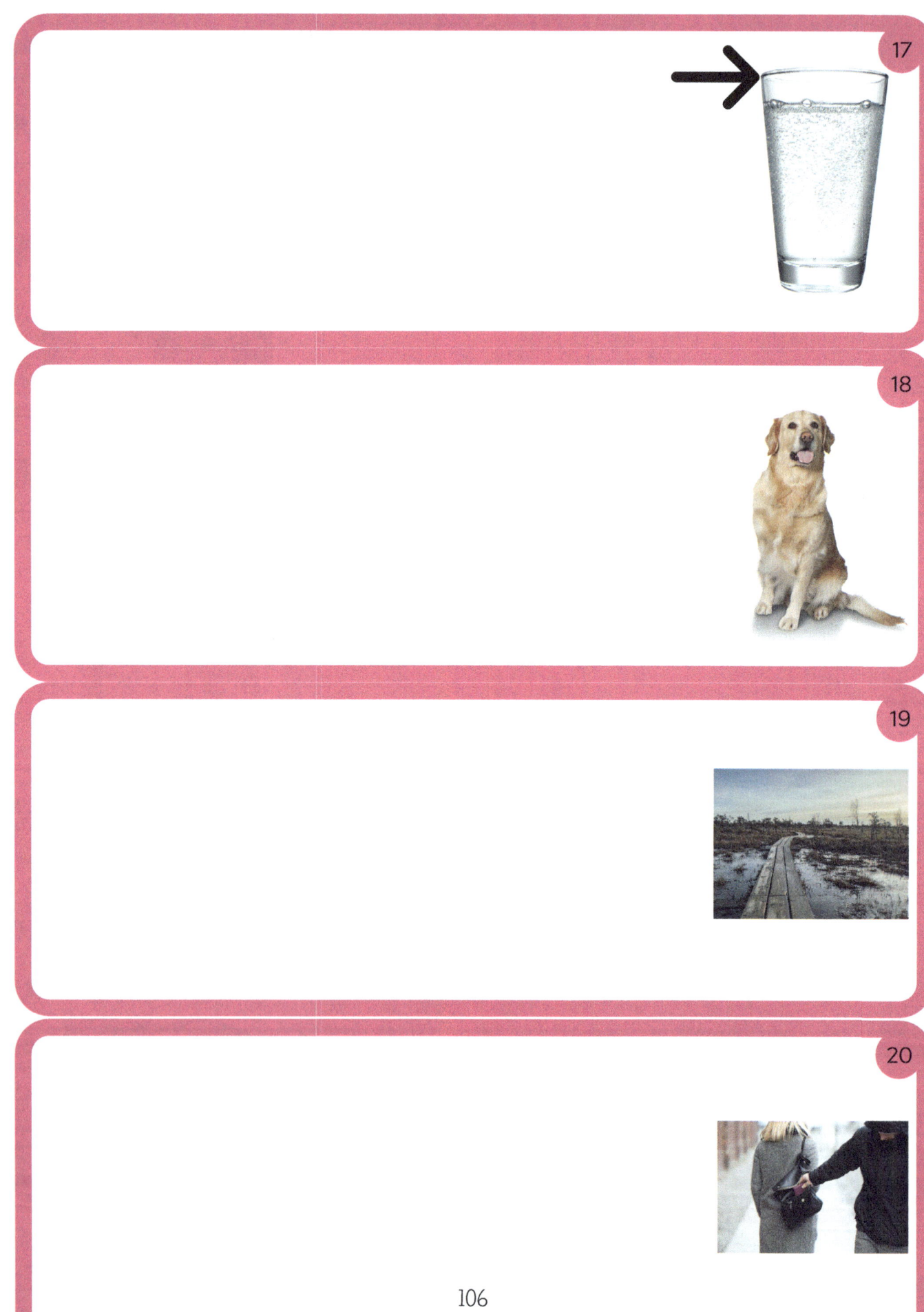

18

19

20

107

25

26

27

28

108

29

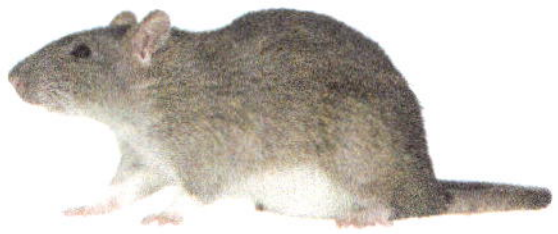

30

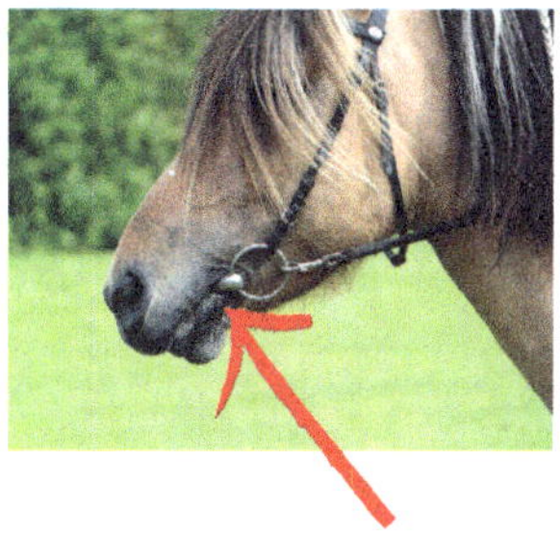

31

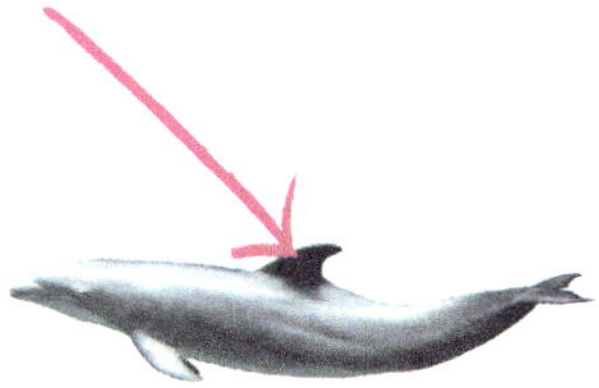

32

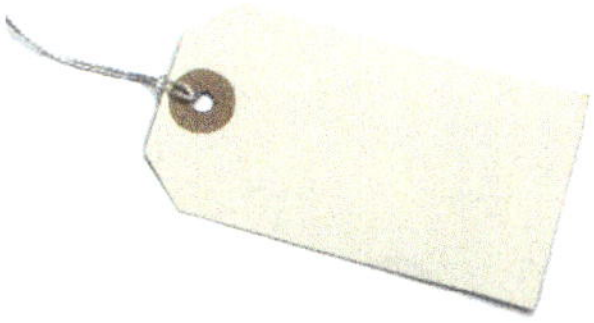

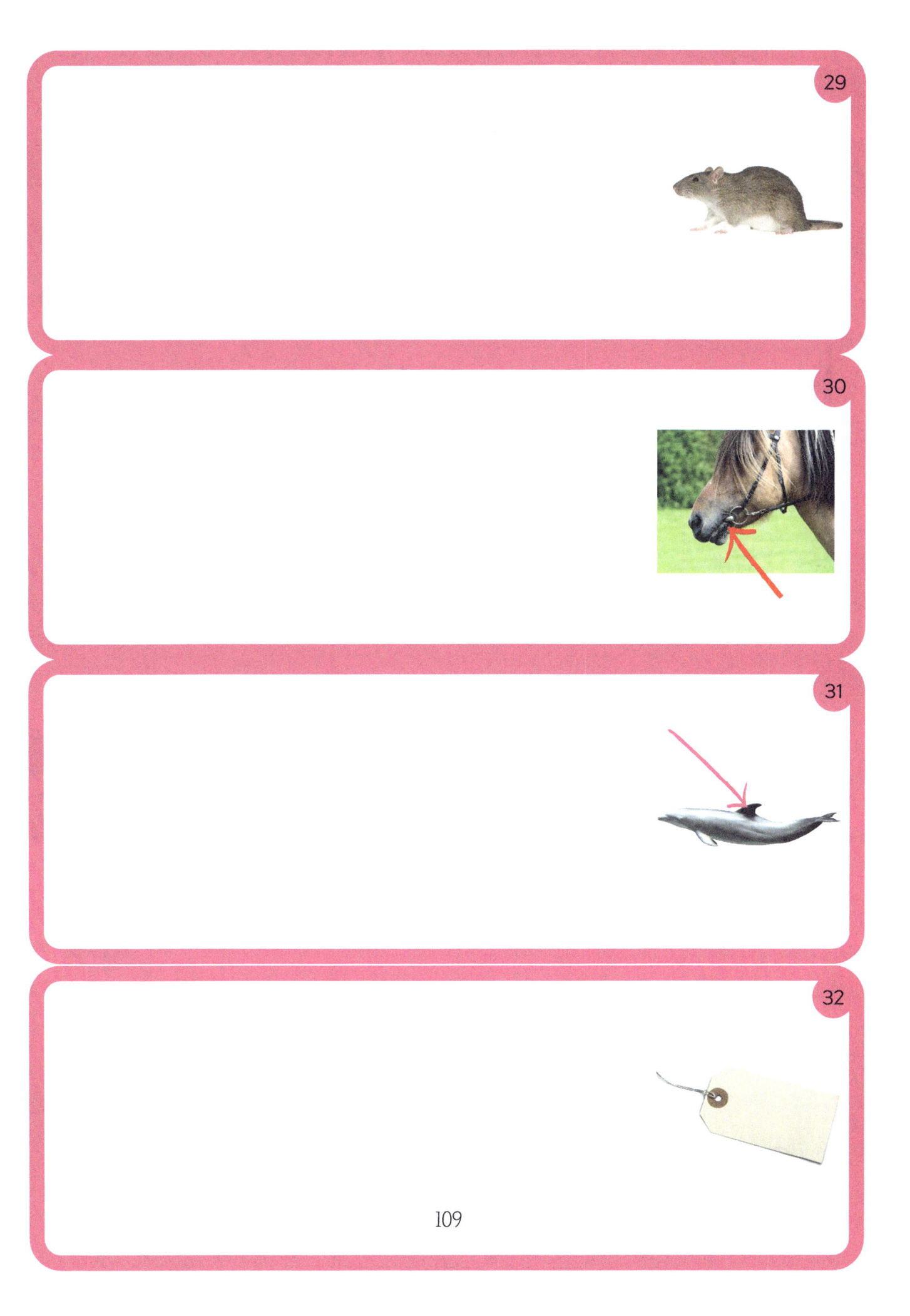

b r i g
☐ sandpaper letters
☐ sensory tray (optional)
☐ movable alphabet

Unit 3 Assessment

Directions:
1. Using the sandpaper letters you made for this unit (b, r, i, and g), invite your child to identify each sound as you hold up one letter at a time.

☐ b   ☐ r   ☐ i   ☐ g

2. Using your sensory tray or the writing lines below, invite your child to write one of each letter.

b   r   i   g

3. Match the letter to the object by its beginning sound.

b

r

i

g

110

Unit 3 Assessment

brig ☐ movable alphabet

4. Build the following words with the movable alphabet by segmenting the words into their individual sounds.

Assessment Results and Next Steps:

Depending on how your child performed on this assessment, you may want to review letter sounds and letter formation before moving on to Unit 4. If your child made minor errors, feel free to move on, as there is review built into the entire program!

For further review if needed, see **Appendix A** for a list of games you can play with your child using the materials in the workbook!

If handwriting is a concern, consider incorporating more fine motor work into your child's day, such as: cutting, sewing, using puzzles with knobs, coloring, tracing, shading, helping in the kitchen, sorting, buttoning, zipping etc. In a Montessori environment, these kinds of activities are usually referred to as "Practical Life" activities and the uses are twofold: teaching practical skills that the child can use each day to help himself, and strengthening the muscles of the hand, wrist, and fingers to prepare for writing. Do not let handwriting prevent you from moving forward. Children can "write" with the movable alphabet for the duration of this program.

Unit 4

p n u w

Pronunciation Guide

In traditional Montessori education settings, only **one sound** is used when introducing each letter. We all know there is more than one sound for the letter "a," but we only use the short sound /ă/ like in alligator in this Reading Games curriculum. Later on, in the Green Reading material, a child is learned multiple pronunciations for letters. For example, a child will learn that when adding a silent e, the letter a makes the long /ā/ sound.

For now, stick with the sounds represented in each pronunciation guide.

Note: All vowels will be pronounced with their short sounds in this curriculum.

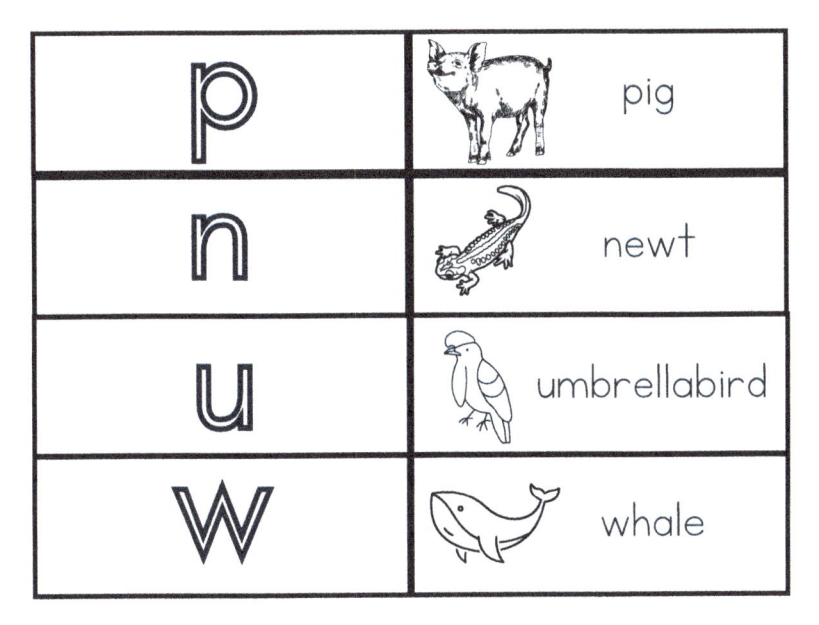

p	pig
n	newt
u	umbrellabird
w	whale

Handwriting Guide

We won't be doing too much handwriting on paper, but every time you show your child how to write a letter by tracing a sandpaper letter, you need to be sure to use the proper handwriting strokes.

Most of the time, you will not pick up your pencil from the paper (or fingers from the sandpaper letter). The only time you will pick up your hand is when you see a **red number 2**.

Important: If your child is left-handed, show her the strokes using your left hand. If your child is right-handed, show her the strokes with your right hand.

p	n	u	w
Start at the midline and draw a straight line down under the baseline. Without picking up your pencil, trace that line back up almost all the way to the midline, then curve up to the midline, circling around and down to the baseline, ending back at the original vertical line.	Start at the midline and draw a straight line down to the baseline. Without picking up your pencil, trace that line back almost to the midline, curving up to the midline, then down to the baseline.	Start at the midline and curve down to the baseline, then back up to the midline. Without picking up your pencil, draw a straight line down to the baseline.	Start at the midline and draw a slanted line down to the baseline, then up to the midline with another slanted line, then down, then up, making two "v" shapes.

p n u w
☐ crayons

Lesson 4.1

Directions:
1. Say, "We are going to play *I Spy*. Listen carefully and follow my directions."
2. "I spy something that starts with /p/ and makes a delicious dessert, especially when eaten hot right out of the oven. It is often filled with fruit. Can you put your finger on it? What is it?" [Pie.] "What sound do you hear at the beginning of *pie*?" [/p/] "Circle the pie."
3. "I spy something that starts with /p/ that you put food on. It needs to be washed after meals. Can you put your finger on it? What is it?" [Plate.] "What sound do you hear at the beginning of *plate*?" [/p/] "Draw your favorite food on the plate."
4. "I spy something that starts with /p/. You can use it to write, and it can be sharpened. Can you put your finger on it? What is it?" [Pencil.] "What sound do you hear at the beginning of *pencil*?" [/p/] "Color the pencil yellow."
5. "I spy something that starts with /p/ that has cheese, sauce, and sometimes other toppings. Put your finger on it. What is it?" [Pizza.] "What sound do you hear at the beginning of *pizza*?" [/p/] "Draw a box around the pizza."
6. "I spy something that starts with /p/ and you can use it to make pie or carve a face into it. Put your finger on it. What is it?" [Pumpkin.] "What sound do you hear at the beginning of *pumpkin*?" [/p/] "Color the pumpkin orange."

Directions:
1. Say, "We are going to play *I Spy*. Listen carefully and follow my directions."
2. "I spy something that starts with /n/ and is hammered into wood to hold it together. Can you put your finger on it? What is it?" [Nail.] "What sound do you hear at the beginning of *nail*?" [/n/] "Circle the nail."
3. "I spy something that starts with /n/ and is used to fetch objects out of water. Can you put your finger on it? What is it?" [Net.] "What sound do you hear at the beginning of *net*?" [/n/] "Draw something inside the net."
4. "I spy something that starts with /n/. You can write or draw inside it. Can you put your finger on it? What is it?" [Notebook.] "What sound do you hear at the beginning of *notebook*?" [/n/] "Color the notebook blue."
5. "I spy something that starts with /n/ and holds birds and their eggs. Put your finger on it. What is it?" [Nest.] "What sound do you hear in the beginning of *nest*?" [/n/] "Color nest brown."
6. "I spy something that starts with /n/ and is used to wipe food from fingers and faces. These are made of paper, but sometimes they can be made of cloth. Put your finger on them. What are they?" [Napkins.] "What sound do you hear at the beginning of *napkins*?" [/n/] "Put an X through the napkins."

114

Lesson 4.2

p n u w
☐ orange and purple crayons

Directions: Color the objects that begin with **/p/ purple** and **/n/ orange**.

115

o p n u w

☐ 3 small objects each that begin with /p/ and /n/
☐ and/or cut-and-paste sound cards from Appendix F

Lesson 4.3

Head's up!: Prep sandpaper letters for tomorrow's lesson.

Directions - Option #1:
1. Gather 3 objects for each sound that are small enough to fit (or roughly fit) onto this page. (pencil, paper, paperclip, putty, paint, pin, nuts, necklace, newspaper clipping, net, nectarine, napkin, or see Appendix D for more ideas.)
2. Place objects in a basket or on the table in mixed order.
3. Name each picture ("pillow" and "necklace.")
4. Invite your child to sort the objects into the boxes with the same beginning sound.

Directions - Option #2:
1. Locate the proper sound group sorting cards in Appendix F. Cut apart (or invite your child to cut apart) the sound cards.
2. Sort then save for the upcoming sandpaper letter sorting lesson.

116

Lesson 4.4

p n u w
- ☐ glitter glue
- ☐ 3+ objects for each sound

☐ **Part 1 Directions:**
1. Make the sandpaper letters. See Appendix E.
2. Introduce the sandpaper letters. Show one at a time and follow the script below.

   Sandpaper Letter Script:
   1. Pick up the *p* in the opposite of your child's dominant hand. (If your child is right-handed, pick up the letter with your left hand. If your child is left-handed, pick up the letter with your right hand.)
   2. Say, "This says /p/."
   3. With the pointer and middle fingers of your other hand (matching child's dominant hand), trace the letter the same way you would write it as you say the sound /p/. Do this 3 times.
   4. Invite your child to say the sound while tracing the letter three times.
   5. Repeat for the next sound.

☐ **Part 2 Directions:**
Sort the household objects used in the previous lesson underneath each sandpaper letter.

Lesson 4.5

o p n u w
☐ crayons

Directions:
1. Say, "We are going to play *I Spy*. Listen carefully and follow my directions."
2. "I spy something that starts with /u/ and represents the opposite of down. Can you put your finger on it? What is it?" [Up.] "What sound do you hear at the beginning of *up*?" [/u/] "Color the "up" arrow blue."
3. "I spy something that starts with /u/. It is a person who makes sure that rules are followed in a game. Can you put your finger on him? What is he?" [Umpire.] "What sound do you hear at the beginning of *umpire*?" [/u/] "Draw a circle around the umpire."
4. "I spy something that starts with /u/. It is the act of pulling a plug out of something. Can you put your finger on the picture? What is this called??" [Unplug.] "What sound do you hear at the beginning of *unplug*?" [/u/] "Put a box around the cords that are being unplugged."
5. "I spy something that starts with /u/ and keeps the rain off of one's head. Put your finger on it. What is it?" [Umbrella.] "What sound do you hear at the beginning of *umbrella*?" [/u/] "Color the umbrella your favorite color."
6. "I spy something that starts with /u/ and it is a word that tells us where the cat is in relation to the table. Put your finger on the cat. Where is the cat?" [Under the table.] "What sound do you hear at the beginning of *under*?" [/u/] "Draw a book on top of the table."

Directions:
1. Say, "We are going to play *I Spy*. Listen carefully and follow my directions."
2. "I spy something that starts with /w/ and is used to build things. It comes from a tree. Can you put your finger on it? What is it?" [Wood.] "What sound do you hear at the beginning of *wood*?" [/w/] "Color the piece of wood brown"
3. "I spy something that starts with /w/ and is found in the ocean. It can be large or small and when i reaches shore, it crashes on the beach. Can you put your finger on it? What is it?" [Wave.] "What sound do you hear at the beginning of *wave*?" [/w/] "Color the wave blue."
4. "I spy something that starts with /w/. It is a fruit that is green on the outside and red on the inside. Can you put your finger on it? What is it?" [Watermelon.] "What sound do you hear at the beginning of *watermelon*?" [/w/] "Color the watermelon red and green."
5. "I spy something that starts with /w/ and is used to tell time. Put your finger on it. What is it?" [Watch.] "What sound do you hear in the beginning of *watch*?" [/w/] "Draw a box around the watch."
6. "I spy something that starts with /w/ and is transparent, which means you can see through it. It has panels made of glass. Put your finger on it. What is it?" [Window.] "What sound do you hear at the beginning of *window*?" [/w/] "Trace the outside of the window."

p n **u** **w**
☐ *gray and yellow crayons*

Lesson 4.6

Directions: Color the objects that begin with /u/ gray and /w/ yellow.

KEY: upside down, wheel, up, web, umbrella, whale

Head's up!:
Prep sandpaper letters for tomorrow's lesson.

Lesson 4.7

p n u w

- ☐ 3+ objects for each sound /u/ and /w/
- ☐ and/or cut-and-paste sound cards from Appendix F

Directions - Option #1:
1. Gather 3 objects for each sound that are small enough to fit (or roughly fit) onto this page. (umbrella, underwear, up arrow, water, wax, wipes, watch or see Appendix D for more ideas.)
2. Place objects in a basket or on the table in mixed order.
3. Name each picture ("umbrella" and "web.")
4. Invite your child to sort the objects into the boxes with the same beginning sound.

Directions - Option #2:
1. Locate the proper sound group sorting cards in Appendix F. Cut apart (or invite your child to cut apart) the sound cards.
2. Sort then save for the upcoming sandpaper letter sorting lesson.

Lesson 4.8

p n u w
- ☐ glitter glue
- ☐ 3+ objects for each sound /u/ and /w/

☐ **Part 1 Directions:**
1. Make the sandpaper letters. See Appendix E.
2. Introduce the sandpaper letters. Show one at a time and follow the script below.

   Sandpaper Letter Script:
   1. Pick up the *u* in the opposite of your child's dominant hand. (If your child is right-handed, pick up the letter with your left hand. If your child is left-handed, pick up the letter with your right hand.)
   2. Say, "This says /u/."
   3. With the pointer and middle fingers of your other hand (matching child's dominant hand), trace the letter the same way you would write it as you say the sound /u/. Do this 3 times.
   4. Invite your child to say the sound while tracing the letter three times.
   5. Repeat for the next sound.

☐ **Part 2 Directions:**
Sort the objects used in the previous lesson underneath each sandpaper letter.

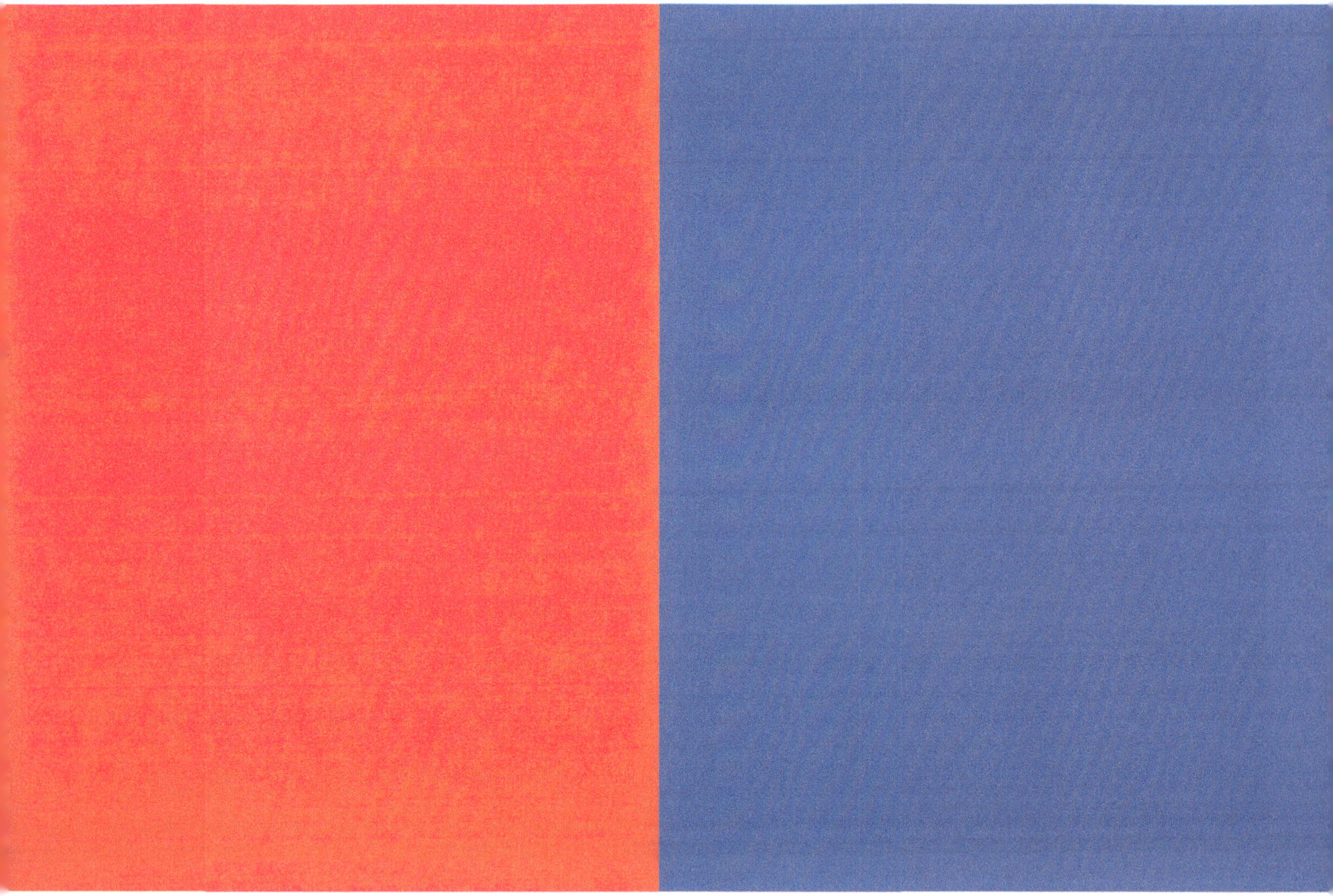

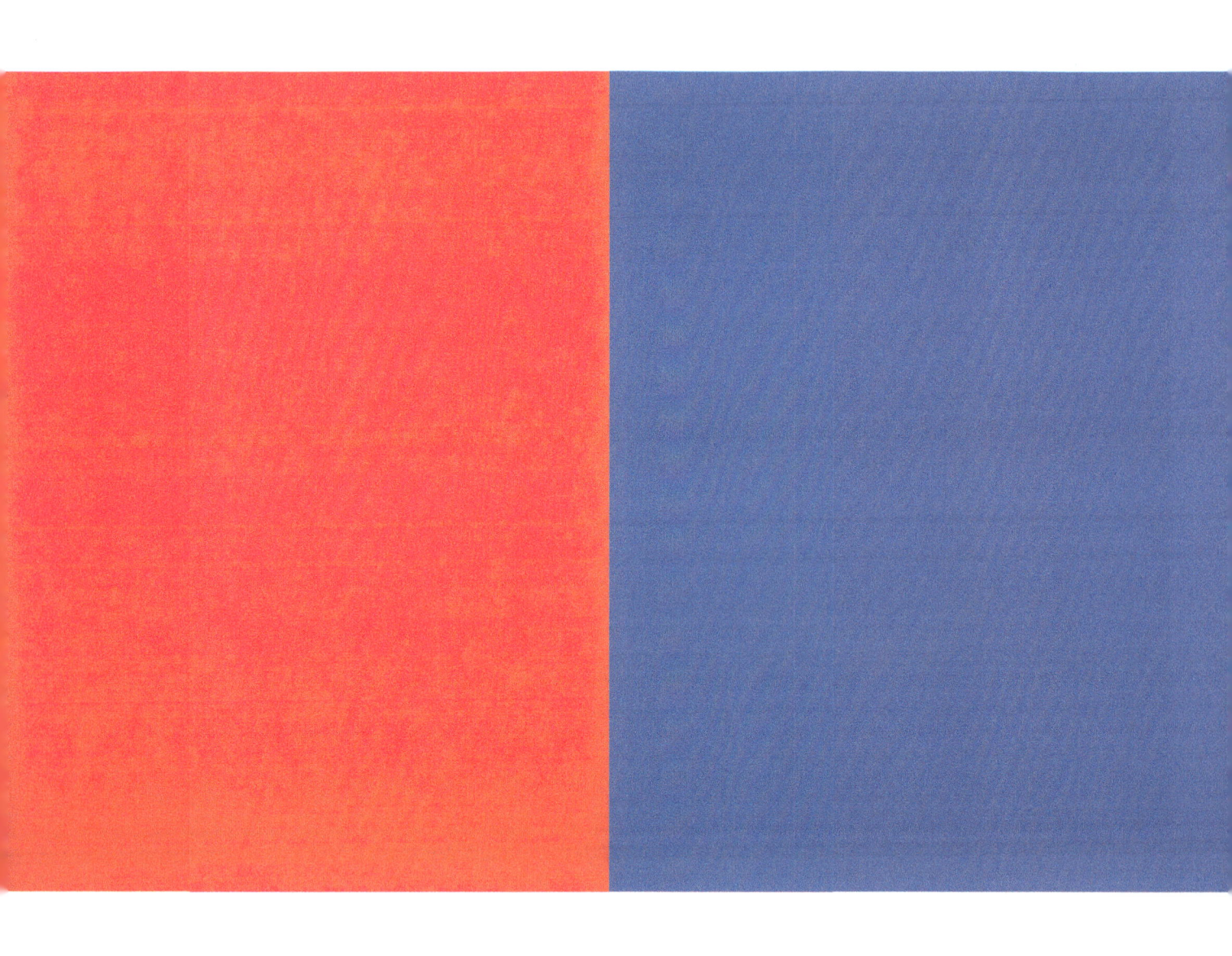

Lesson 4.9

p n u w
☐ counters/chips

Directions:
1. Cut out the BINGO cards.
2. Choose a game board and play with your student(s). Cut them from the workbook or leave them attached.
3. Shuffle and place cards face down in a single pile.
4. Take turns drawing one card at a time. Each player places a chip (any counter will work) on top of the matching letter on his/her BINGO game board.
5. Each player should cover his/her entire board.

Optional Extra Game: Go Fish
See Appendix E for directions.

KEY:
p: pumpkin, pie, pig
n: napkin, nail, nickel
u: umbrella, up, untied
w: water, waffles, wig

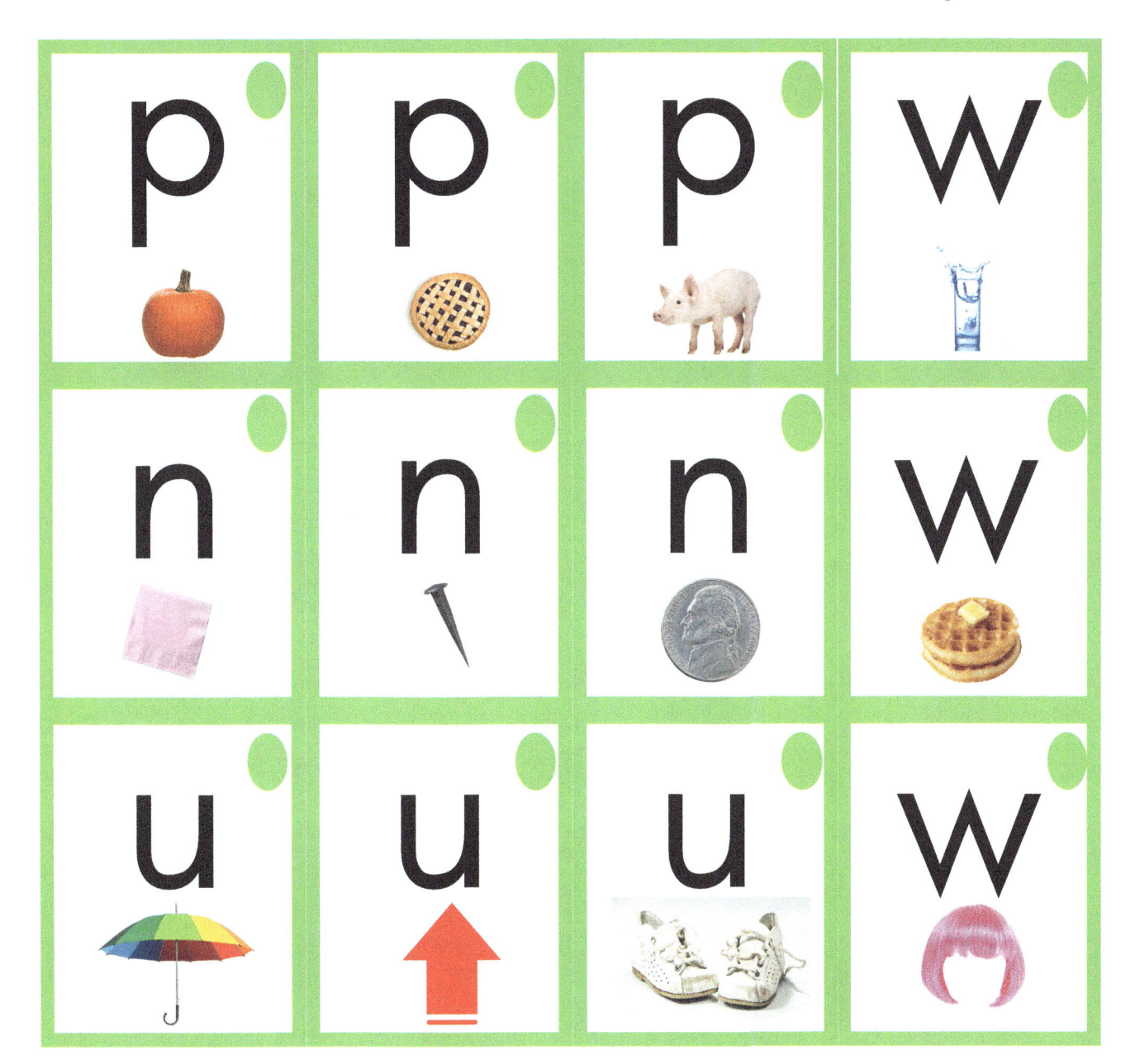

125

p	n	u
w	u	n
p	w	w

n	u	w
p	u	p
n	w	u

p	n	n
w	u	p
u	n	w

u	p	w
w	p	u
n	n	u

Directions: Play one round of the **"My Letter Sound Adventure Game."** Here are the new cards for your **My Letter Sound Adventure Game.** See Appendix B for directions on *how* to play the game and the removable game board.

Lesson 4.10

p n u w

☐ My Letter Sound Adventure Game (Appendix B)

129

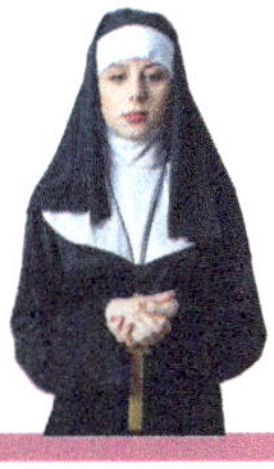
82

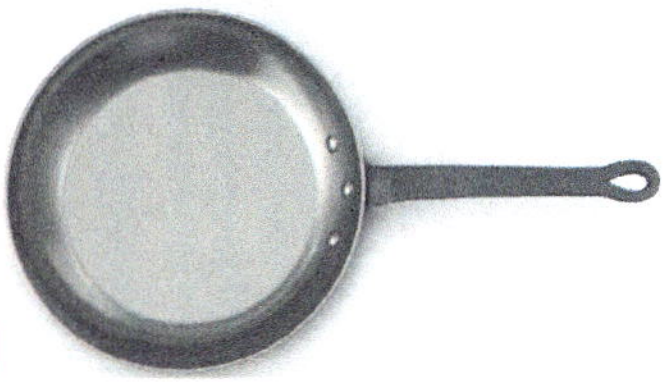
83

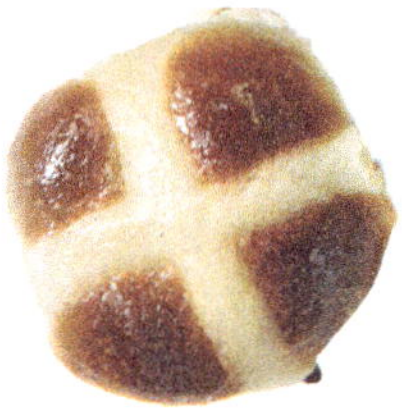
84

85

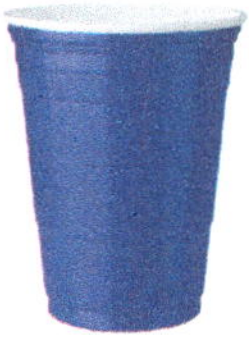
86

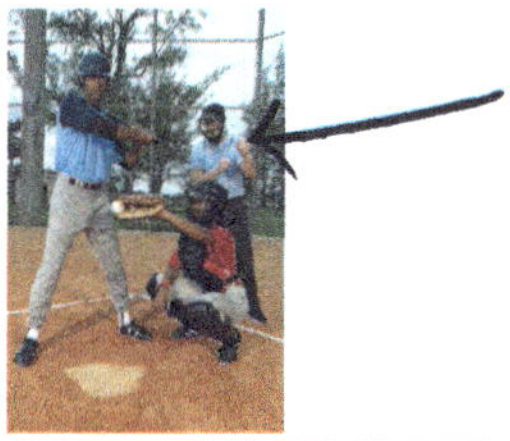
87

88

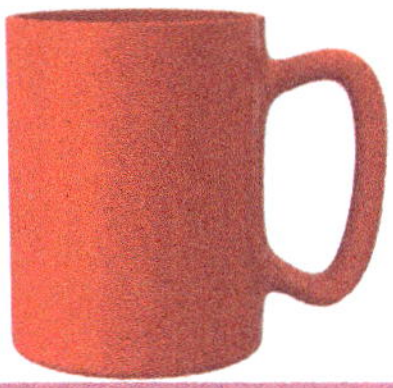
89

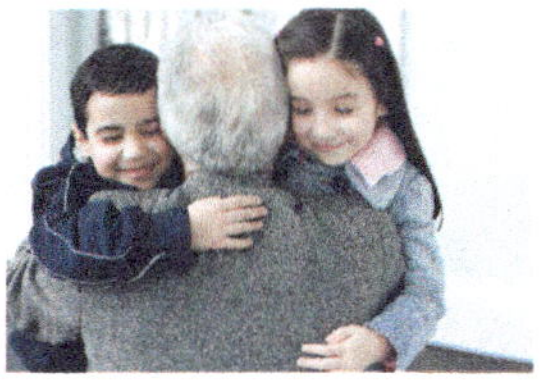
90

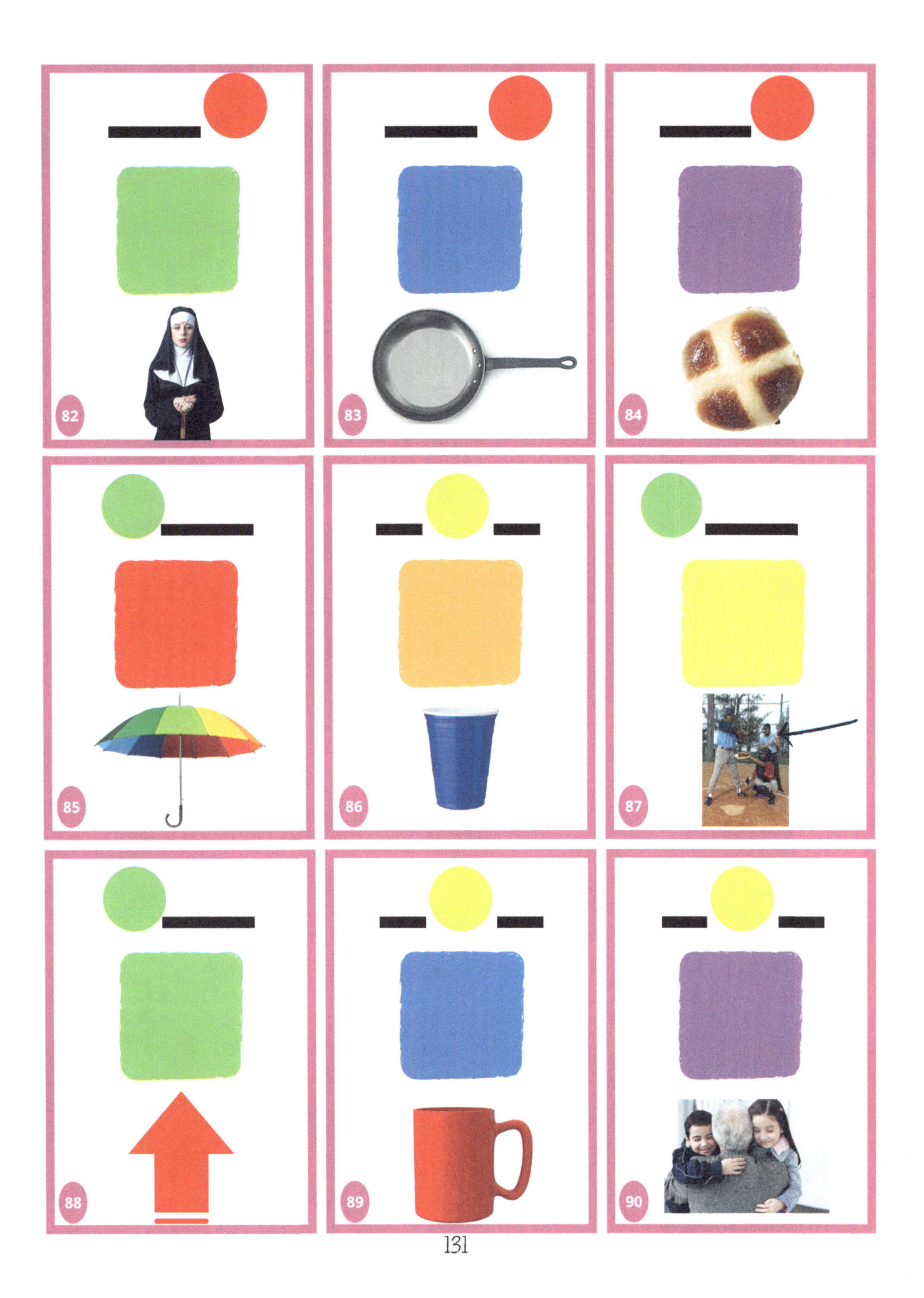

Key 73-96

73. penny
74. pig
75. paperclip
76. sap
77. sip
78. stop
79. nest
80. numbers
81. nail polish
82. nun
83. pan
84. bun
85. umbrella
86. cup
87. umpire
88. up
89. mug
90. hug
91. water
92. whale
93. cow
94. bow
95. worm
96. mow

133

p n u w
☐ fly swatter

Lesson 4.11

☐ **Part 1 Directions:**
1. Laminate page (optional) then cut apart individual cards.
2. Invite your student to spread the letter cards out across the top of his/her work space horizontally.
3. Shuffle the picture cards and invite your child to look at the picture, say the name of the object, and identify the beginning sound. Then place the picture card underneath the proper letter, making a column. There is a control of error on the back of each card so your child can learn to do this activity independently. See Appendix A for a visual.

☐ **Part 2 Directions:**
Make this into a game! Play "**Swat the Sound.**" See game instructions and other game ideas in Appendix A.

p n u w

p: pencil, parrot, pineapple
n: noodles, nuts, nose

u: umpire, umbrella, ultrasound
w: whale, watermelon, wagon

nose   parrot   noodles   pencil

watermelon   ultrasound   nuts   pineapple

bat   inch   whale   umpire

Lesson 4.12

p n u w
- ☐ sensory tray
- ☐ optional: laminating sheet
- ☐ scissors, stapler

Part 1 Directions:
1. Prepare a shallow tray and fill it with salt, sand, or cornmeal.
2. Review the sandpaper letter /s/. Trace three times while saying the sound, then invite your child to do the same.
3. Show your child how to write the letter in the sensory tray with your finger after tracing the sandpaper letter. Show your child how to gently shake the tray to redistribute the material to give a clean writing surface. Invite your child to write the letter with her finger.
4. Repeat with the other three letters in this sound group.

Part 2 Directions:
1. Invite your child to make a book out of the letters by cutting apart the strips on this page, stacking them, and stapling the booklet on the left-hand side.
2. Your child should be able to identify the letter sound and connect the letter sound to the beginning sound in each picture.
3. On the back of each strip, your child can practice writing with a pencil.
4. NOTE: To make these re-usable, laminate then cut, and use a dry-erase marker for tracing and writing.

p: pizza, pumpkin, porcupine   n: nail polish, nest, nuts   u: ultrasound, umbrella, umpire.   w: whale, world, wand p

n

u

w

Lesson 4.13

p n u w
☐ pencil or counters
☐ optional: laminating sheet + 4 clothes pins

Directions:
Invite your child to circle or place a counter on top of the correct picture to match each beginning letter sound.

Re-Usable Shelf Work:
Laminate sheet. Cut individual cards. Place clothespins in a basket next to the cards and invite your child to clip the clothespin on the correct picture to match each beginning sound.
On the back of each card, place a dot behind the correct picture as a control of error.

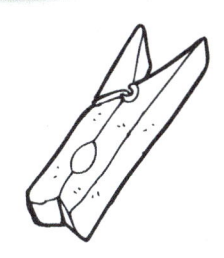

KEY: pineapple, necklace, waffles, umbrella

139

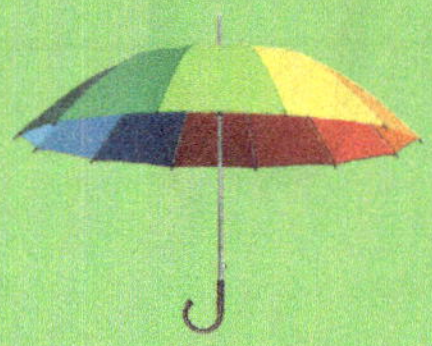

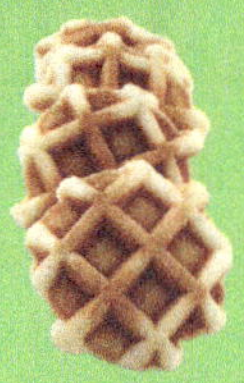

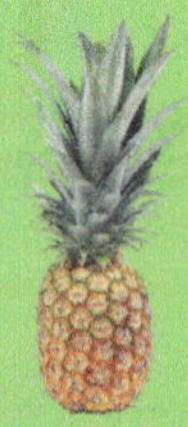

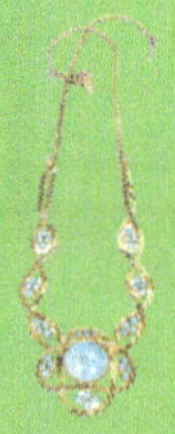

Lesson 4.14

Directions:
1. Laminate (optional, but recommended), cut, and add the alphabet tiles to your organizer.
2. Read each new letter sound.
3. Build the word, "pot" together on the first Pink Series Word Building Card for this unit.
4. Invite our child to build as many of the words as he shows interest on the Pink Series Word Cards pages.

p n u w
☐ movable alphabet organizer

u	p	n	w
u	p	n	w
u	p	n	w
u	p	n	w
u	p	n	w

Lesson 4.14
continued

p n u w
☐ movable alphabet organizer

Directions:
1. Build the first card together, segmenting each sound slowly.
2. Invite your child to build as many words as he shows interest and/or as time permits.
3. See **Appendix C** for visual step-by-step instructions and a KEY.

Note:
There are many CVC words your child will now be able to sound out. (There are 30 words in just this lesson!) You may want to set a goal for your child to write *3 words* in one sitting, allowing your child to pick which words she writes. You may also want to invite your child to spell words at non-school times if she shows interest. You can also start each Reading Games lesson by inviting your child to write one or two words with the movable alphabet.

Please do not feel that you need to have your child write every single one of these words!

33

34

35

143

36.

37.

38.

39.

40

41

42

43

145

44

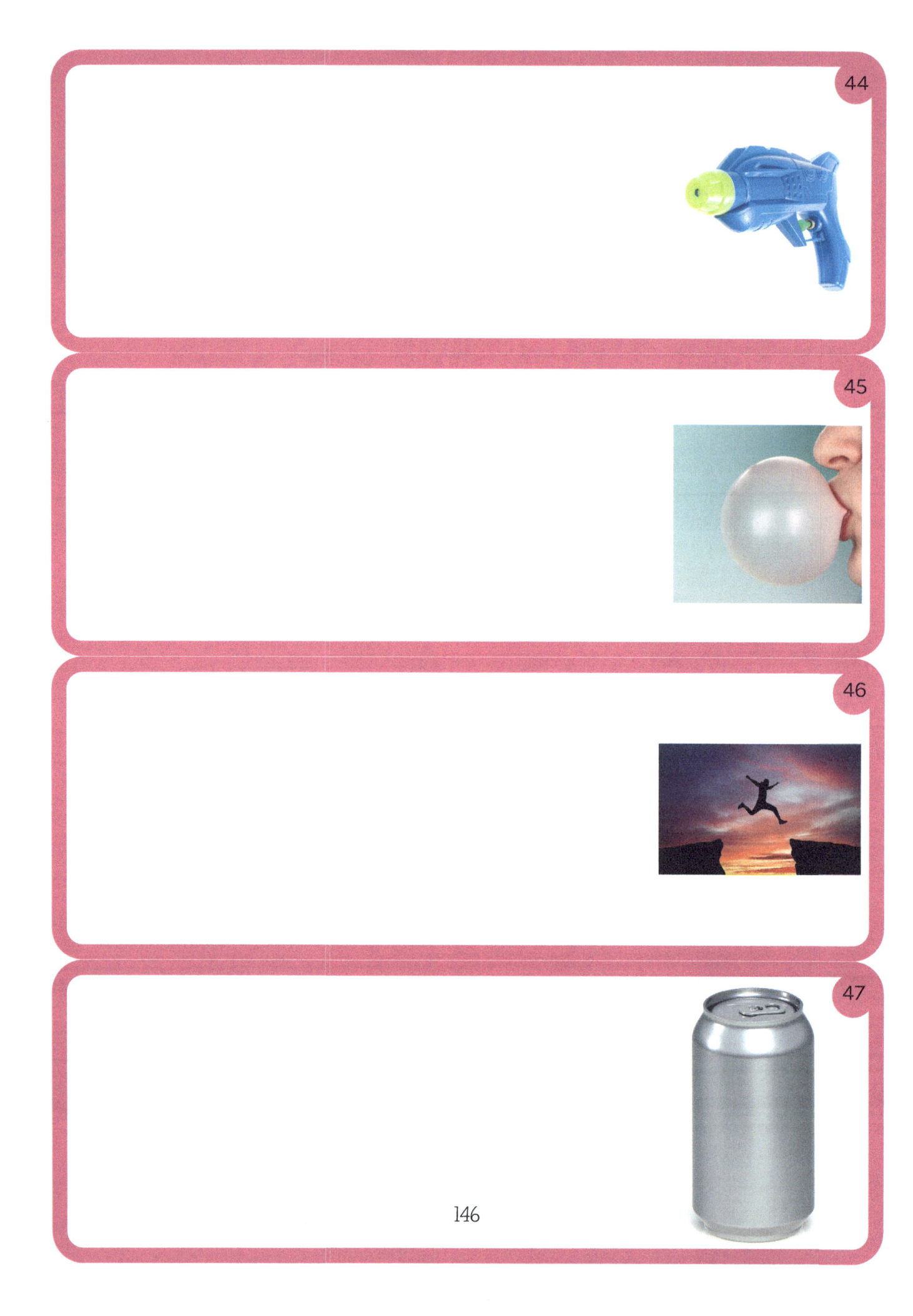

45

46

47

48.

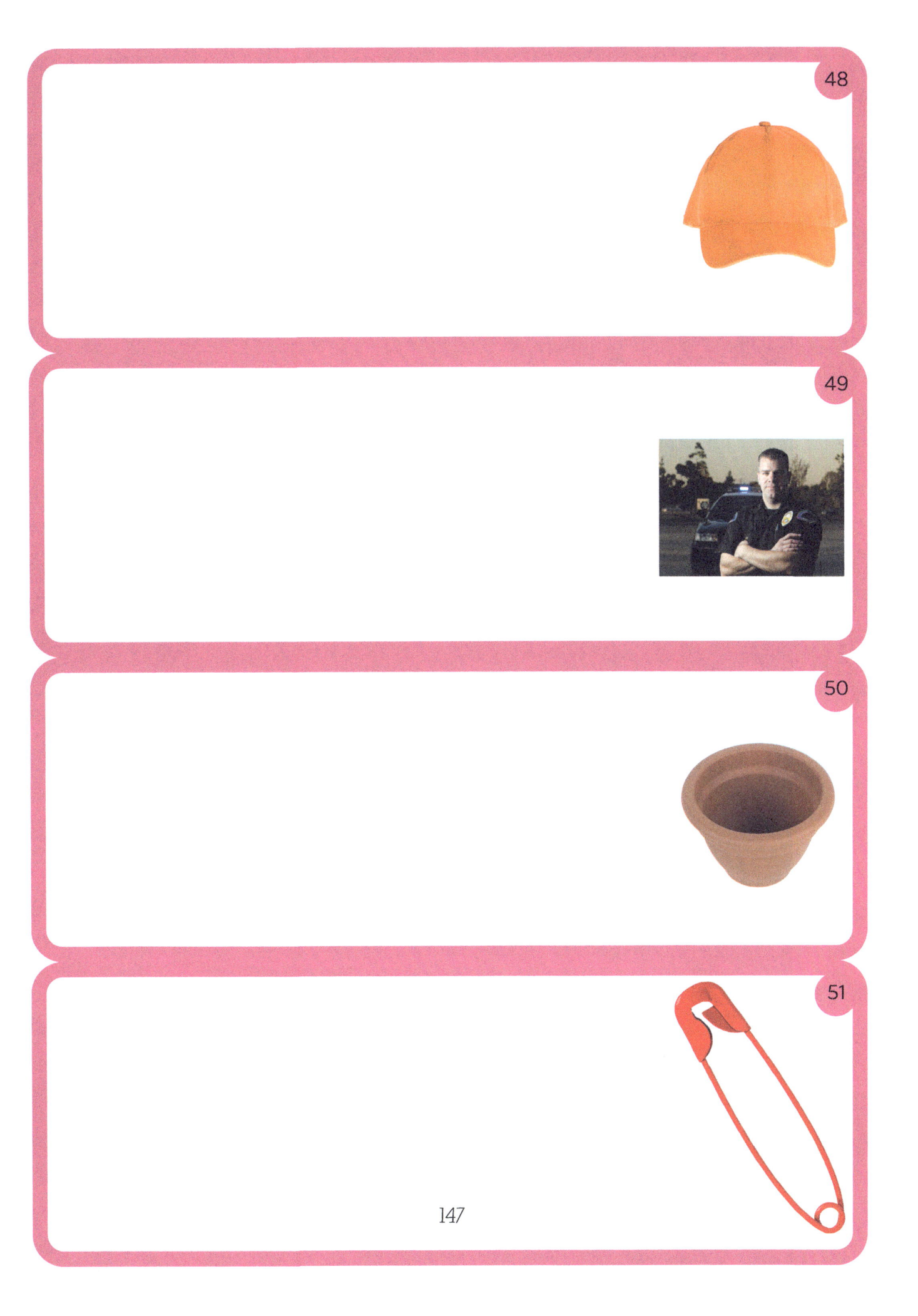

49.

50.

51.

52

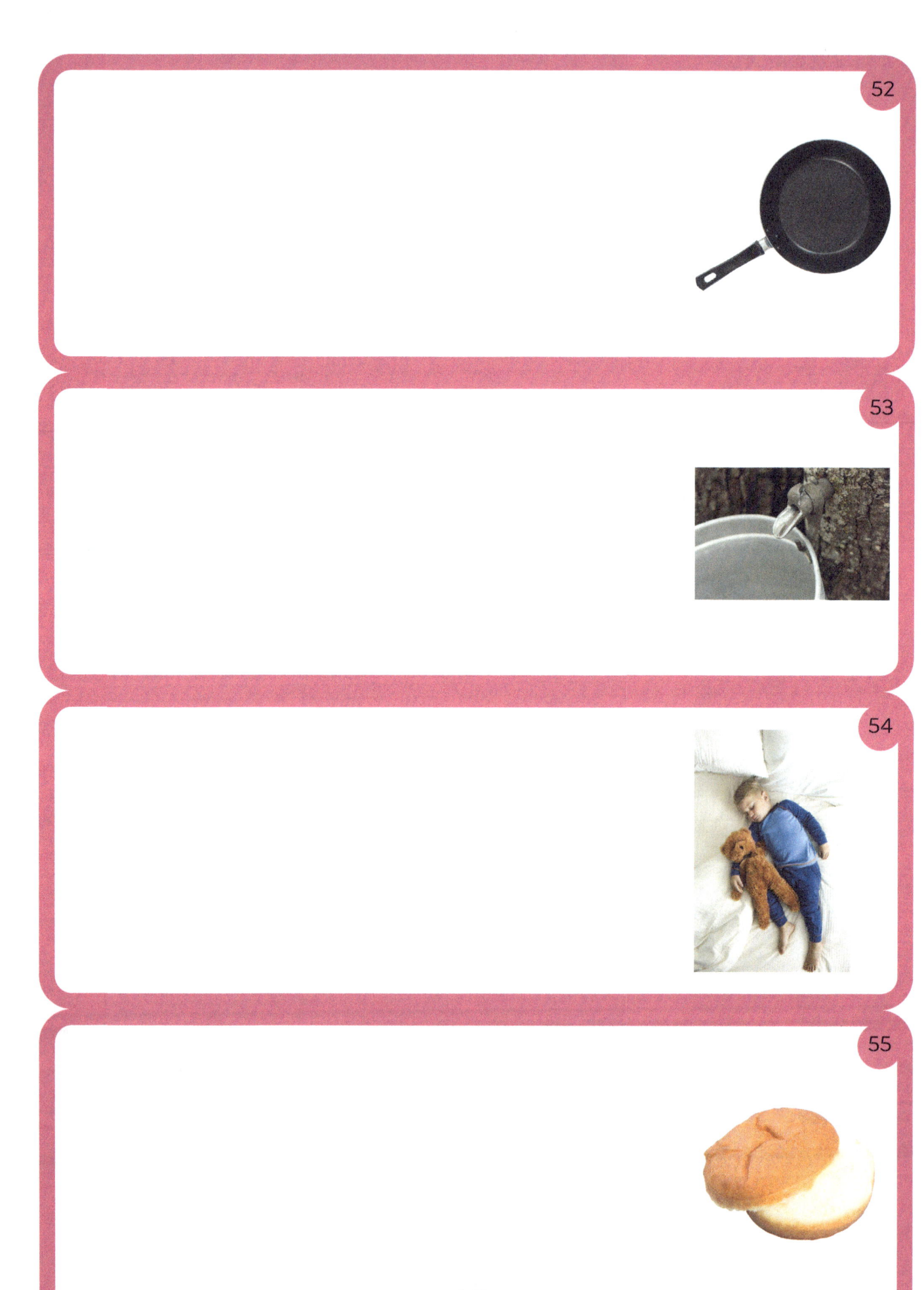

53

54

55

56

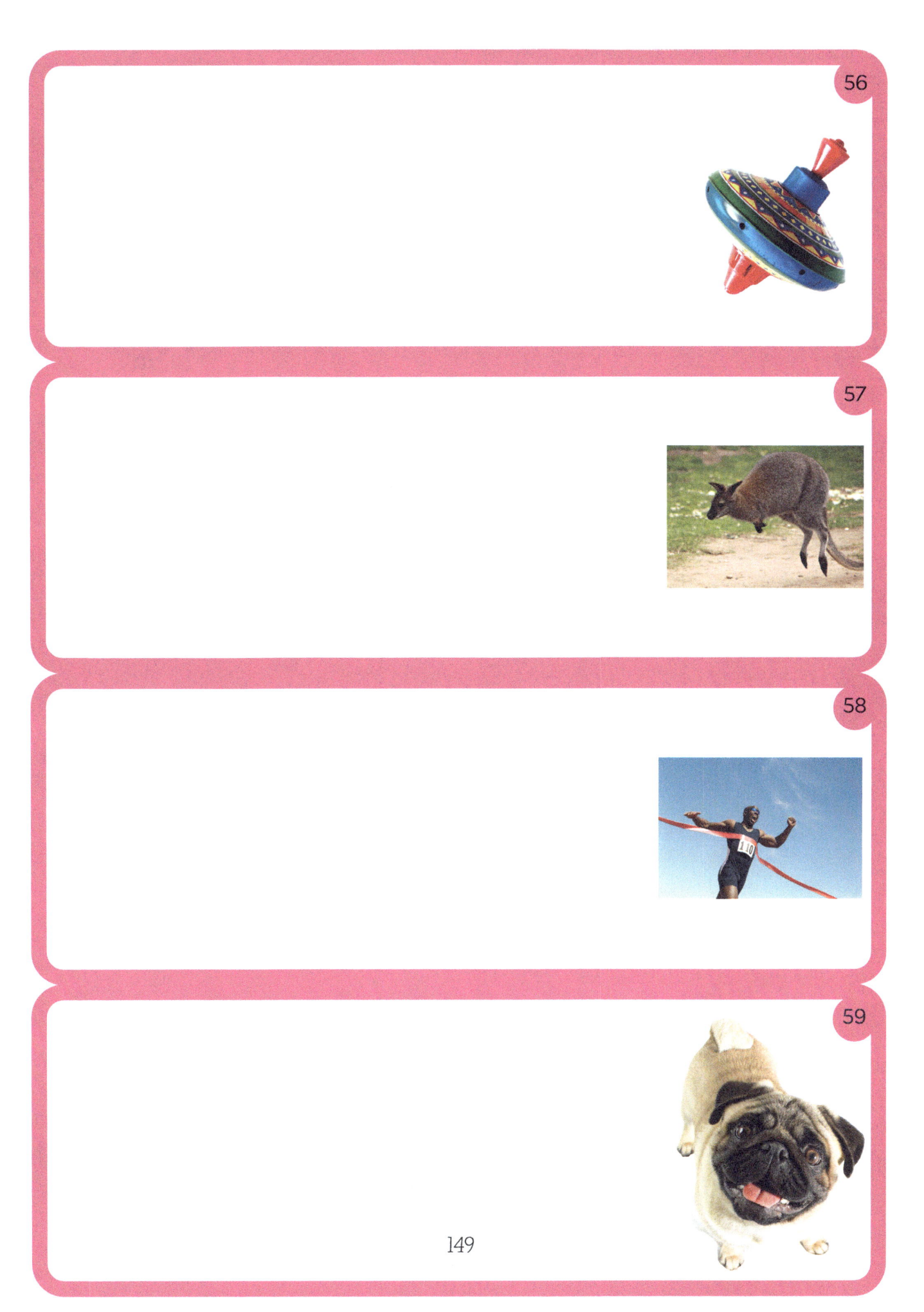

57

58

59

60

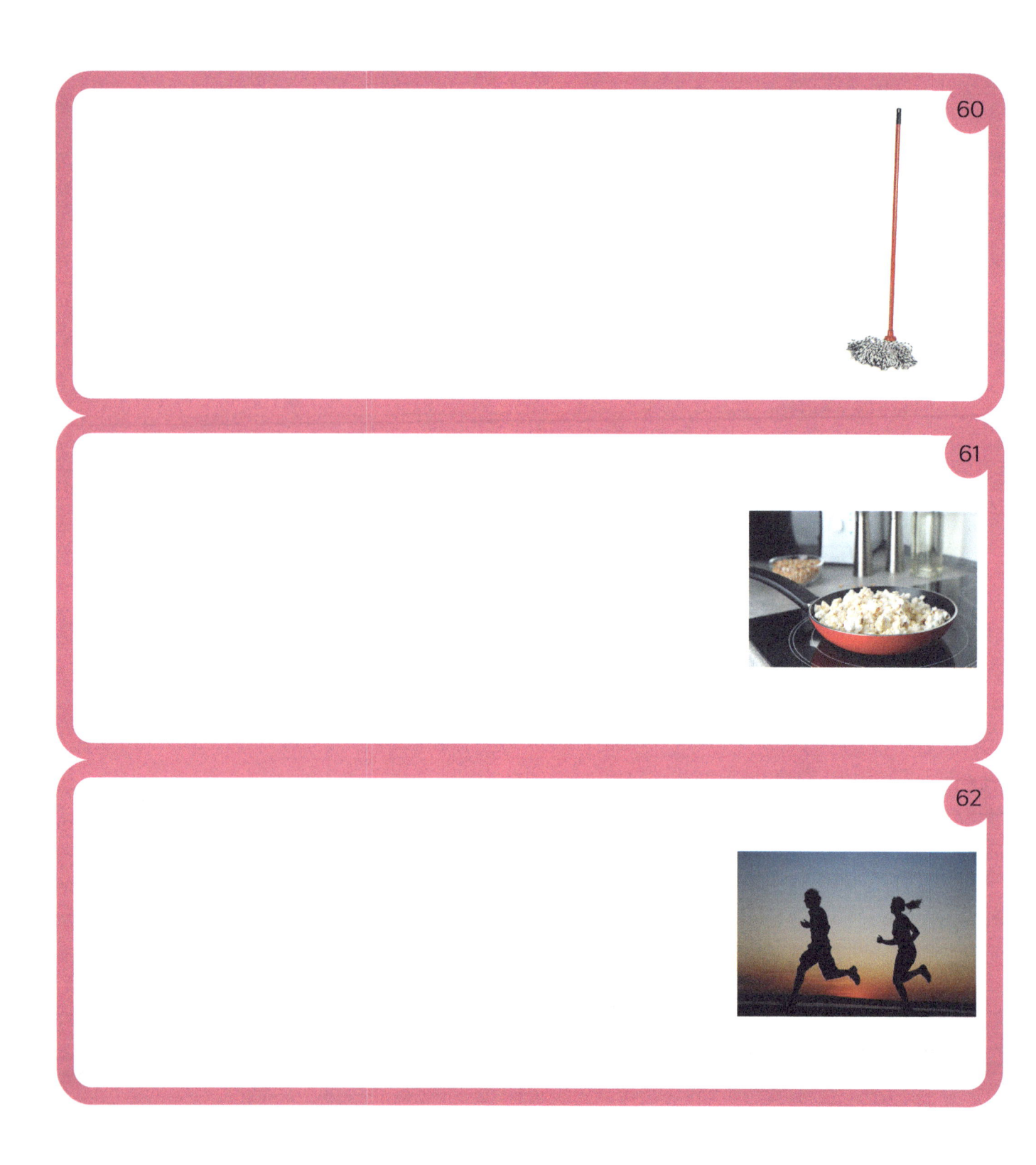

61

62

p n u w
☐ sandpaper letters
☐ sensory tray (optional)
☐ movable alphabet

Unit 4 Assessment

Directions:
1. Using the sandpaper letters you made for this unit (p, n, u, and w), invite your child to identify each sound as you hold up one letter at a time.

☐ p   ☐ n   ☐ u   ☐ w

2. Using your sensory tray or the writing lines below, invite your child to write one of each letter.

p   n   u   w

3. Match the letter to the object by its beginning sound.

p

n

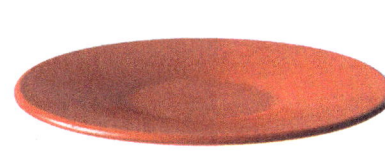

u

w

151

O p n u w

☐ 'sandpaper letters

Unit 4 Assessment

4. Build the following words with the movable alphabet by segmenting the words into their individual sounds.

    🟥   🟦   🟥

    🟥   🟦   🟥

Assessment Results and Next Steps:

Depending on how your child performed on this assessment, you may want to review letter sounds and letter formation before moving on to Unit 5. If your child made minor errors, feel free to move on, as there is review built into the entire program!

For further review if needed, see **Appendix A** for a list of games you can play with your child using the materials in the workbook!

If handwriting is a concern, consider incorporating more fine motor work into your child's day, such as: cutting, sewing, using puzzles with knobs, coloring, tracing, shading, helping in the kitchen, sorting, buttoning, zipping etc. In a Montessori environment, these kinds of activities are usually referred to as "Practical Life" activities and the uses are twofold: teaching practical skills that the child can use each day to help himself, and strengthening the muscles of the hand, wrist, and fingers to prepare for writing. Do not let handwriting prevent you from moving forward. Children can "write" with the movable alphabet for the duration of this program.

Unit 5

j f e l

Pronunciation Guide

In traditional Montessori education settings, only **one sound** is used when introducing each letter. We all know there is more than one sound for the letter "a," but we only use the short sound /ă/ like in alligator in this Reading Games curriculum. Later on, in the Green Reading material, a child is learned multiple pronunciations for letters. For example, a child will learn that when adding a silent e, the letter a makes the long /ā/ sound.

For now, stick with the sounds represented in each pronunciation guide.

Note: All vowels will be pronounced with their short sounds in this curriculum.

j	jaguar
f	fish
e	elephant
l	lion

Handwriting Guide

We won't be doing too much handwriting on paper, but every time you show your child how to write a letter by tracing a sandpaper letter, you need to be sure to use the proper handwriting strokes.

Most of the time, you will not pick up your pencil from the paper (or fingers from the sandpaper letter). The only time you will pick up your hand is when you see a **red number 2**.

Important: If your child is left-handed, show her the strokes using your left hand. If your child is right-handed, show her the strokes with your right hand.

Start at the midline and draw a straight line to the baseline, going through the baseline then hooking up and to the left. Then pick up your pencil and place the dot above the midline.

Start halfway between the midline and top line. Curve up and to the left, then back down to the baseline. Pick up your pencil and cross the first line at the midline from left to right.

Start halfway between the midline and the baseline, then draw a straight line to the right and curve up and around to the left, touching the starting point, and finishing the curve by touching the baseline.

Start at (or near) the top line, and draw a single line straight down to the baseline.

Lesson 5.1

j f e l

☐ crayons

Directions:
1. Say, "We are going to play *I Spy*. Listen carefully and follow my directions."
2. "I spy something that starts with /j/ and is a face carved into a pumpkin. A light is placed inside it. What is it called?" [Jack-o-lantern.] "Put your finger on the jack-o-lantern. What sound do you hear at the beginning of *jack-o-lantern*?" [/j/] "Color the jack-o-lantern orange."
3. "I spy something that starts with /j/ that lives in the ocean and does not have bones. It has long tentacles. Can you put your finger on it? What is it?" [Jellyfish.] "What sound do you hear at the beginning of *jellyfish*?" [/j/] "Color the jellyfish purple."
4. "I spy something that starts with /j/. You can put stuff inside it, and it has a lid. Can you put your finger on it? What is it?" [Jar.] "What sound do you hear at the beginning of *jar*?" [/j/] "Fill the jar with your favorite flavor of jam."
5. "I spy something that starts with /j/ that you can drink. It is made from apples or other fruit. Put your finger on it. What is it?" [Juice.] "What sound do you hear at the beginning of *juice*?" [/j/] "Draw a box around the juice."
6. "I spy something that starts with /j/ and you wear it when it is cold outside. Put your finger on it. What is it?" [Jacket.] "What sound do you hear at the beginning of *jacket*?" [/j/] "Circle the jacket."

Directions:
1. Say, "We are going to play *I Spy*. Listen carefully and follow my directions."
2. "I spy something that starts with /f/ and grows from the ground. There are many, many varieties of these, and they are beautiful. Can you put your finger on it? What is it?" [Flower.] "What sound do you hear at the beginning of *flower*?" [/f/] "Circle the flower."
3. "I spy something that starts with /f/ and can hop. It is an amphibian Can you put your finger on it? What is it?" [Frog.] "What sound do you hear at the beginning of *frog*?" [/f/] "Color the frog green."
4. "I spy something that starts with /f/. It is very hot and indicates that something is burning. Can you put your finger on it? What is it?" [Fire.] "What sound do you hear at the beginning of *fire*?" [/f/] "Color the fire orange and yellow."
5. "I spy something that starts with /f/ and has blades that spin around. It is very useful on a hot day. Put your finger on it. What is it?" [Fan.] "What sound do you hear in the beginning of *fan*?" [/f/] "Draw an X on the fan."
6. "I spy something that starts with /f/ and humans have two of them. They are at the end of your legs. Put your finger on them. What are they?" [Feet.] "What sound do you hear at the beginning of *feet*?" [/f/] "Color the feet your favorite color."

j f e l
☐ brown and blue crayons

Lesson 5.2

Directions: Color the objects that begin with **/j/ brown** and **/f/ blue.**

155

Head's up!:
Prep sandpaper letters for tomorrow's lesson.

Lesson 5.3

j f e l

☐ 3 small objects each that begin with /j/ and /f/
☐ and/or cut-and-paste sound cards from Appendix F

Directions - Option #1:
1. Gather 3 objects for each sound that are small enough to fit (or roughly fit) onto this page. (jar, jacks, juice, jelly/jam, joker/Jack cards, figs, fruit, fan, fox, fish, or see Appendix D for more ideas.)
2. Place objects in a basket or on the table in mixed order.
3. Name each picture ("jeans" and "frog.")
4. Invite your child to sort the objects into the boxes with the same beginning sound.

Directions - Option #2:
1. Locate the proper sound group sorting cards in Appendix F. Cut apart (or invite your child to cut apart) the sound cards.
2. Sort then save for the upcoming sandpaper letter sorting lesson.

Lesson 5.4

j f e l
☐ glitter glue
☐ 3+ objects for each sound /f/ and /j/

☐ **Part 1 Directions:**
1. Make the sandpaper letters. See Appendix E.
2. Introduce the sandpaper letters. Show one at a time and follow the script below.

   Sandpaper Letter Script:
   1. Pick up the *j* in the opposite of your child's dominant hand. (If your child is right-handed, pick up the letter with your left hand. If your child is left-handed, pick up the letter with your right hand.)
   2. Say, "This says /j/."
   3. With the pointer and middle fingers of your other hand (matching child's dominant hand), trace the letter the same way you would write it as you say the sound /j/. Do this 3 times.
   4. Invite your child to say the sound while tracing the letter three times.
   5. Repeat for the next sound.

☐ **Part 2 Directions:**
Sort the objects used in the previous lesson underneath each sandpaper letter.

Lesson 5.5

j f e l

☐ crayons

Directions:
1. Say, "We are going to play *I Spy*. Listen carefully and follow my directions."
2. "I spy something that starts with /e/ and people do this activity to stay healthy. Can you put your finger on it? What is it?" [Exercise.] "What sound do you hear at the beginning of *exercise*?" [/e/] "Color the person exercising red."
3. "I spy something that starts with /e/. Chickens lay these, and they make a great breakfast. Can you put your finger on them? What are they?" [Eggs.] "What sound do you hear at the beginning of *eggs*?" [/e/] "Draw a circle around the eggs."
4. "I spy something that starts with /e/. It means the same as leaving. There are usually signs with this word above the doors that lead outdoors in public buildings. Can you put your finger on the picture? What is this called?" [Exit.] "What sound do you hear at the beginning of *exit*?" [/e/] "Put a box around the picture of a person leaving out the exit from a building."
5. "I spy something that starts with /e/ and helps you bend your arm. Put your finger on it. What is it?" [Elbow.] "What sound do you hear at the beginning of *elbow*?" [/e/] "Circle the elbow."
6. "I spy something that starts with /e/ and it makes a loud trumpeting sound. It is the tallest living land mammal and has big ears. Put your finger on it. What is it?" [Elephant.] "What sound do you hear at the beginning of *elephant*?" [/e/] "Color the elephant gray."

Directions:
1. Say, "We are going to play *I Spy*. Listen carefully and follow my directions."
2. "I spy something that starts with /l/ and is very sour. You can squeeze it and add water and sugar to make lemonade. Can you put your finger on it? What is it?" [Lemon.] "What sound do you hear at the beginning of *lemon*?" [/l/] "Color the lemon yellow."
3. "I spy something that starts with /l/ and is found above your foot. It enables you to stand. Can you put your finger on it? What is it?" [Leg.] "What sound do you hear at the beginning of *leg*?" [/l/] "Circle just the leg."
4. "I spy something that starts with /l/. It gives light and is placed on a tabletop. Can you put your finger on it? What is it?" [Lamp.] "What sound do you hear at the beginning of *lamp*?" [/l/] "Color the lampshade and draw a design on the base of the lamp."
5. "I spy something that starts with /l/ and is a part of a plant. Put your finger on it. What is it?" [Leaf.] "What sound do you hear in the beginning of *leaf*?" [/l/] "Color the leaf a color it might be in autumn."
6. "I spy something that starts with /l/ and is usually sent in the mail inside an envelope. Put your finger on it. What is it?" [Letter.] "What sound do you hear at the beginning of *letter*?" [/l/] "Draw a box around the letter."

159

j f e l
☐ green and pink crayons

Lesson 5.6

Directions: Color the objects that begin with **/e/ green** and **/l/ pink**.

KEY: envelope, elephant, lightbulb, lips, egg, log

160

Head's up!:
Prep sandpaper letters for tomorrow's lesson.

Lesson 5.7

j f e l
- [ ] 3+ objects each that begin with /e/ and /l/
- [ ] and/or cut-and-paste sound cards from Appendix F

Directions:
1. Gather 3 objects for each sound that are small enough to fit (or roughly fit) onto this page. (eggs, eggplant, elephant, elk, empty (box), lightbulb, lamp, lock, lunchbox, lace, or see Appendix D for more ideas.)
2. Place objects in a basket or on the table in mixed order.
3. Name each picture ("igloo" and "glue.")
4. Invite your child to sort the objects into the boxes with the same beginning sound.

Directions - Option #2:
1. Locate the proper sound group sorting cards in Appendix F. Cut apart (or invite your child to cut apart) the sound cards.
2. Sort then save for the upcoming sandpaper letter sorting lesson.

Lesson 5.8

☐ **Part 1 Directions:**
1. Make the sandpaper letters. See Appendix E.
2. Introduce the sandpaper letters. Show one at a time and follow the script below.

   Sandpaper Letter Script:
   1. Pick up the *e* in the opposite of your child's dominant hand. (If your child is right-handed, pick up the letter with your left hand. If your child is left-handed, pick up the letter with your right hand.)
   2. Say, "This says /e/."
   3. With the pointer and middle fingers of your other hand (matching child's dominant hand), trace the letter the same way you would write it as you say the sound /e/. Do this 3 times.
   4. Invite your child to say the sound while tracing the letter three times.
   5. Repeat for the next sound.

☐ **Part 2 Directions:**
Sort the household objects used in the previous lesson underneath each sandpaper letter.

j f e l
☐ glitter glue
☐ 3+ objects each that begin with /e/ and /l/

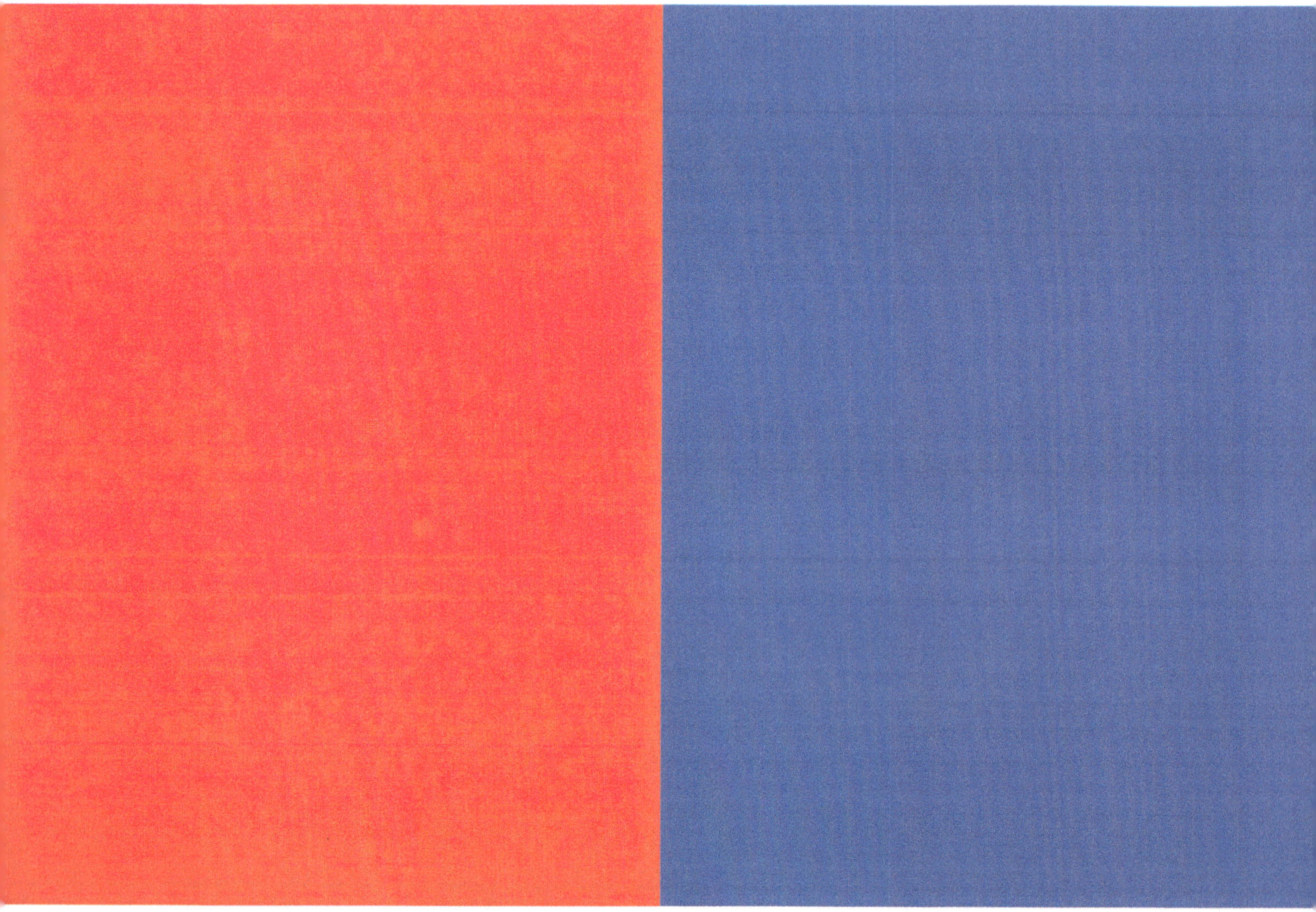

Lesson 5.9

j f e l
☐ counters/chips

Directions:
1. Cut out the BINGO cards.
2. Choose a game board and play with your student(s). Cut them from the workbook or leave them attached.
3. Shuffle and place cards face down in a single pile.
4. Take turns drawing one card at a time. Each player places a chip (any counter will work) on top of the matching letter on his/her BINGO game board.
5. Each player should cover his/her entire board.

Optional Extra Game: Go Fish
See Appendix E for directions.

KEY:
j: jet, jump rope, jacks
f: flowers, fist, fire
e: exit, eggs, elephant
l: lips, legs, lightbulb

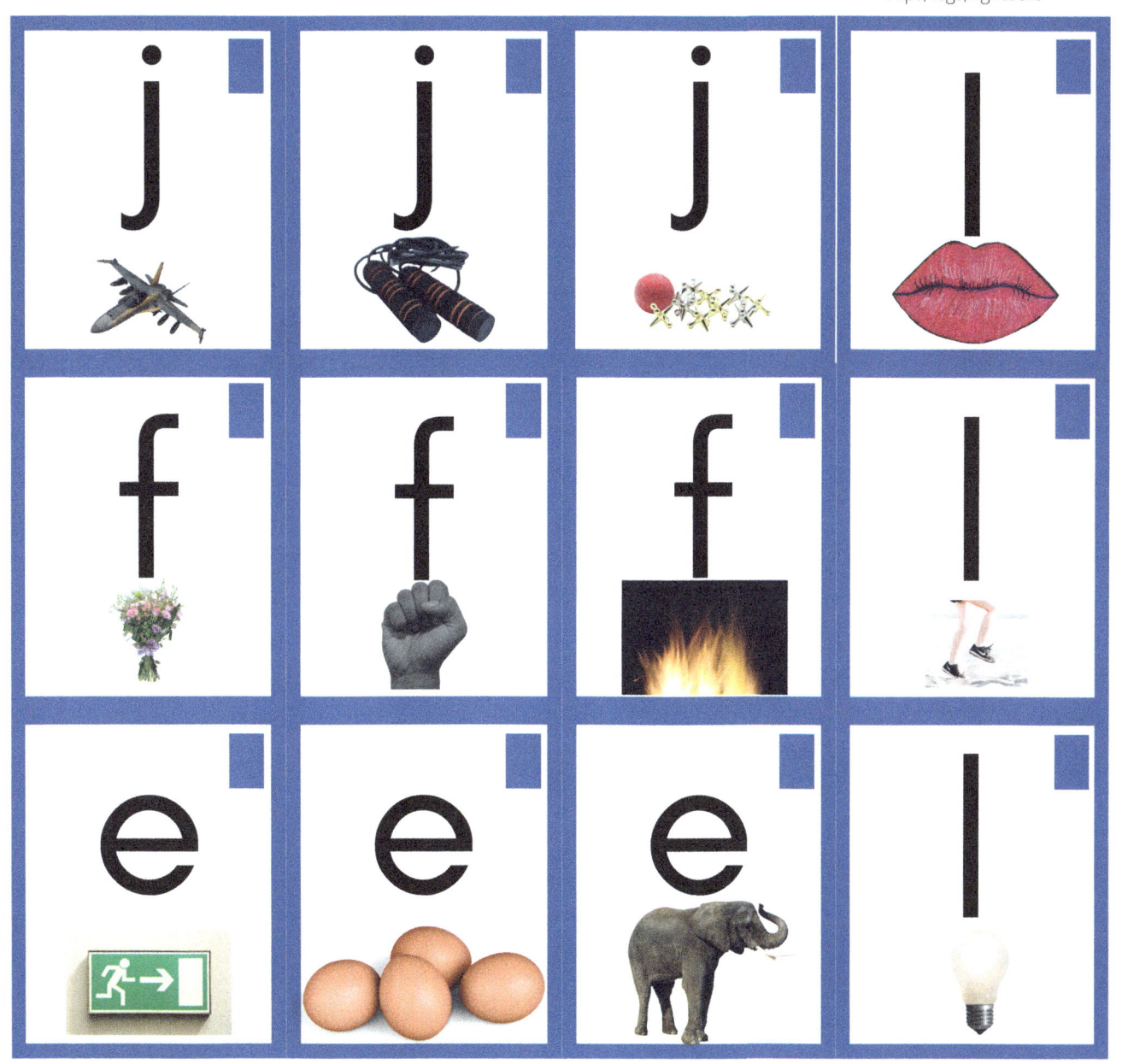

j	f	e
l	e	f
j	l	l

f	e	l
j	e	j
f	l	e

j	f	f
l	e	j
e	f	l

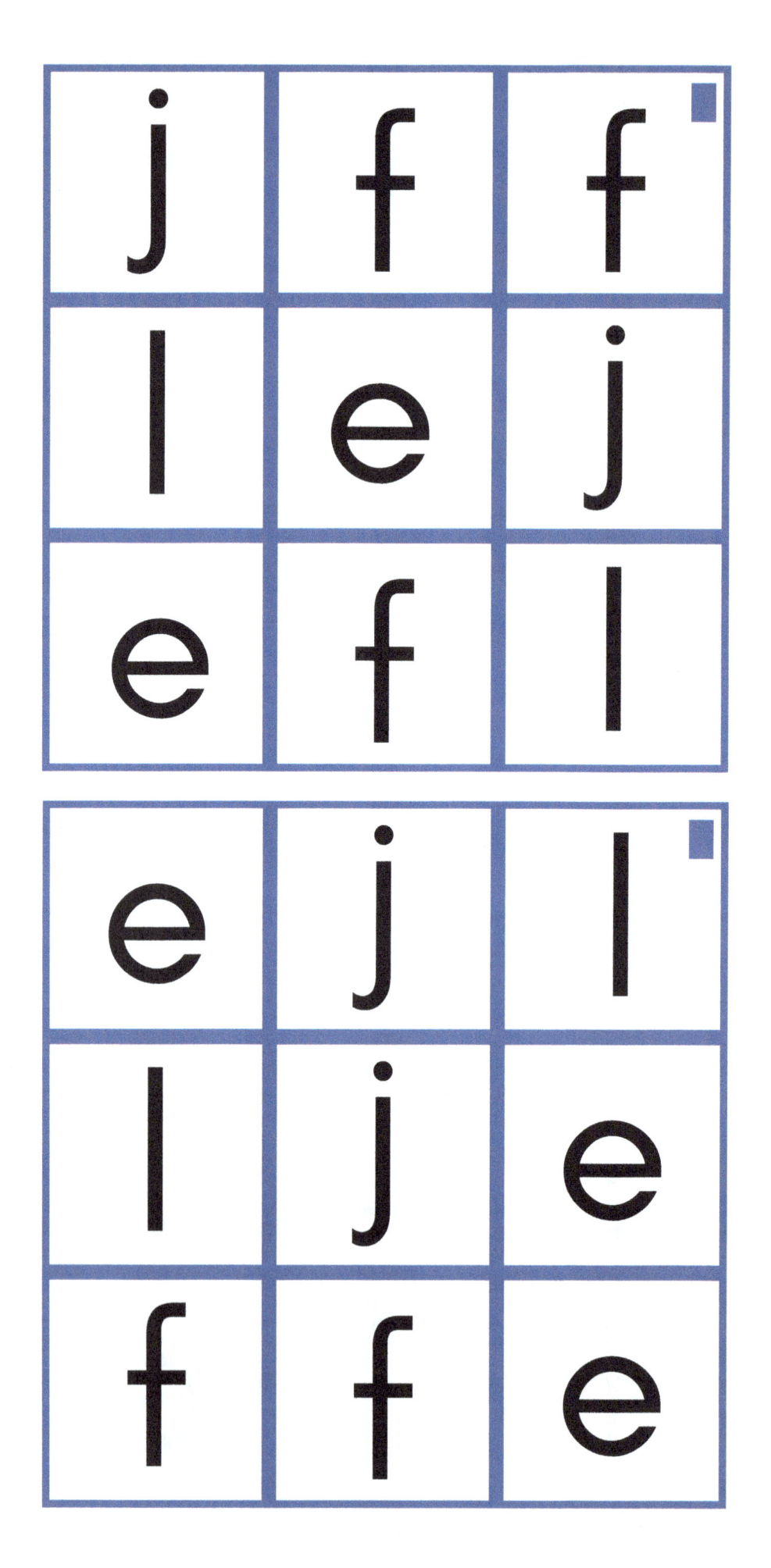

e	j	l
l	j	e
f	f	e

Directions: Play one round of the **"My Letter Sound Adventure Game."** Here are the new cards for your **My Letter Sound Adventure Game.** See Appendix B for directions on *how* to play the game and the removable game board.

Lesson 5.10

j f e l
☐ My Letter Sound Adventure Game (Appendix B)

97
98
99
100
101
102
103
104
105

169

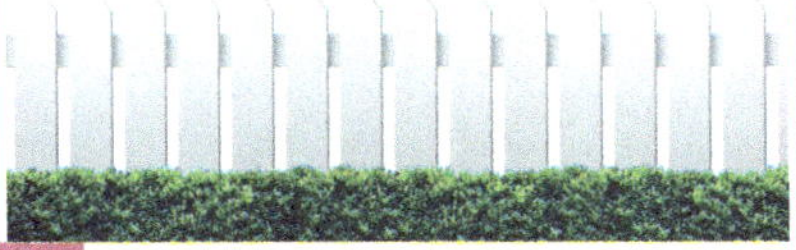

106

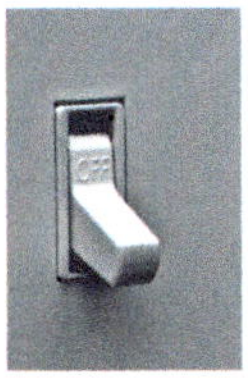

107

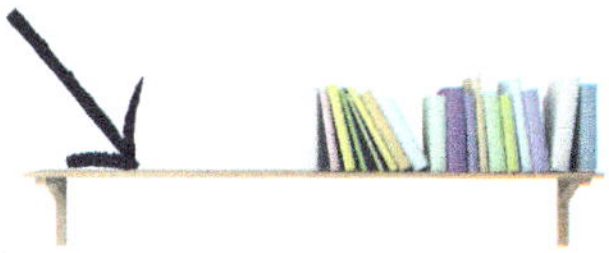

108

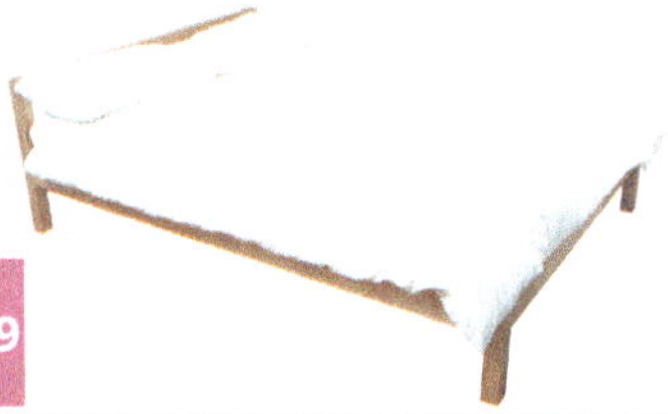

109

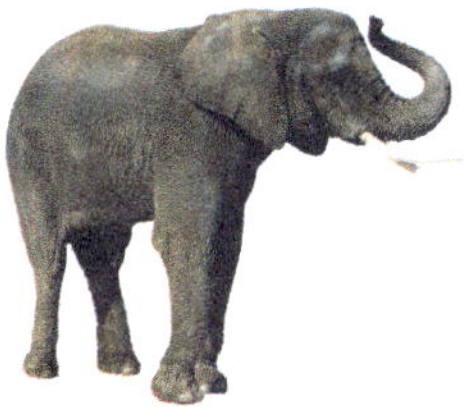

110

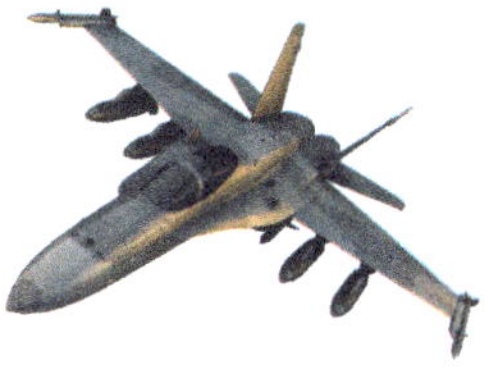

111

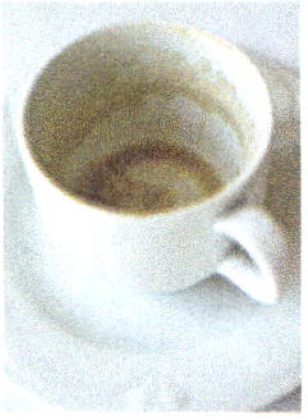

112

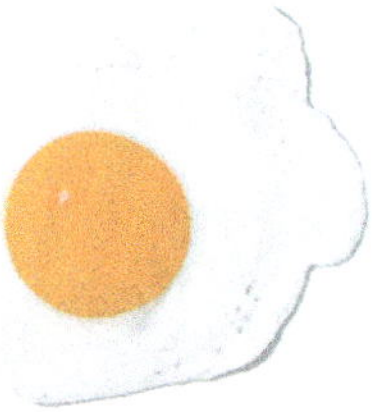

113

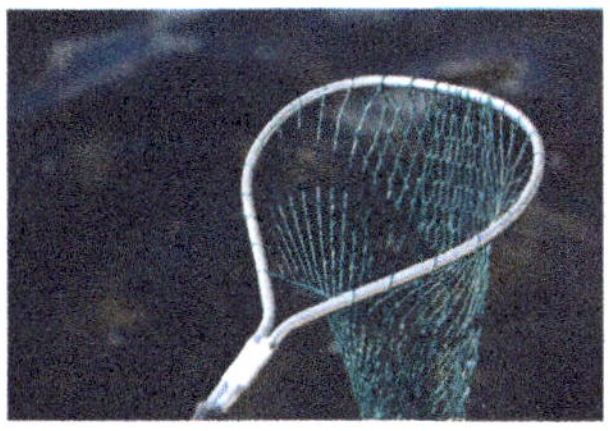

114

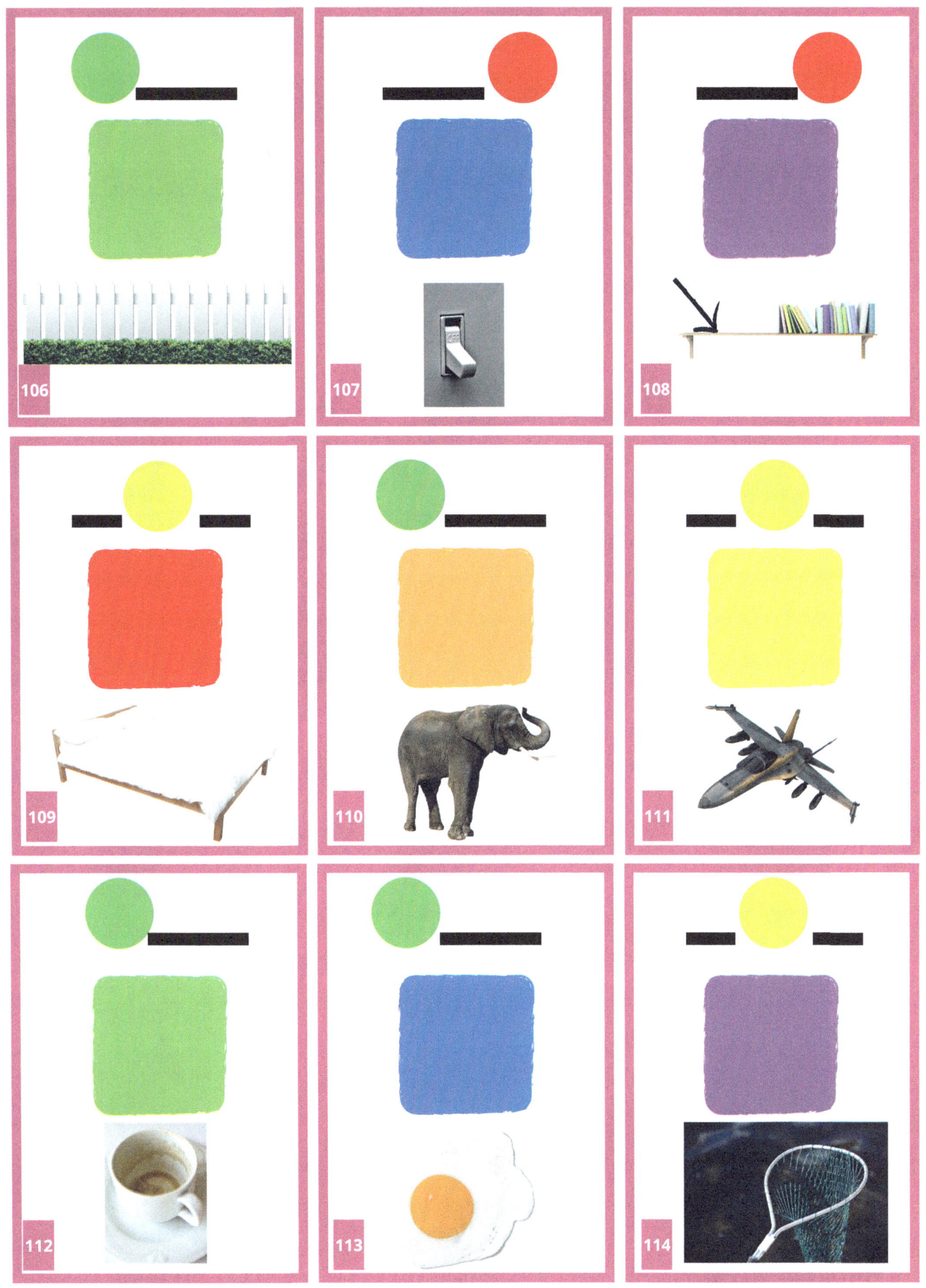

Key 97-108

97. badge ("j" sound at end)
98. wedge ("j" sound at end)
99. jam
100. hedge ("j" sound at end)
101. juice
102. Jack-o-lantern
103. feather
104. half
105. fire
106. fence
107. off
108. shelf

Key 108-120

109. bed
110. elephant
111. jet
112. empty
113. egg
114. net
115. ball
116. lamp
117. lake
118. waterfall
119. well
120. lightbulb

173

Lesson 5.11

j f e l
☐ sidewalk chalk

☐ **Part 1 Directions:**
1. Laminate page (optional) then cut apart individual cards.
2. Invite your student to spread the letter cards out across the top of his/her work space horizontally.
3. Shuffle the picture cards and invite your child to look at the picture, say the name of the object, and identify the beginning sound. Then place the picture card underneath the proper letter, making a column. There is a control of error on the back of each card so your child can learn to do this activity independently. See Appendix A for a visual.

☐ **Part 2 Directions:**
Make this into a game! Play "**Hopscotch**." See game instructions and other game ideas in **Appendix A.**

j f e l

j: jam, juice, joker.　　f: frog, fruit, fish　　　　175　　　e: elephant, egg, envelope.　　l: lamp, ladder, lion

fish	juice	frog	joker
fruit	jam	lamp	egg
lion	envelope	ladder	elephant

Lesson 5.12

j f e l
- stapler
- scissors
- pencil or laminating sheet + marker

Part 1 Directions:
1. Prepare a shallow tray and fill it with salt, sand, or cornmeal.
2. Review the sandpaper letter /s/. Trace three times while saying the sound, then invite your child to do the same.
3. Show your child how to write the letter in the sensory tray with your finger after tracing the sandpaper letter. Show your child how to gently shake the tray to redistribute the material to give a clean writing surface. Invite your child to write the letter with her finger.
4. Repeat with the other three letters in this sound group.

Part 2 Directions:
1. Invite your child to make a book out of the letters by cutting apart the strips on this page, stacking them, and stapling the booklet on the left-hand side.
2. Your child should be able to identify the letter sound and connect the letter sound to the beginning sound in each picture.
3. On the back of each strip, your child can practice writing with a pencil.
4. NOTE: To make these re-usable, laminate then cut, and use a dry-erase marker for tracing and writing.

j: jam, joker, juice.   f: fox, fence, fire   e: eggplant, elephant, elevator.   l: lamb, lollipop, lobster

j

f

e

l

Lesson 5.13

j f e l
- [ ] 4 clothespins OR
- [ ] pencil

Directions:
Invite your child to circle or place a counter on top of the correct picture to match each beginning letter sound.

Re-Usable Shelf Work:
Laminate sheet. Cut individual cards. Place clothespins in a basket next to the cards and invite your child to clip the clothespin on the correct picture to match each beginning sound.
Show your child how to check the answer on the back as a control of error.

KEY: jaguar, frog, lightbulb, egg

179

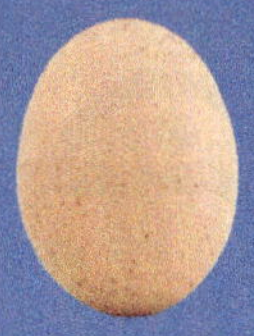

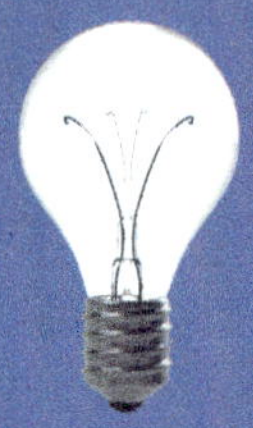

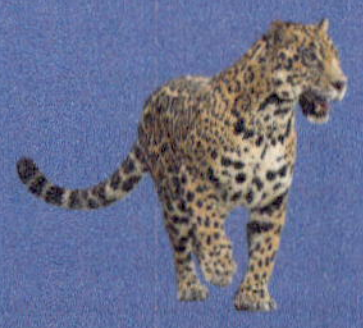

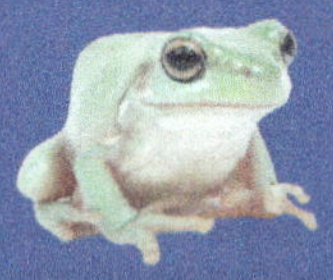

Lesson 5.14

Directions:
1. Laminate (optional, but recommended), cut, and add the alphabet tiles to your organizer.
2. Read each new letter sound.
3. Build the word, "set" together on the first Pink Series Word Building Card for this unit.
4. Invite our child to build as many of the words as he shows interest on the Pink Series Word Cards pages.

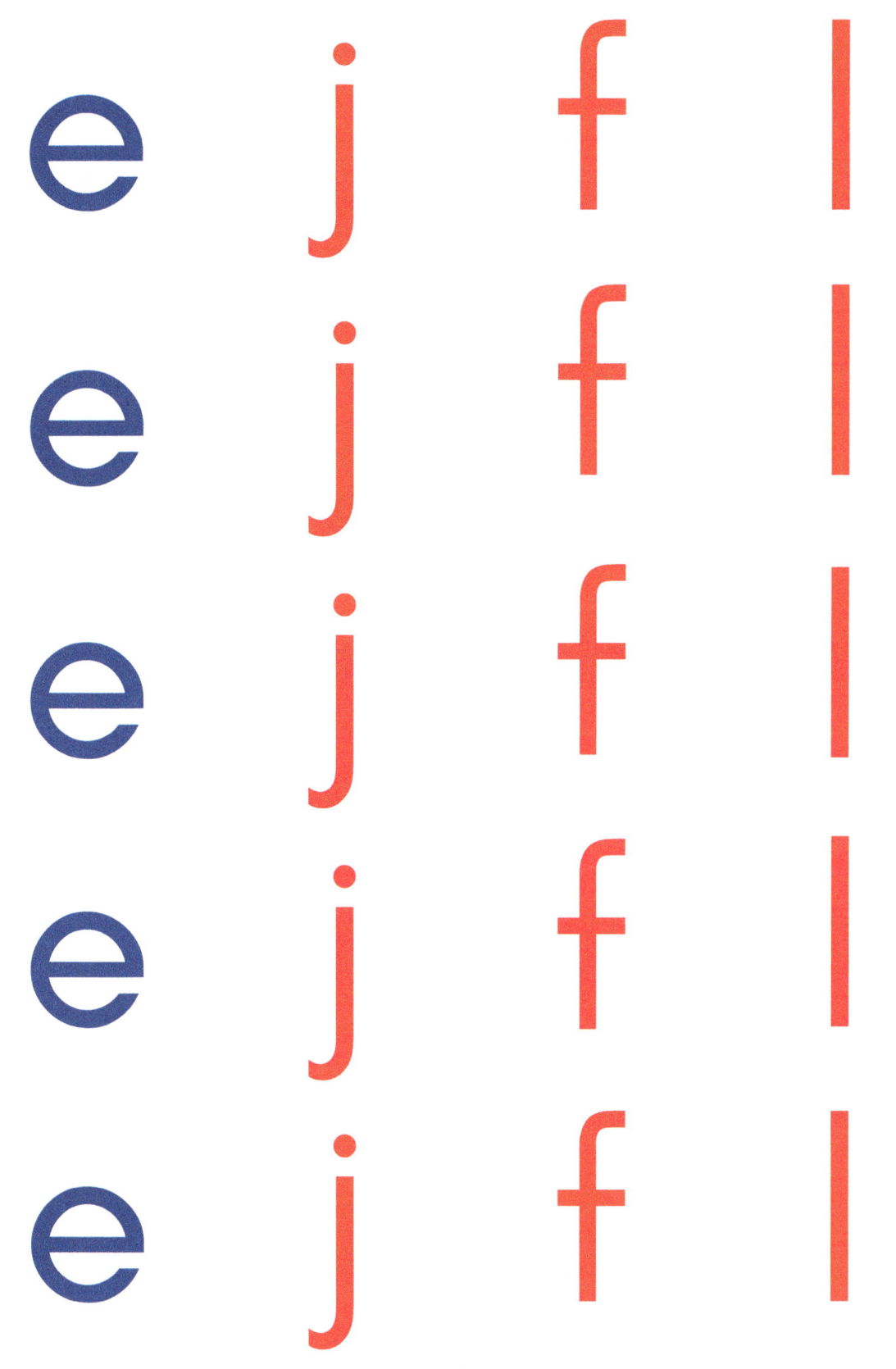

j f e l

movable alphabet organizer

e	j	f	l
e	j	f	l
e	j	f	l
e	j	f	l
e	j	f	l

Lesson 5.14
continued

Directions:
1. Build the first card together, segmenting each sound slowly.
2. Invite your child to build as many words as he shows interest and/or as time permits.
3. See **Appendix C** for visual step-by-step instructions and a KEY.

Note:
There are many CVC words your child will now be able to sound out. You may want to set a goal for your child to write *3 words* in one sitting, allowing your child to pick which words she writes. You may also want to invite your child to spell words at non-school times if she shows interest. You can also start each Reading Games lesson by inviting your child to write one or two words with the movable alphabet.

Please do not feel that you need to have your child write every single one of these words!

66

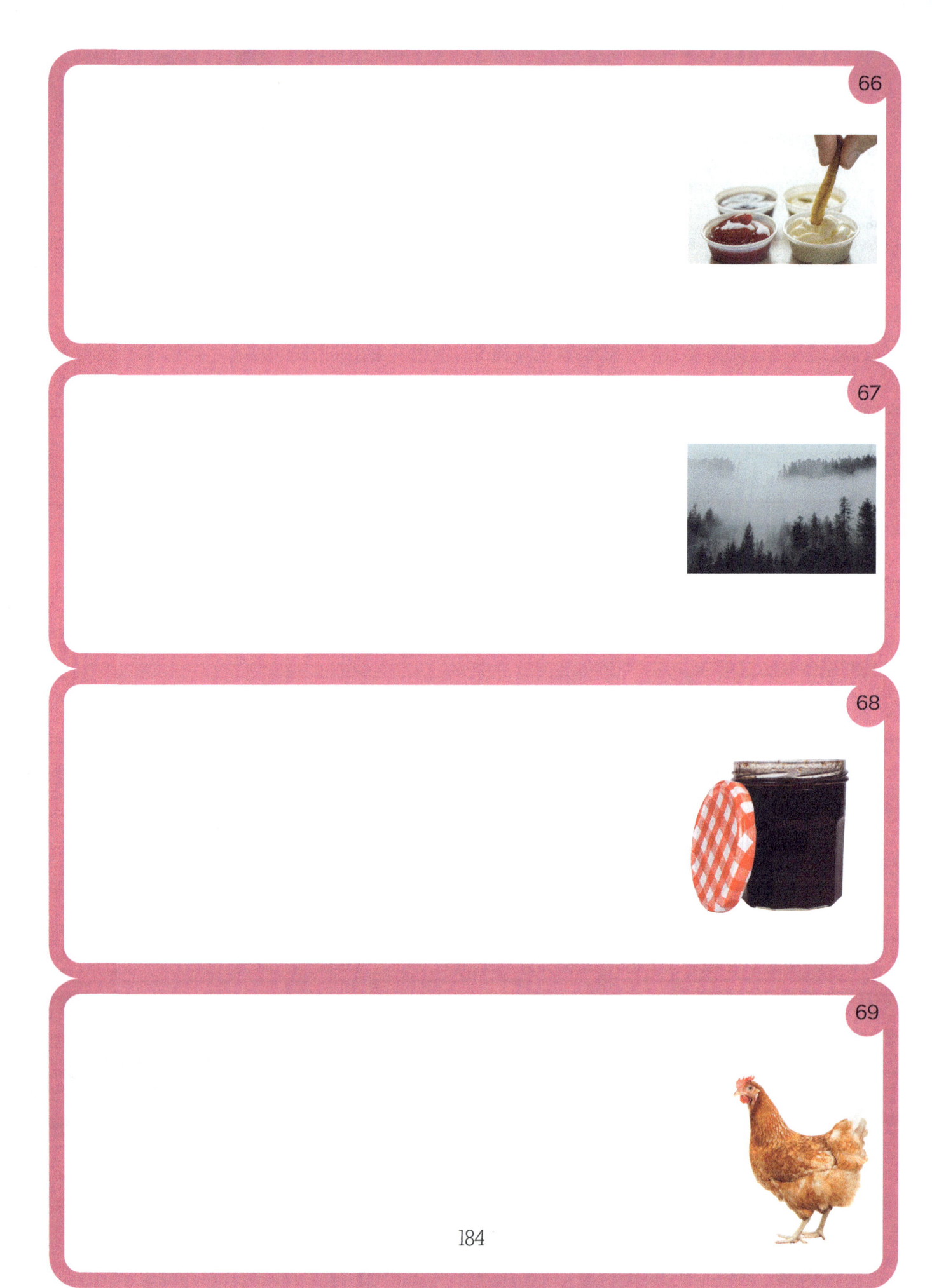

67

68

69

70

71

72

73

74.

75.

76.

77.

78

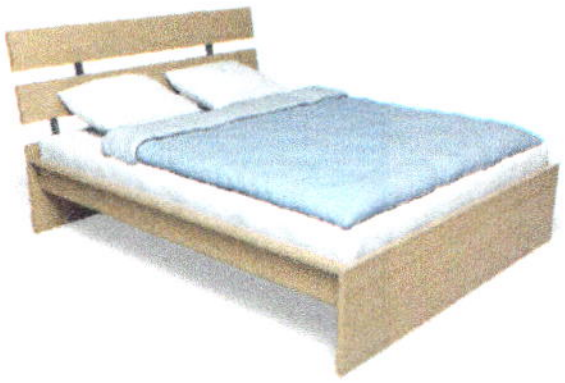

79

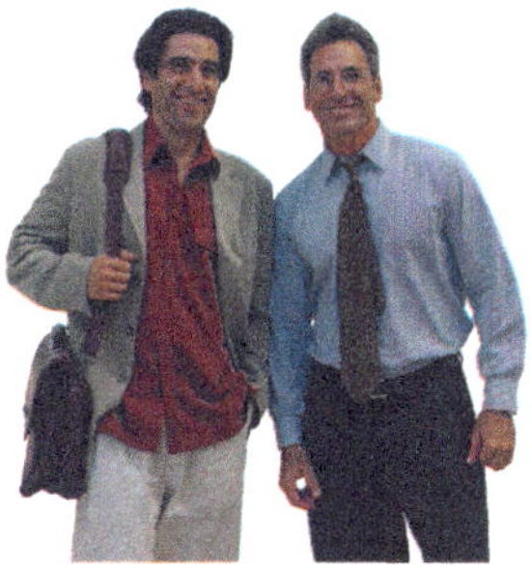

80

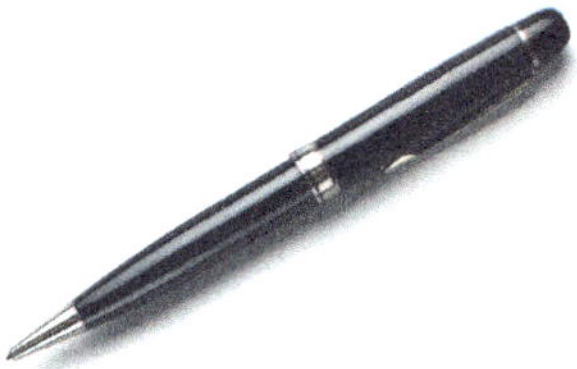

81

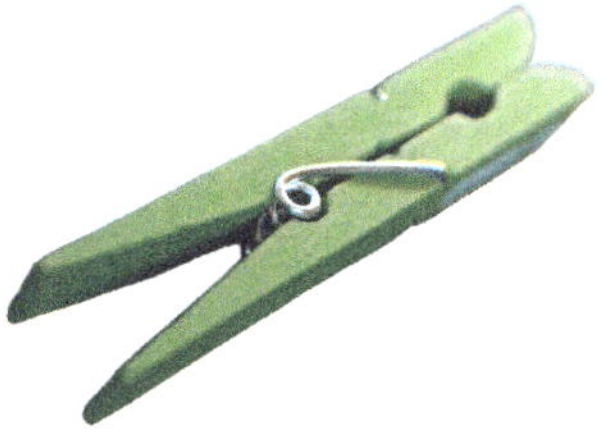

82

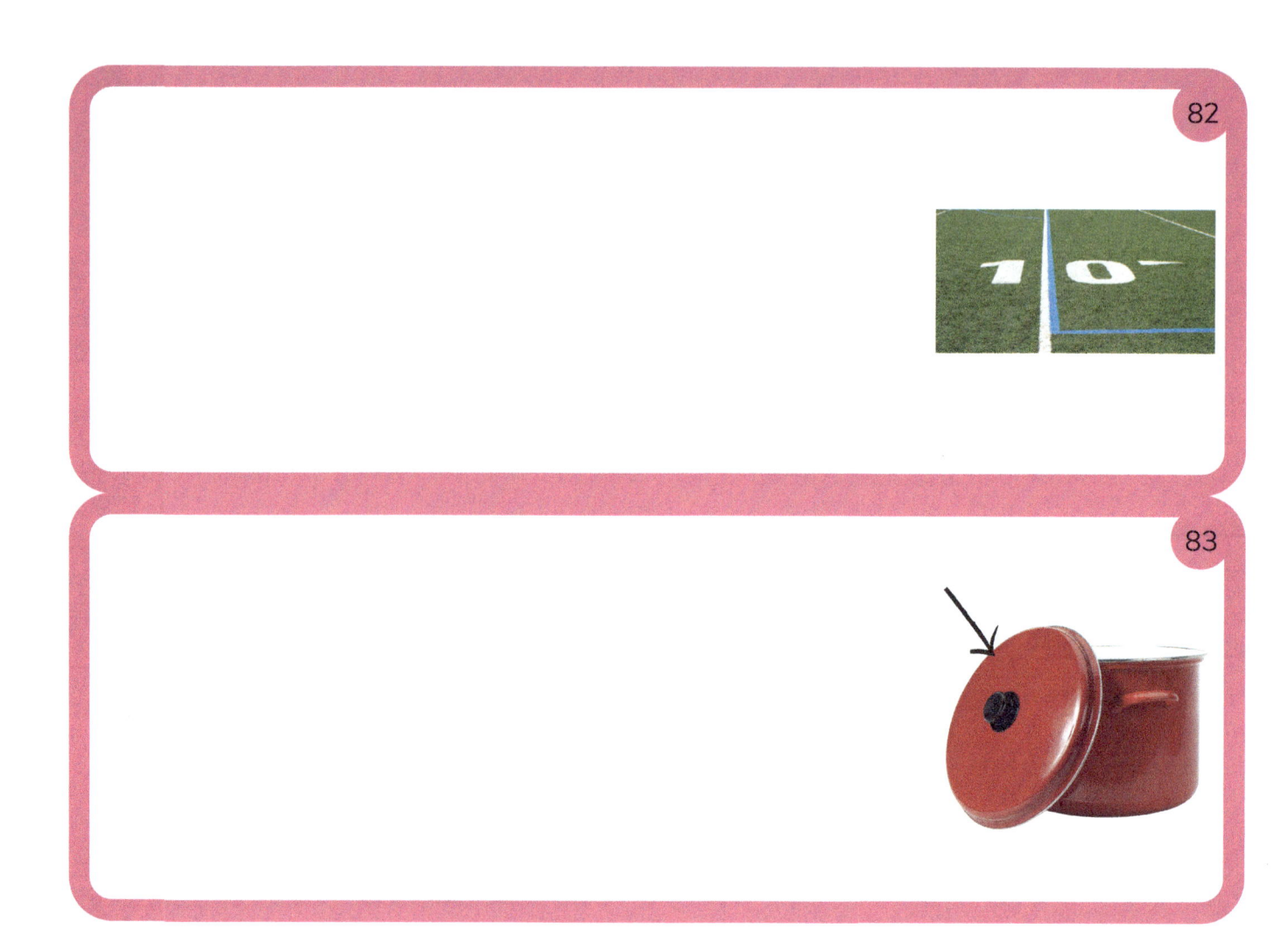

83

Unit 5 Assessment

j f e l

☐ sandpaper letters
☐ sensory tray (optional)
☐ movable alphabet

Directions:

1. Using the sandpaper letters you made for this unit (j, f, e, and l), invite your child to identify each sound as you hold up one letter at a time.

☐ j ☐ f ☐ e ☐ l

2. Using your sensory tray or the writing lines below, invite your child to write one of each letter.

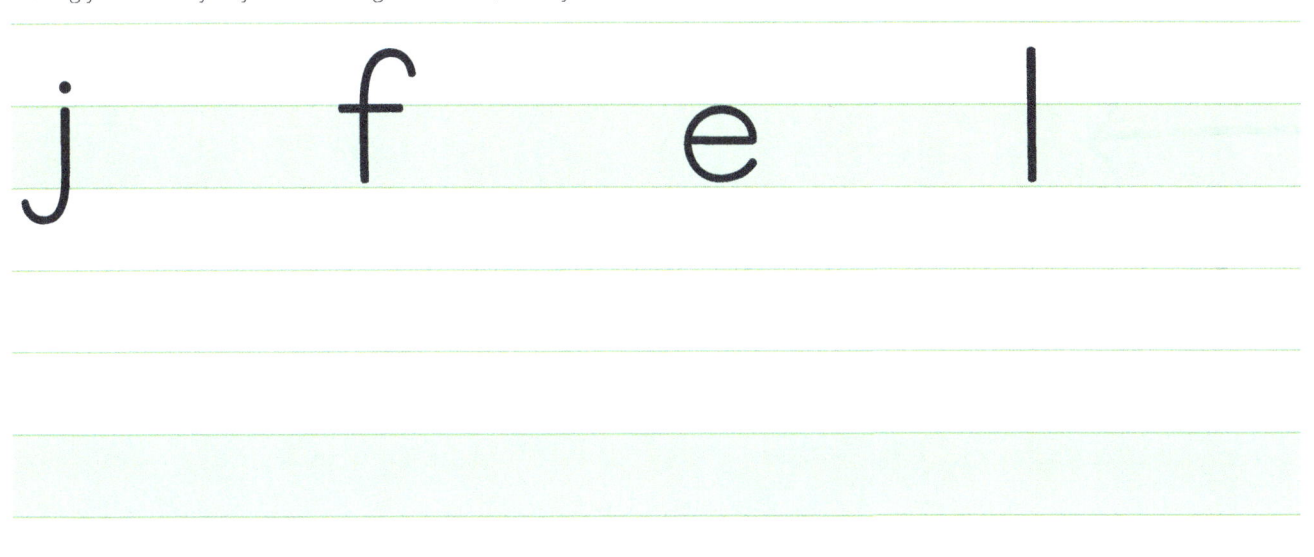

j   f   e   l

3. Draw a line from the letter to the object that has its beginning sound.

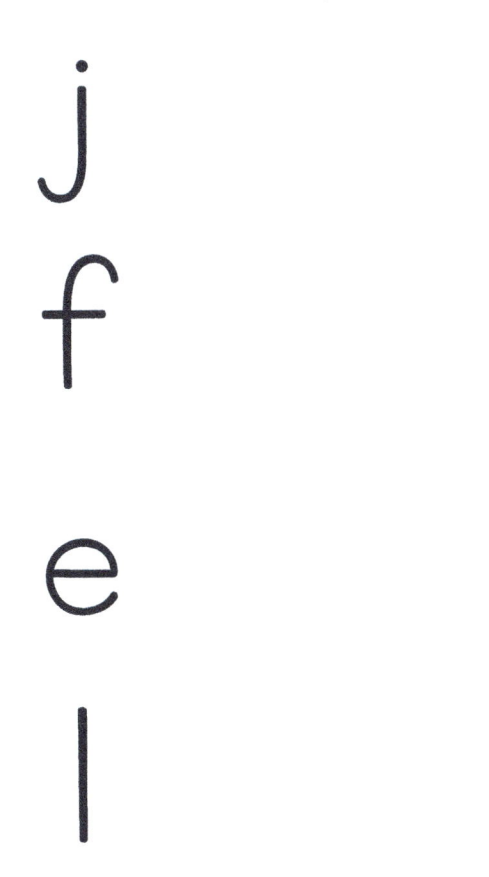

j

f

e

l

189

Unit 5 Assessment

☐ movable alphabet

j f e l

4. Build the following words with the movable alphabet by segmenting the words into their individual sounds.

___ ___ ___

___ ___ ___

Assessment Results and Next Steps:

Depending on how your child performed on this assessment, you may want to review letter sounds and letter formation before moving on to Unit 6. If your child made minor errors, feel free to move on, as there is review built into the entire program!

For further review if needed, see **Appendix A** for a list of games you can play with your child using the materials in the workbook!

If handwriting is a concern, consider incorporating more fine motor work into your child's day, such as: cutting, sewing, using puzzles with knobs, coloring, tracing, shading, helping in the kitchen, sorting, buttoning, zipping etc. In a Montessori environment, these kinds of activities are usually referred to as "Practical Life" activities and the uses are twofold: teaching practical skills that the child can use each day to help himself, and strengthening the muscles of the hand, wrist, and fingers to prepare for writing. Do not let handwriting prevent you from moving forward. Children can "write" with the movable alphabet for the duration of this program.

Unit 6

kqvxyz

k	kangaroo
q	quail
v	vulture
x	fox
y	yak
z	zebra

Pronunciation Tip: Be careful introducing /k/ and /qu/. By clearly pronouncing the /w/ sound in /qu/, like "qw," you will help your child distinguish when a qu- needs to be used instead of the k-.

Handwriting Guide

We won't be doing too much handwriting on paper, but every time you show your child how to write a letter by tracing a sandpaper letter, you need to be sure to use the proper handwriting strokes.

Most of the time, you will not pick up your pencil from the paper (or fingers from the sandpaper letter). The only time you will pick up your hand is when you see a **red number 2**.

Important: If your child is left-handed, show her the strokes using your left hand. If your child is right-handed, show her the strokes with your right hand.

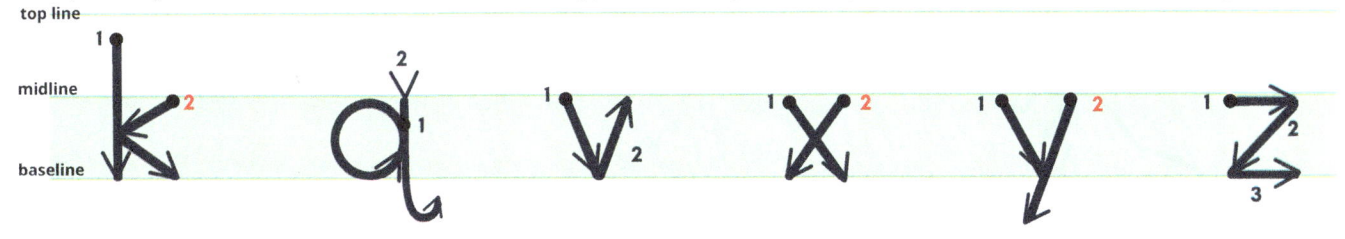

Start at (or near) the top line and draw a straight line down to the baseline. Pick up your pencil and draw a line from the midline to the halfway point between the midline and baseline, then back to the right slanted down to meet the baseline.

Start just below the midline and curve left up to the midline and circle around down to the baseline, then back up through the starting point and straight up to the midline. Without picking up your pencil, draw a line straight down to under the baseline and draw a small hook up to the right.

Start at the midline and draw a slanted line down to the right to touch the baseline. Then from that point, without picking up your pencil, draw another slanted line up to the right to touch the midline.

Start at the midline and draw a slanted line down to the right to touch the baseline. Pick up your pencil and start again at the midline above where your first line ended. Draw a slanted line down to the left to touch the baseline.

Start at the midline and draw a lanted line down to the right to touch the baseline. Pick up your pencil and start at the midline again, but to the right of where your first line ended. Draw a slanted line down to the left to meet the end of your first line at the baseline, and keep going underneath the baseline.

Start at the midline and draw a line to the right, then a slanted line to the left, down to the baseline, ending where your first stroke began, then finish with a horizontal line to the right that ends at the same place as your upper horizontal line.

191

kqvxyz
☐ crayons

Lesson 6.1

Directions:
1. Say, "We are going to play *I Spy*. Listen carefully and follow my directions."
2. "I spy something that starts with /k/ and is used to heat water for tea. What is it called?" [Jack-o-lantern.] "Put your finger on the kettle. What sound do you hear at the beginning of *kettle*?" [/k/] "Color the kettle black."
3. "I spy something that starts with /k/ that climbs eucalyptus trees and eats their leaves. It is a mammal. Can you put your finger on it? What is it?" [Koala.] "What sound do you hear at the beginning of *koala*?" [/k/] "Color the koala gray."
4. "I spy something that starts with /k/. It attaches to a string and can be flown in the air on a windy day. Can you put your finger on it? What is it?" [Kite.] "What sound do you hear at the beginning of *kite*?" [/k/] "Make a design on the kite."
5. "I spy something that starts with /k/ that you can eat. It is made from tomatoes and is used as a dip or sauce. Put your finger on it. What is it?" [Ketchup.] "What sound do you hear at the beginning of *ketchup*?" [/k/] "Draw a box around the ketchup."
6. "I spy something that starts with /k/ and is the baby version of a cat. Put your finger on it. What is it?" [Kitten.] "What sound do you hear at the beginning of *kitten*?" [/k/] "Circle the kitten."

Directions:
1. Say, "We are going to play *I Spy*. Listen carefully and follow my directions."
2. "I spy something that starts with /qu/ and can keep you warm. There are many varieties of these, and they are often homemade. Can you put your finger on it? What is it?" [Quilt.] "What sound do you hear at the beginning of *quilt*?" [/qu/] "Color the quilt using several different colors."
3. "I spy something that starts with /qu/ and has a black plume on its head. It is the state bird of California Can you put your finger on it? What is it?" [Quail.] "What sound do you hear at the beginning of *quail*?" [/qu/] "Draw feathers on the quail."
4. "I spy something that starts with /qu/. It is a feather that is dipped in in and used as a writing pen. Can you put your finger on it? What is it?" [Quill.] "What sound do you hear at the beginning of *quill*?" [/qu/] "Draw a box around the quill."
5. "I spy something that starts with /qu/ and is used as punctuation at the end of a sentence when something is being asked. Put your finger on it. What is it?" [Question mark.] "What sound do you hear in the beginning of *question mark*?" [/qu/] "Color in the question mark with red. ."
6. "I spy something that starts with /qu/. This person is a female ruler. She usually wears a crown. Put your finger on her. What is she?" [Queen.] "What sound do you hear at the beginning of *queen*?" [/qu/] "Color the queen's crown."

Lesson 6.2

kqvxyz
☐ yellow and pink crayons

Directions: Color the objects that begin with /k/ yellow and /qu/ pink.

193

kqvxyz

- ☐ 3 small objects each that begin with /k/ and /qu/
- ☐ and/or cut-and-paste sound cards from Appendix F

Lesson 6.3

Head's up!: Prep sandpaper letters for tomorrow's lesson.

Directions - Option #1:
1. Gather 3 objects for each sound that are small enough to fit (or roughly fit) onto this page. (kitten, kit, kite, keys, kiwi, ketchup; quarter, quill, question mark, quilt square, or see Appendix D for more ideas.)
2. Place objects in a basket or on the table in mixed order.
3. Name each picture ("**k**itten" and "**qu**arter.")
4. Invite your child to sort the objects into the boxes with the same beginning sound.

**Note: *These are hard sounds to distinguish, so make sure to enunciate the hard /k/ and the /qw/ sounds clearly.*

Directions - Option #2:
1. Locate the proper sound group sorting cards in Appendix F. Cut apart (or invite your child to cut apart) the sound cards.
2. Sort then save for the upcoming sandpaper letter sorting lesson.

Lesson 6.4

kqvxyz
- ☐ glitter glue
- ☐ 3+ small objects for each sound /k/ and /qu/

☐ **Part 1 Directions:**
1. Make the sandpaper letters. See Appendix E.
2. Introduce the sandpaper letters. Show one at a time and follow the script below.

Sandpaper Letter Script:
1. Pick up the *k* in the opposite of your child's dominant hand. (If your child is right-handed, pick up the letter with your left hand. If your child is left-handed, pick up the letter with your right hand.)
2. Say, "This says /k/."
3. With the pointer and middle fingers of your other hand (matching child's dominant hand), trace the letter the same way you would write it as you say the sound /k/. Do this 3 times.
4. Invite your child to say the sound while tracing the letter three times.
5. Repeat for the next sound. (Even though the "q" is by itself, pronounce it as the digraph, "qu" like /qw/.)

☐ **Part 2 Directions:**
Sort the objects used in the previous lesson underneath each sandpaper letter.

195

Lesson 6.5

kqvxyz
☐ crayons

Directions:
1. Say, "We are going to play *I Spy*. Listen carefully and follow my directions."
2. "I spy something that starts with /v/ and can be worn over a shirt. It doesn't have sleeves Can you put your finger on it? What is it?" [Vest.] "What sound do you hear at the beginning of *vest*?" [/v/] "Color the vest red."
3. "I spy something that starts with /v/. It can transport people or things from one place to another. Can you put your finger on it? What is it?" [Van.] "What sound do you hear at the beginning of *van*?" [/v/] "Color the wheels of the van green."
4. "I spy something that starts with /v/. It is a bird that helps keep the earth healthy by eating dead animals. Can you put your finger on the picture? What is this bird called?" [Vulture.] "What sound do you hear at the beginning of *vulture*?" [/v/] "Color the vulture brown."
5. "I spy something that starts with /v/ and can make beautiful music when a person runs the bow across the strings. Put your finger on it. What is it?" [Violin.] "What sound do you hear at the beginning of *violin*?" [/v/] "Circle the violin."
6. "I spy something that starts with /v/ and can be used to hold cut flowers. Put your finger on it. What is it?" [Vase.] "What sound do you hear at the beginning of *vase*?" [/v/] "Color the vase with any design you choose."

Directions:
1. Say, "We are going to play *I Spy*. Listen carefully and follow my directions."
2. "I spy something that ends with /x/ and can make beautiful music when played. It is usually made of brass and has a wood reed at the mouthpiece. Can you put your finger on it? What is it?" [Sax.] "What sound do you hear at the end of *sax*?" [/x/] "Color the sax orange."
3. "I spy something that ends with /x/, and you can put things inside it to store or ship. It is made of cardboard. Can you put your finger on it? What is it?" [Box.] "What sound do you hear at the end of *box*?" [/lx] "Circle the box."
4. "I spy something that ends with /x/. It has a sharp blade on one end and is used to chop down trees. Can you put your finger on it? What is it?" [Ax.] "What sound do you hear at the end of *ax*?" [/x/] "Color the blade of the ax gray."
5. "I spy something that ends with /x/ and makes up most of a candle. This melts when heated by the candle flame. Put your finger on it. What is it?" [Wax.] "What sound do you hear in the end of *wax*?" [/x/] "Color the wax of the candle purple."
6. "I spy something that ends with /x/ and lives in dens in the forest. It is fast and crafty and looks similar to a small dog. Put your finger on it. What is it?" [Fox.] "What sound do you hear at the end of *fox*?" [/x/] "Color the tail of the fox brown."

kqvxyz
☐ blue and orange crayons

Lesson 6.6

Directions: Color the objects that **begin** with /v/ blue and that **end** in /x/ orange.

198

Head's up!:
Prep sandpaper letters for tomorrow's lesson.

Lesson 6.7

kqvxyz

☐ 3 objects that begin with /v/
☐ 3 objects that end in /x/
☐ and/or cut-and-paste sound cards from Appendix F

Directions - Option #1:
1. Gather 3 objects for each sound that are small enough to fit (or roughly fit) onto this page. (vase, vegetables, van, vest; box, fox, wax, ox, or see Appendix D for more ideas.)
2. Place objects in a basket or on the table in mixed order.
3. Name each picture ("vulture" and "ax.")
4. Invite your child to sort the objects into the boxes with the same **beginning sound as** *vulture* and the same **ending sound as** *ax*.

Directions - Option #2:
1. Locate the proper sound group sorting cards in Appendix F. Cut apart (or invite your child to cut apart) the sound cards.
2. Sort then save for the upcoming sandpaper letter sorting lesson.

199

Lesson 6.8

kqvxyz
- ☐ 3 objects that begin with /v/
- ☐ 3 objects that end in /x/
- ☐ glitter glue

☐ **Part 1 Directions:**
1. Make the sandpaper letters. See Appendix E.
2. Introduce the sandpaper letters. Show one at a time and follow the script below.

Sandpaper Letter Script:
1. Pick up the *v* in the opposite of your child's dominant hand. (If your child is right-handed, pick up the letter with your left hand. If your child is left-handed, pick up the letter with your right hand.)
2. Say, "This says /v/."
3. With the pointer and middle fingers of your other hand (matching child's dominant hand), trace the letter the same way you would write it as you say the sound /v/. Do this 3 times.
4. Invite your child to say the sound while tracing the letter three times.
5. Repeat for the next sound.

☐ **Part 2 Directions:**
Sort the objects used in the previous lesson underneath each sandpaper letter.

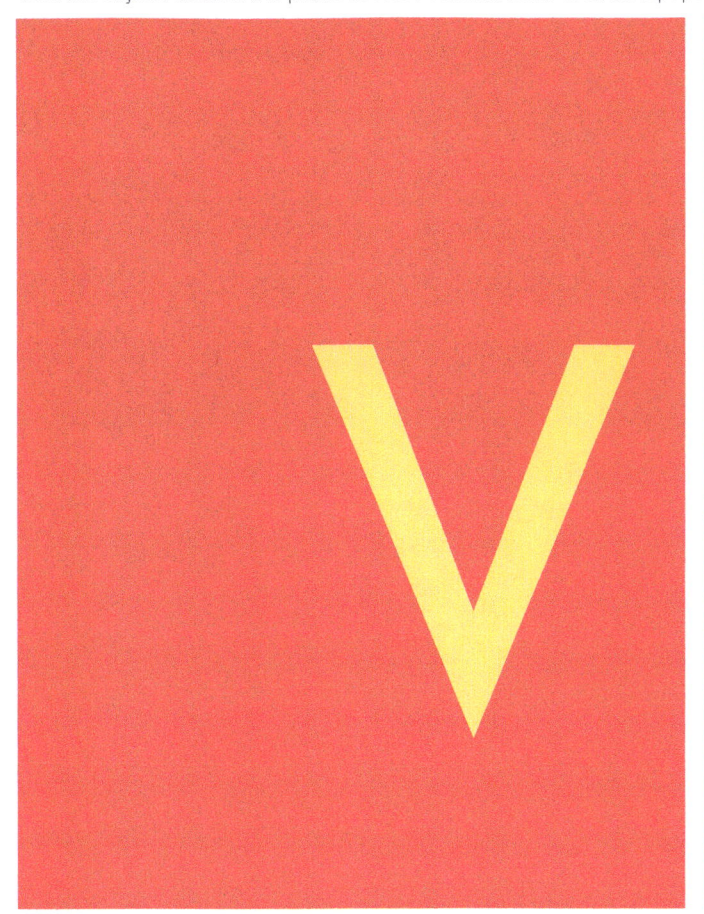

v   x

Lesson 6.9

kqvxyz
☐ crayons

Directions:
1. Say, "We are going to play *I Spy*. Listen carefully and follow my directions."
2. "I spy something that starts with /y/ and can be made into clothing, blankets, or even toys by knitting it together. Can you put your finger on it? What is it?" [Yarn.] "What sound do you hear at the beginning of *yarn*?" [/y/] "Color yarn your favorite color."
3. "I spy something that starts with /y/. They usually have brown skin and an orange interior. These grow grow underground, and sometimes they are called sweet potatoes. Can you put your finger on them? What are they?" [Yams.] "What sound do you hear at the beginning of *yams*?" [/y/] "Color the yams orange."
4. "I spy something that starts with /y/. It is something a person does when he needs to be heard by others. It is like loud talking. Can you put your finger on the picture? What is this called?" [Yell.] "What sound do you hear at the beginning of *yell*?" [/y/] "Put a box around the picture of a person yelling through a megaphone."
5. "I spy something that starts with /y/ and has horns and a long coat. Put your finger on it. What is it?" [Yak.] "What sound do you hear at the beginning of *yak*?" [/y/] "Circle the yak."
6. "I spy something that starts with /y/ and moves in the water. It can hold many passengers. This type of boat is usually large, over 40 feet long, and fancy. Put your finger on it. What is it?" [Yacht.] "What sound do you hear at the beginning of *yacht*?" [/y/] "Color the yacht blue."

Directions:
1. Say, "We are going to play *I Spy*. Listen carefully and follow my directions."
2. "I spy something that starts with /z/, is a line, but is not straight. It is a back and forth pattern. Can you put your finger on it? What is it?" [Zig zag.] "What sound do you hear at the beginning of *zig zag*?" [/z/] "Trace the zig zag."
3. "I spy something that starts with /z/ and is a number that means "nothing." Can you put your finger on it? What is it?" [Zero.] "What sound do you hear at the beginning of *zero*?" [/z/] "Color the zero with red."
4. "I spy something that starts with /z/. It is a green squash. Can you put your finger on it? What is it?" [Zucchini.] "What sound do you hear at the beginning of *zucchini*?" [/z/] "Color the zucchini green."
5. "I spy something that starts with /z/ and is used to fasten clothes. It has little prongs called teeth and a tab to pull. Put your finger on it. What is it?" [Zipper.] "What sound do you hear in the beginning of *zipper*?" [/z/] "Color zipper pull pink."
6. "I spy something that starts with /z/ and has black and white stripes. Put your finger on it. What is it?" [Zebra.] "What sound do you hear at the beginning of *zebra*?" [/z/] "Draw some water for the zebra to drink."

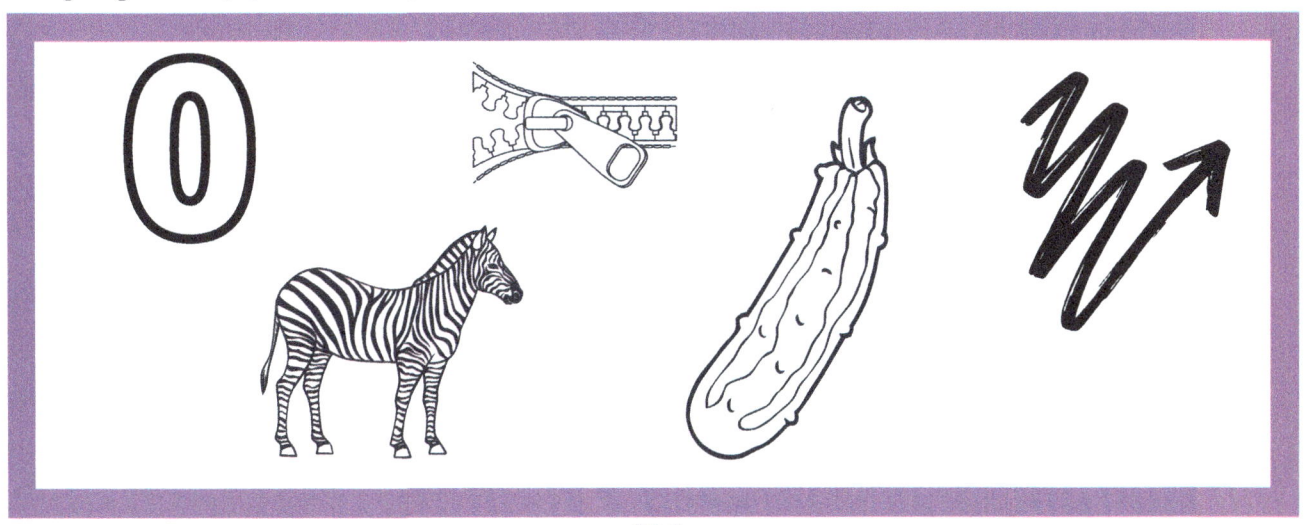

kqvxyz
☐ black and yellow crayons

Lesson 6.10

Directions: Color the objects that begin with **/y/ black** and **/z/ yellow.**

KEY: yo-yo, zero, yak, yarn, zebra, zipper

204

Lesson 6.11

kqvxyz
- ☐ 3 objects each that begin with /y/ and /z/
- ☐ and/or cut-and-paste sound cards from Appendix F

Directions - Option #1:
1. Gather 3 objects for each sound that are small enough to fit (or roughly fit) onto this page. (yellow tablet, yarn, yak, yam, yo-yo; zebra, zero, zipper, or see Appendix D for more ideas.)
2. Place objects in a basket or on the table in mixed order.
3. Name each picture ("yellow" and "zebra.")
4. Invite your child to sort the objects into the boxes with the same beginning sound.

Directions - Option #2:
1. Locate the proper sound group sorting cards in Appendix F. Cut apart (or invite your child to cut apart) the sound cards.
2. Sort then save for the upcoming sandpaper letter sorting lesson.

Lesson 6.12

kqvxyz
☐ 3 objects that begin with /v/
☐ glitter glue

☐ **Part 1 Directions:**
1. Make the sandpaper letters. See Appendix E.
2. Introduce the sandpaper letters. Show one at a time and follow the script below.

Sandpaper Letter Script:
1. Pick up the *y* in the opposite of your child's dominant hand. (If your child is right-handed, pick up the letter with your left hand. If your child is left-handed, pick up the letter with your right hand.)
2. Say, "This says /y/."
3. With the pointer and middle fingers of your other hand (matching child's dominant hand), trace the letter the same way you would write it as you say the sound /y/. Do this 3 times.
4. Invite your child to say the sound while tracing the letter three times.
5. Repeat for the next sound.

☐ **Part 2 Directions:**
Sort the objects used in the previous lesson underneath each sandpaper letter.

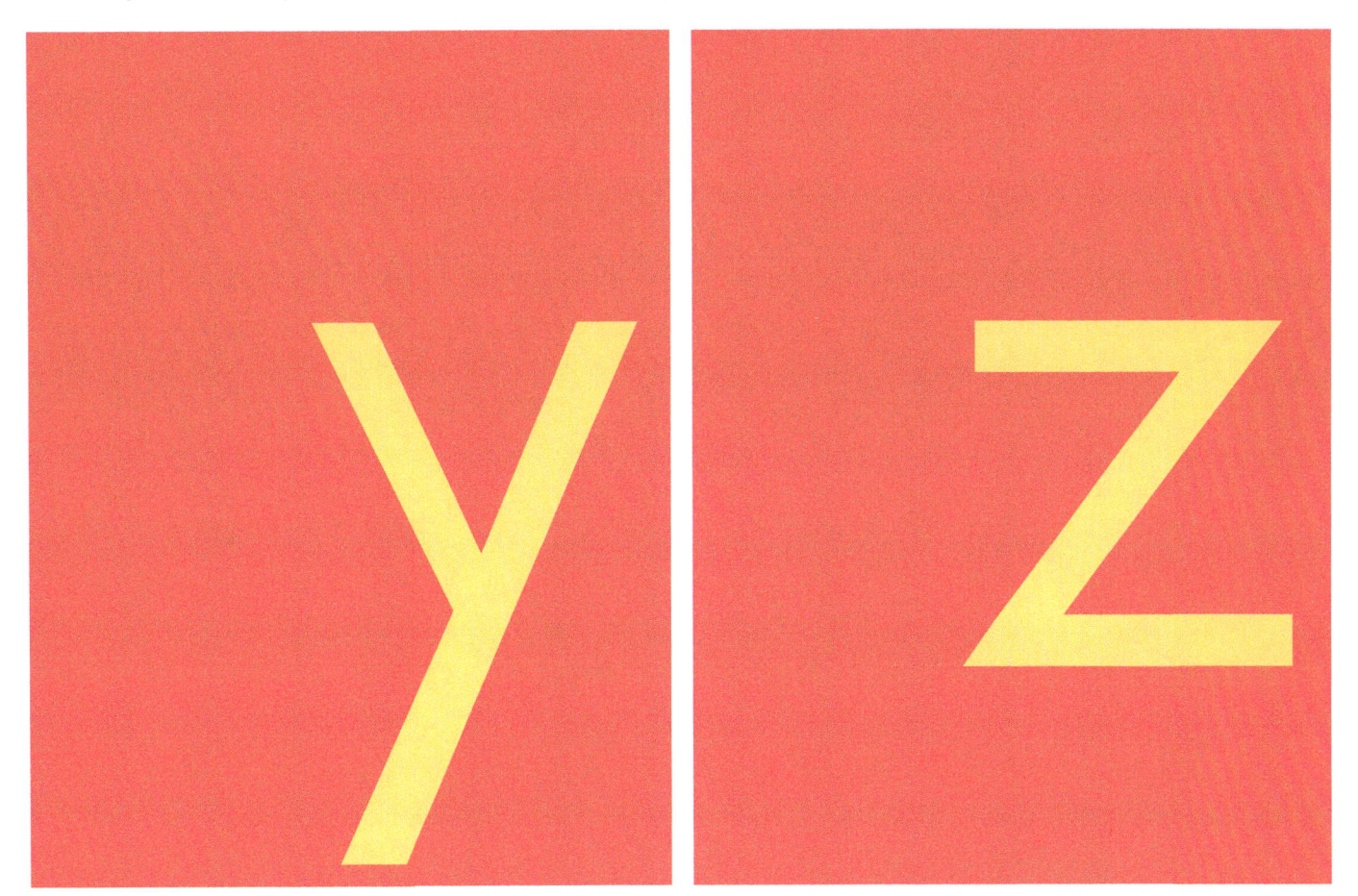

Lesson 6.13

kqvxyz
☐ counters/chips

Directions:
1. Cut out the BINGO cards.
2. Choose a game board and play with your student(s). Cut them from the workbook or leave them attached.
3. Shuffle and place cards face down in a single pile.
4. Take turns drawing one card at a time. Each player places a chip (any counter will work) on top of the matching letter on his/her BINGO game board.
5. Each player should cover his/her entire board.

Optional Extra Game: Go Fish
See Appendix E for directions.

KEY:
k: kettle, kitchen, kite
q; queen, quarter, quiet
x: six, x-ray, box
v: violin, vulture, vase

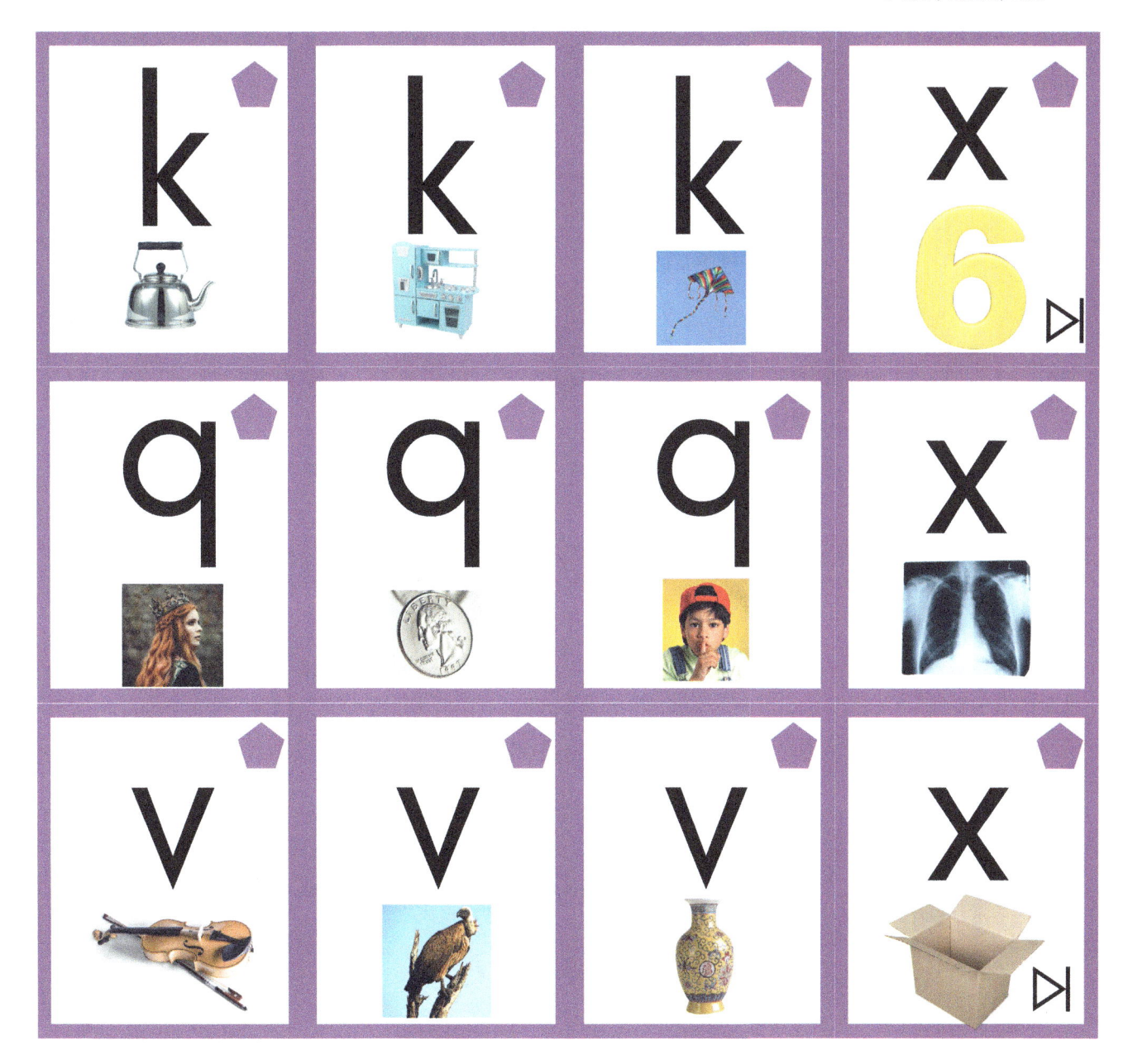

209

KEY:
y: yolk, yak, yarn
z: zebra, zipper, zucchini

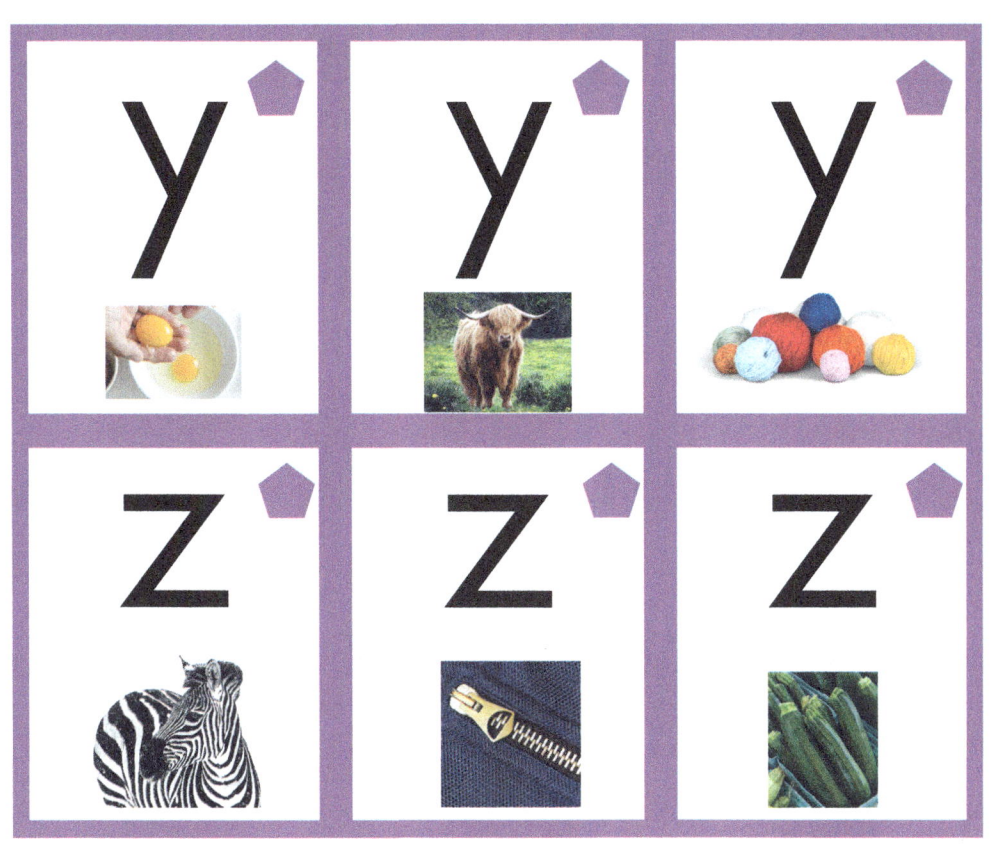

k	z	y
z	x	v
q	v	q

q	y	k
x	z	z
v	v	y

v	y	y
x	z	k
x	q	v

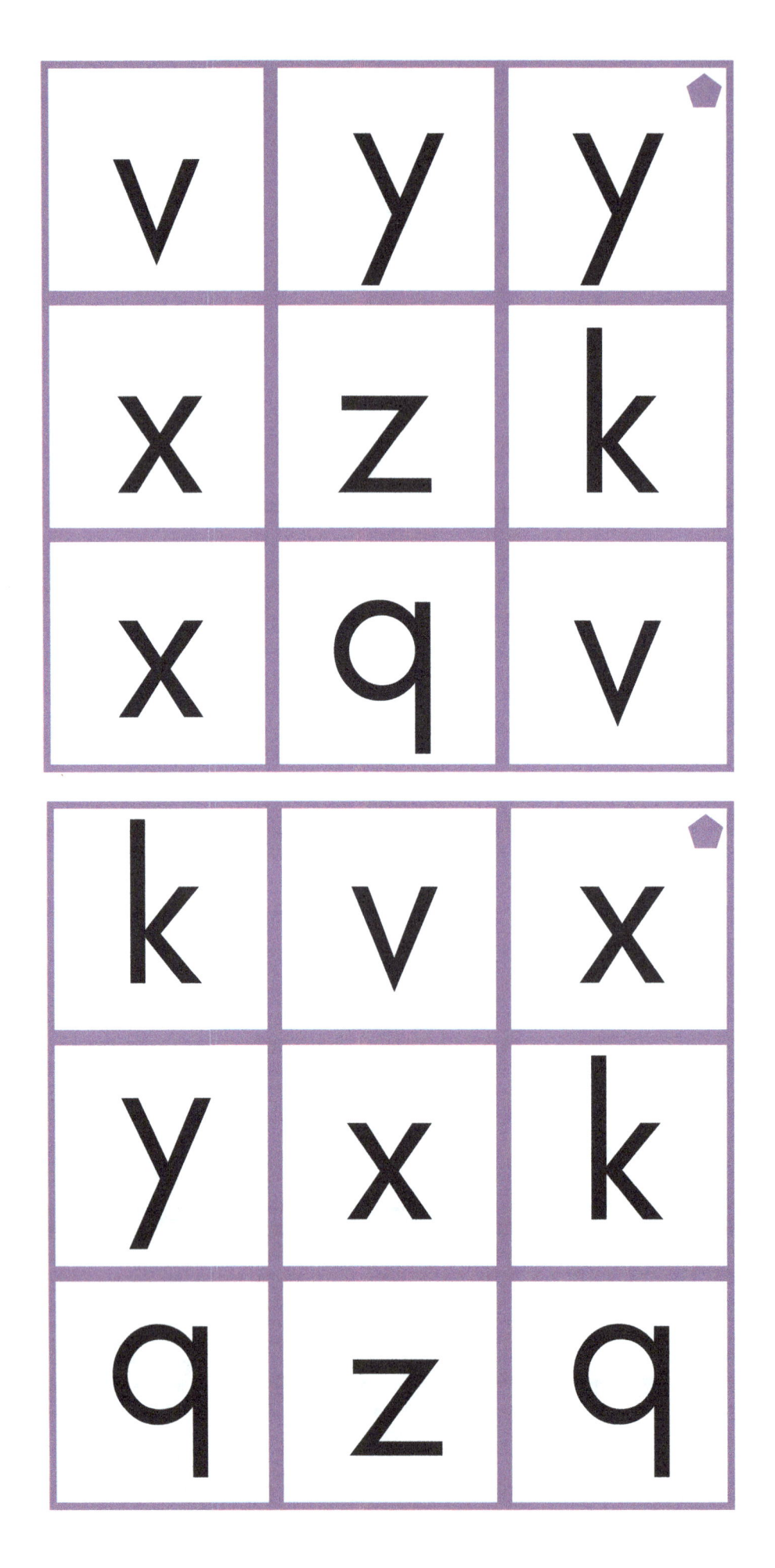

k	v	x
y	x	k
q	z	q

Directions: Play one round of the **"My Letter Sound Adventure Game."** Here are the new cards for your **My Letter Sound Adventure Game.** See Appendix B for directions on *how* to play the game and the removable game board.

Lesson 6.14

kqvxyz

☐ My Letter Sound Adventure Game (Appendix B)

121	122	123
124	125	126
127	128	129

215

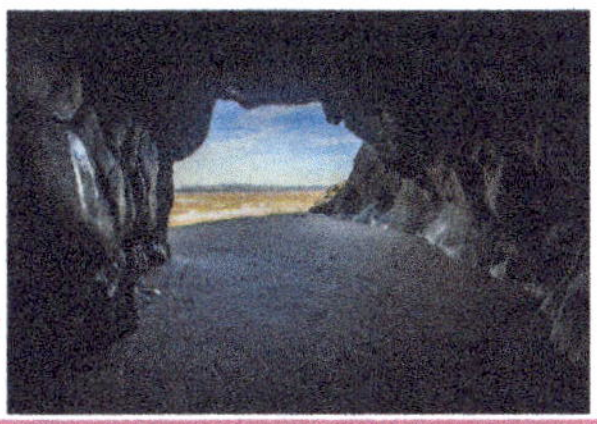

130

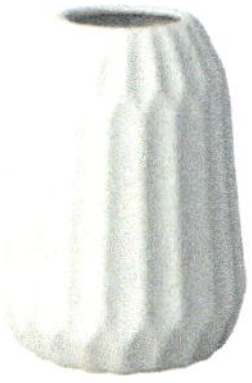

131

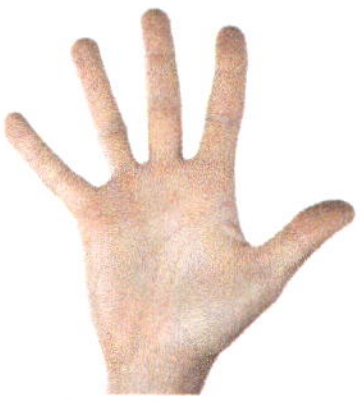

132

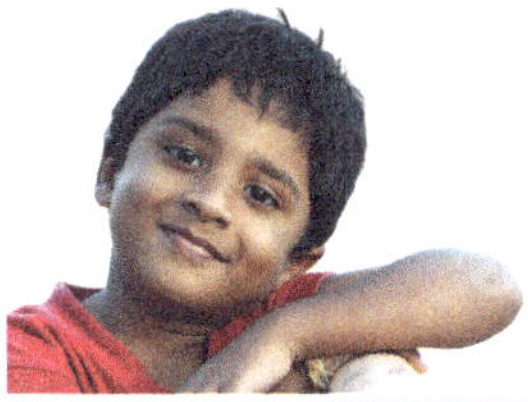

133

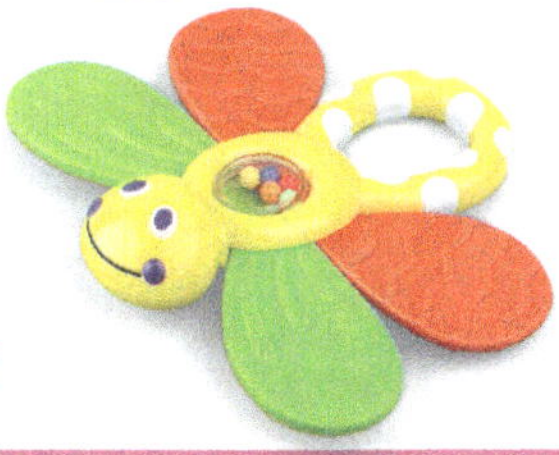

134

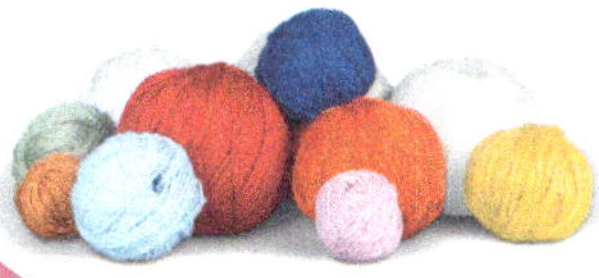

135

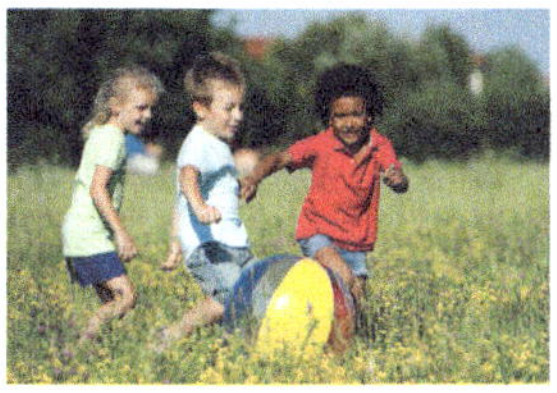

136

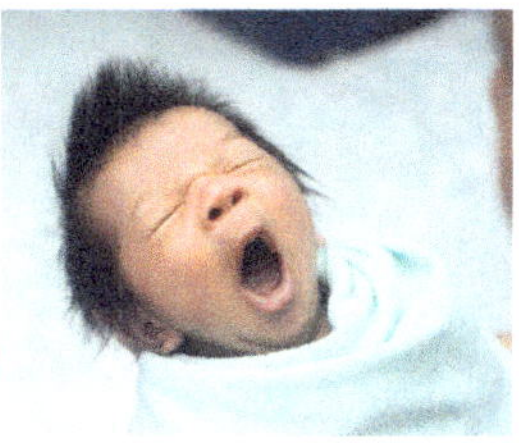

137

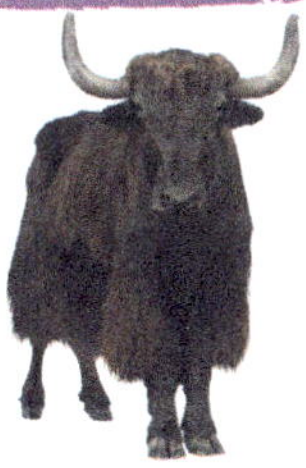

138

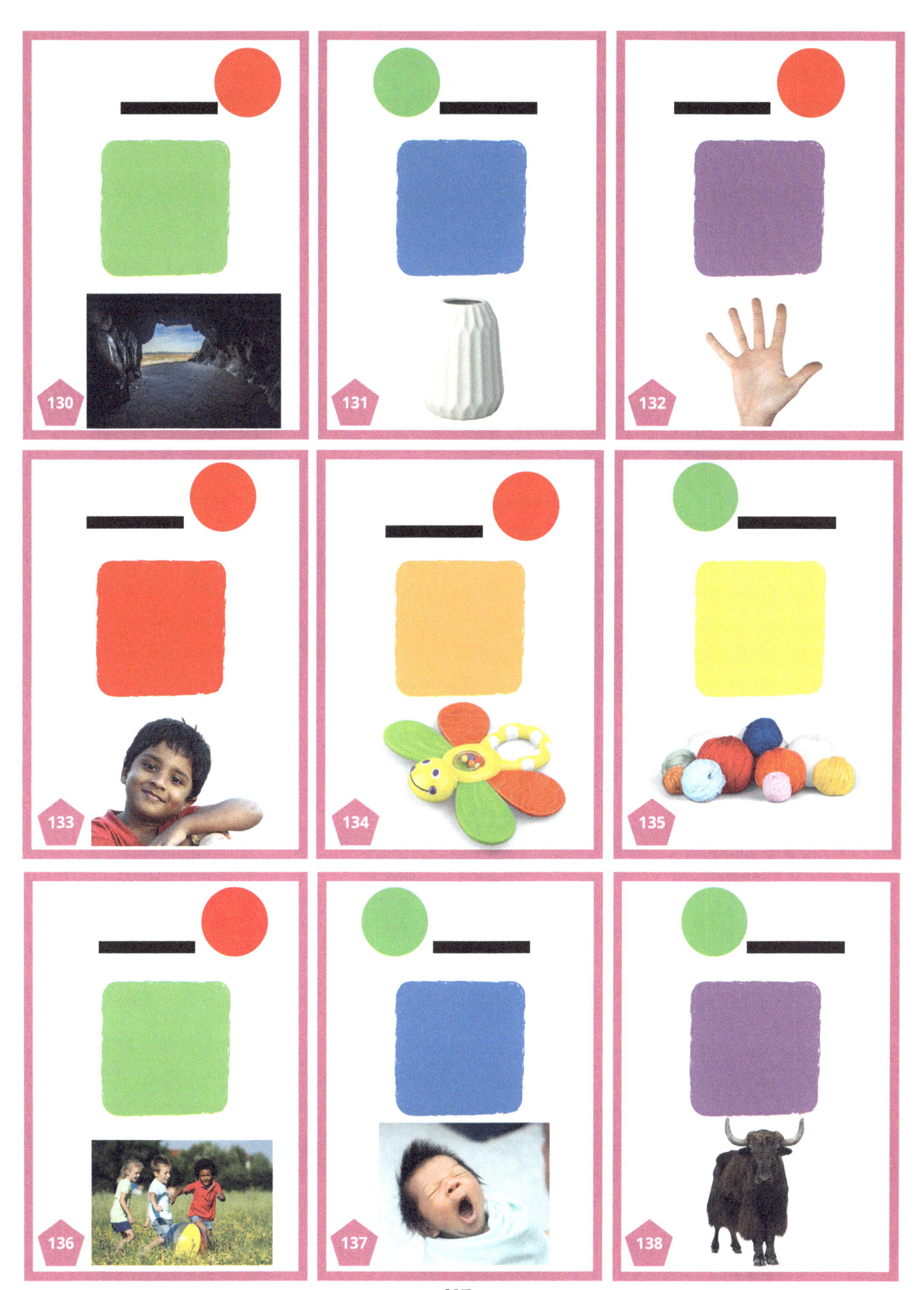

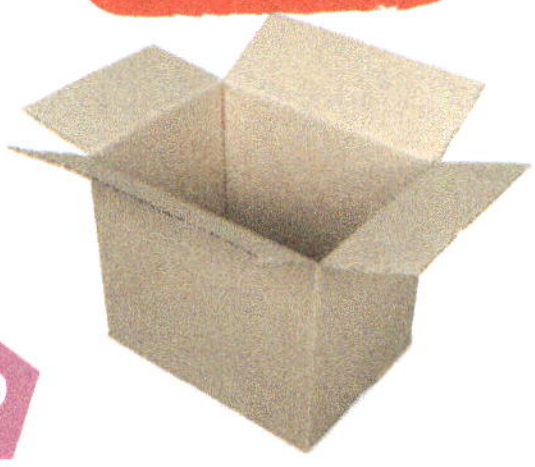

139

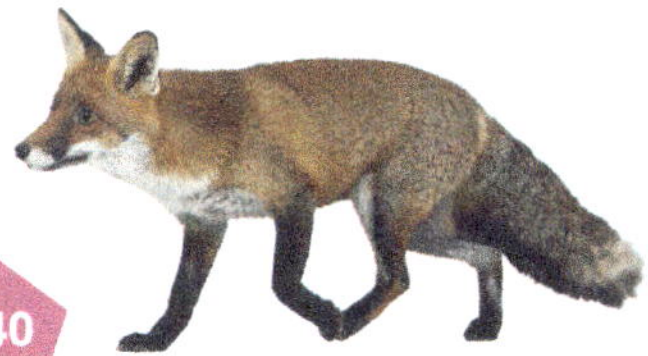

140

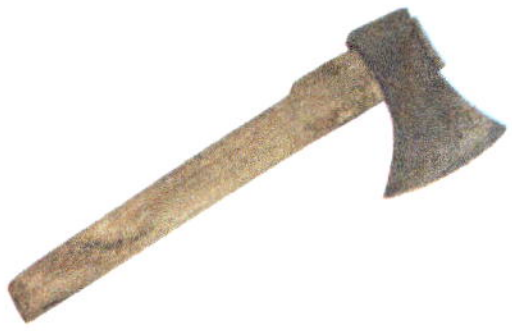

141

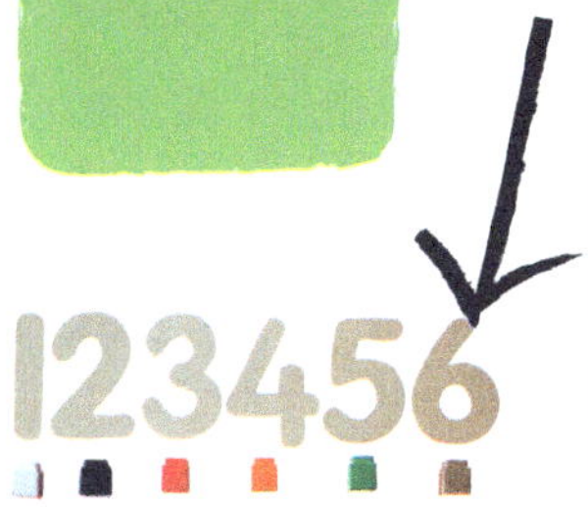

142

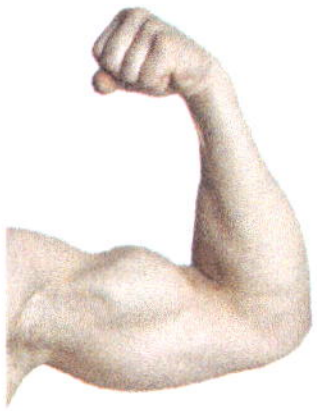

143

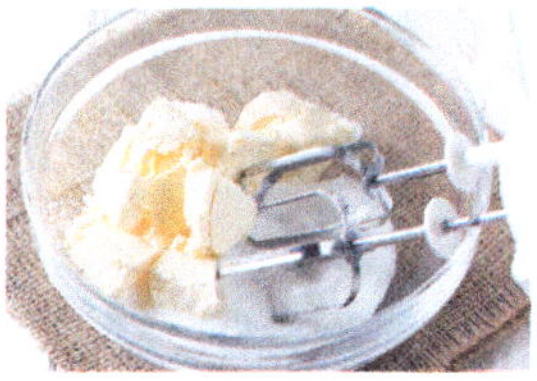

144

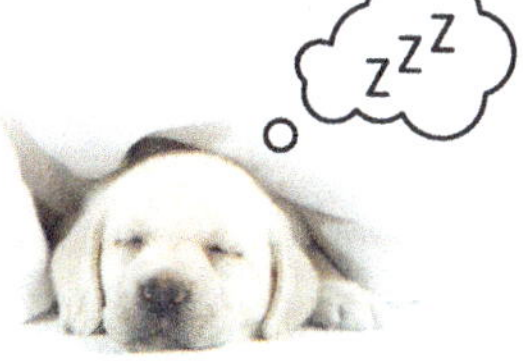

145

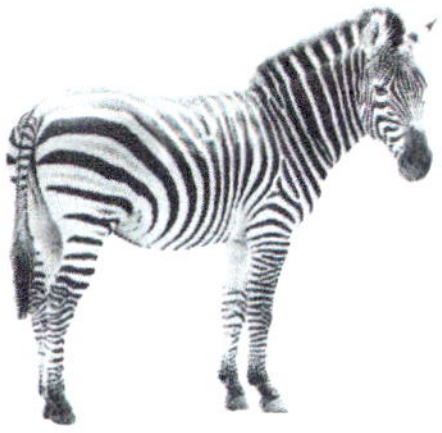

146

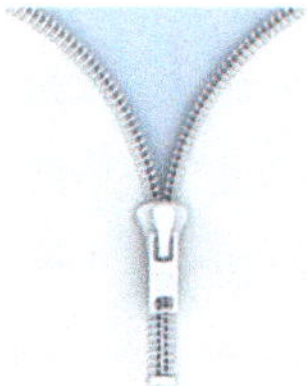

147

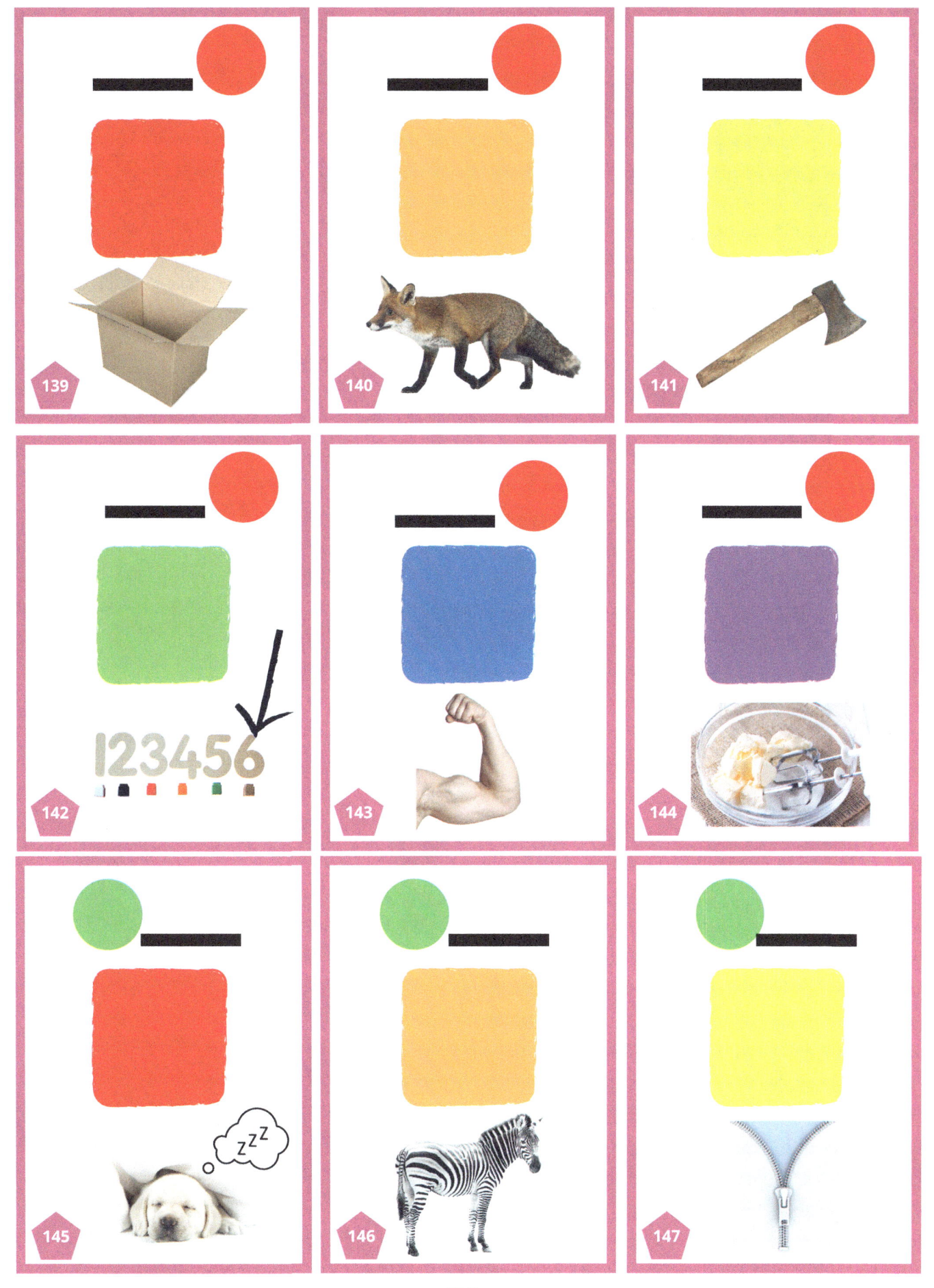

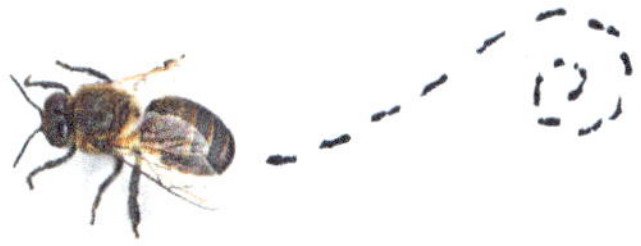

148

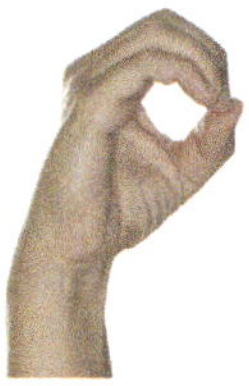

149

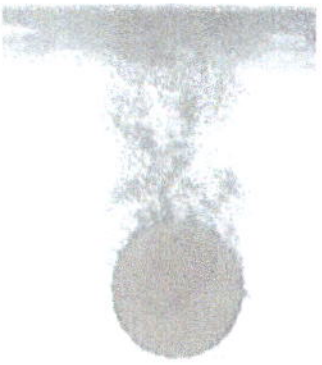

150

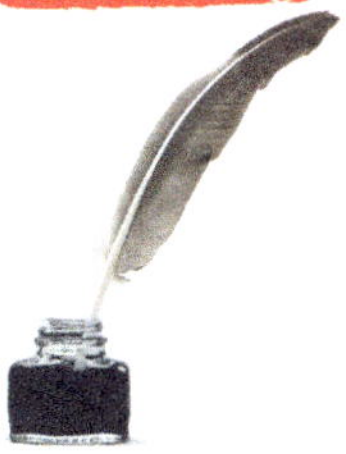

151

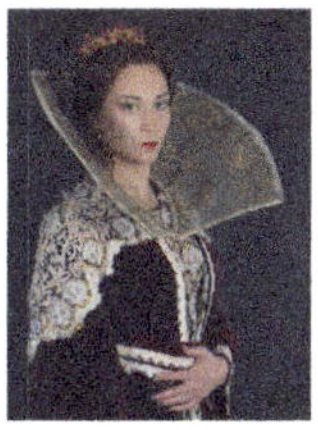

152

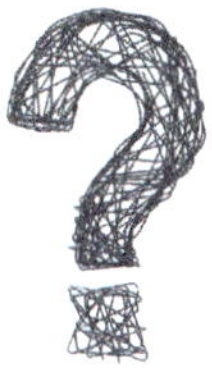

153

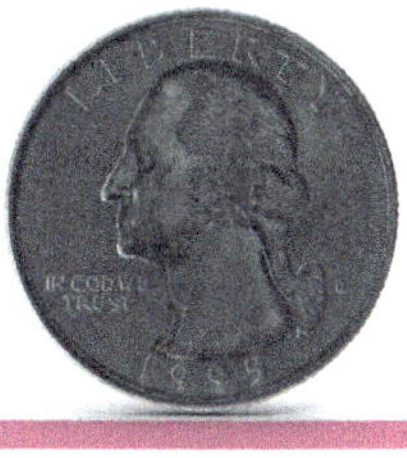

154

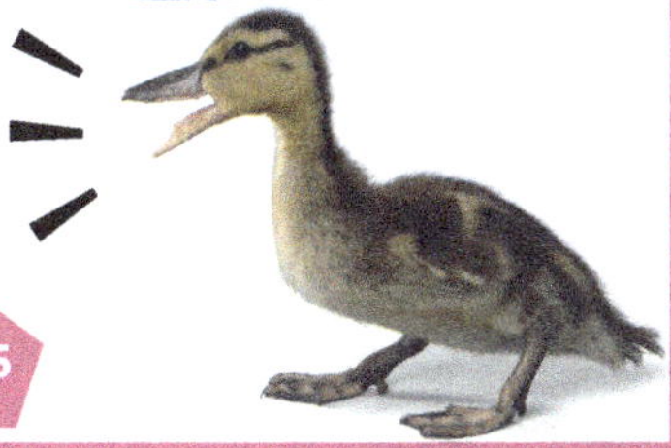

155

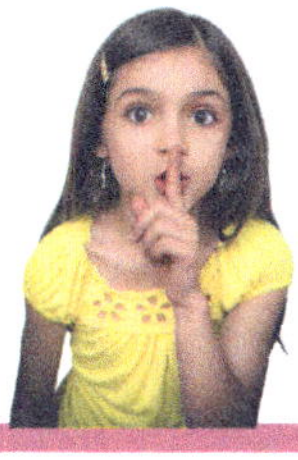

156

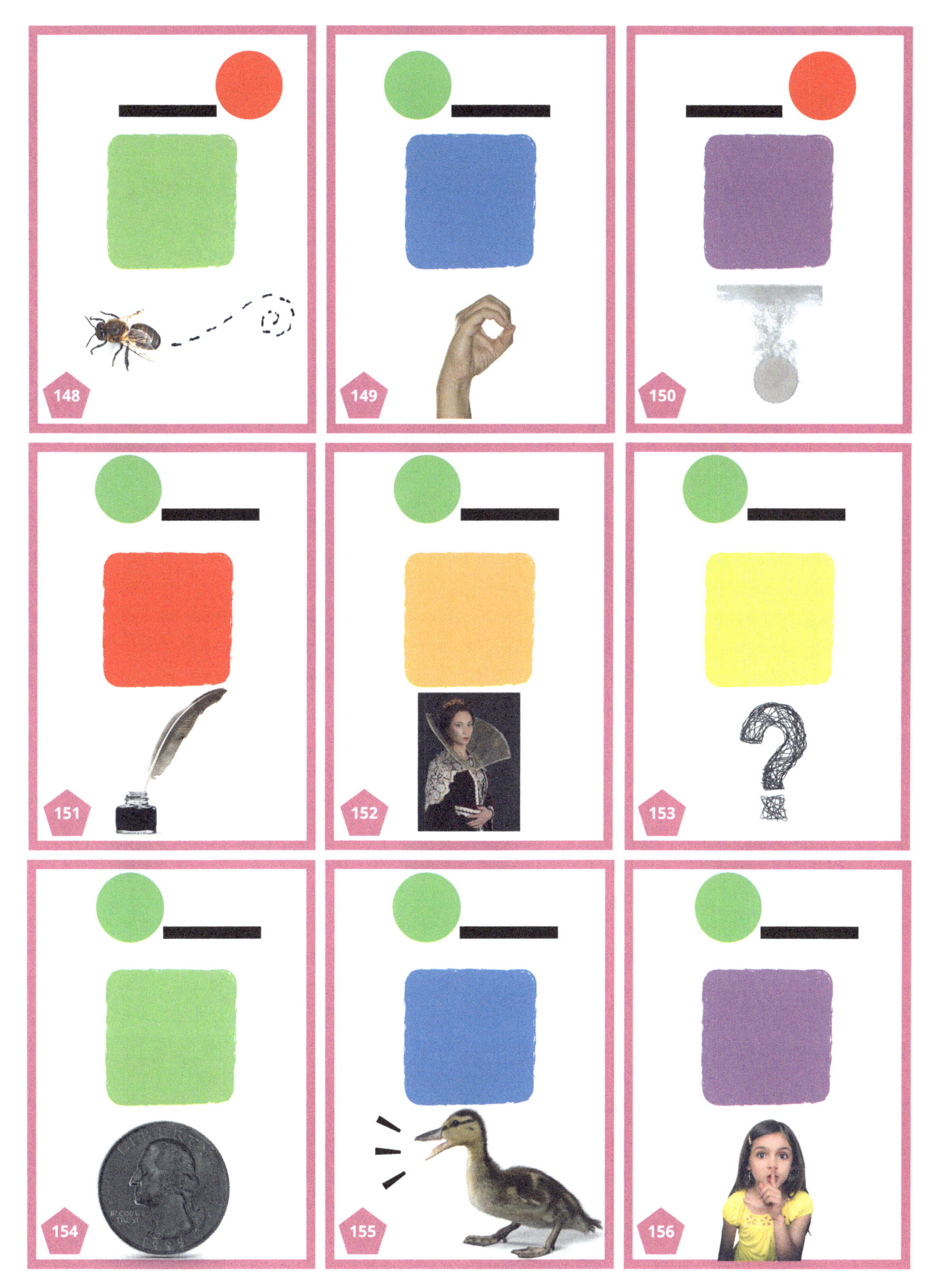

Key 121-144

121. kite
122. bark
123. kale
124. kangaroo
125. ark
126. fork
127. vacuum
128. violin
129. dove
130. cave
131. vase
132. five
133. boy
134. toy
135. yarn
136. play
137. yawn
138. yak
139. box
140. fox
141. ax
142. six
143. flex
144. mix

Key 145-156

145. z's
146. zebra
147. Zipper
148. buzz
149. zero
150. fizz
151. quill
152. queen
153. question
154. quarter
155. quack
156. quiet

"My Letter Sound Adventure" Word List

1. cat
2. apple
3. llama
4. bat
5. ax
6. soda/cola
7. bus
8. snail
9. snake
10. ask
11. salt
12. gas
13. mop
14. ram
15. emu
16. mail
17. amp
18. jam
19. hat
20. bat
21. tie
22. rat
23. turtle
24. tiger
25. act
26. candy
27. music
28. car
29. camera
30. arc
31. dog
32. bed
33. ads
34. door
35. sad
36. dolphin
37. mop
38. octopus
39. olive
40. off
41. ostrich
42. fog
43. hands
44. heart
45. hat
46. hockey stick
47. helmet
48. house
49. gold
50. hog
51. bag
52. grass
53. log
54. gate
55. rake
56. rabbit
57. car
58. star
59. rocks
60. door
61. chip
62. lip
63. igloo
64. inchworm
65. pin
66. iguana
67. bottle
68. cub
69. ball
70. bubbles
71. cab
72. books
73. penny
74. pig
75. paperclip
76. sap
77. sip
78. stop
79. nest
80. numbers
81. nail polish
82. nun
83. pan
84. bun
85. umbrella
86. cup
87. umpire
88. up
89. mug
90. hug
91. water
92. whale
93. cow
94. bow
95. worm
96. mow
97. badge ("j" sound at end)
98. wedge ("j" sound at end)
99. jam
100. hedge ("j" sound at end)
101. juice
102. Jack-o-lantern
103. feather
104. half
105. fire
106. fence
107. off
108. shelf
109. bed
110. elephant
111. jet
112. empty
113. egg
114. net
115. ball
116. lamp
117. lake
118. waterfall
119. well
120. lightbulb
121. kite
122. bark
123. kale
124. kangaroo
125. ark
126. fork
127. vacuum
128. violin
129. dove
130. cave
131. vase
132. five
133. boy
134. toy
135. yarn
136. play
137. yawn
138. yak
139. box
140. fox
141. ax
142. six
143. flex
144. mix
145. z's
146. zebra
147. Zipper
148. buzz
149. zero
150. fizz
151. quill
152. queen
153. question
154. quarter
155. quack
156. quiet

223

Lesson 6.15

kqvxyz
☐ tape

☐ **Part 1 Directions:**
1. Laminate page (optional) then cut apart individual cards. (Note: There are two pages of cards for the 6 letter sounds in this unit!)
2. Invite your student to spread the letter cards out across the top of his/her work space horizontally.
3. Shuffle the picture cards and invite your child to look at the picture, say the name of the object, and identify the beginning sound. Then place the picture card underneath the proper letter, making a column. There is a control of error on the back of each card so your child can learn to do this activity independently. See Appendix A for a visual.

☐ **Part 2 Directions:**
Make this into a game! Play "Four Corners." See game instructions and other game ideas in **Appendix A.**

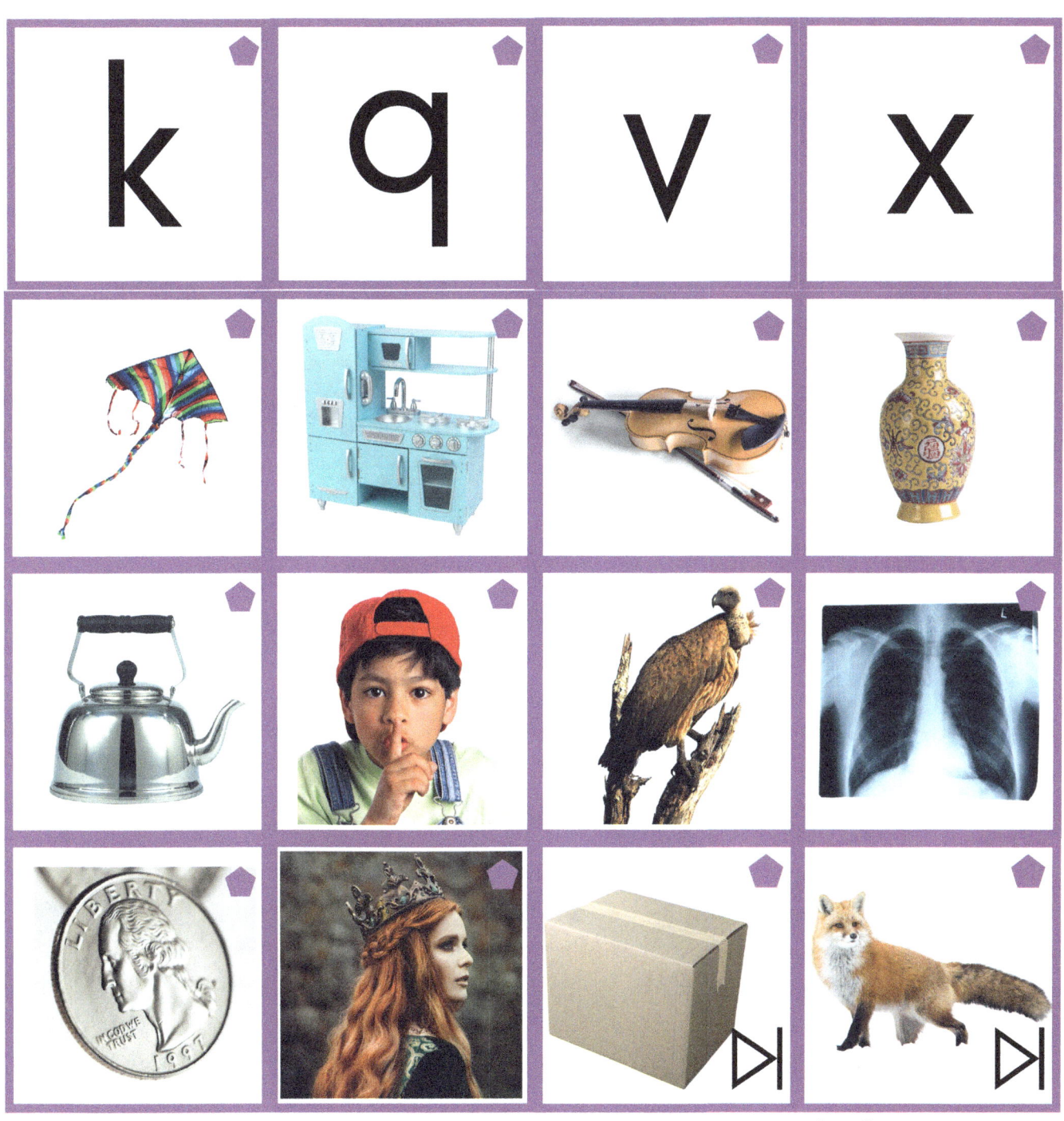

▶▌ = ending sound

225

vase	violin	kitchen	kite
x-ray	vulture	quiet	kettle
fox	box	queen	quarter

Lesson 6.15
continued

kqvxyz
☐ tape

y z

yolk   yak

yarn   zebra

zipper   zucchini

Lesson 6.16

kqvxyz
- ☐ sensory tray
- ☐ laminating sheet + marker OR pencil
- ☐ stapler, scissors

Part 1 Directions:
1. Prepare a shallow tray and fill it with salt, sand, or cornmeal.
2. Review the sandpaper letter /s/. Trace three times while saying the sound, then invite your child to do the same.
3. Show your child how to write the letter in the sensory tray with your finger after tracing the sandpaper letter. Show your child how to gently shake the tray to redistribute the material to give a clean writing surface. Invite your child to write the letter with her finger.
4. Repeat with the other three letters in this sound group.

Part 2 Directions:
1. Invite your child to make a book out of the letters by cutting apart the strips on this page, stacking them, and stapling the booklet on the left-hand side.
2. Your child should be able to identify the letter sound and connect the letter sound to the beginning sound in each picture.
3. On the back of each strip, your child can practice writing with a pencil.
4. NOTE: To make these re-usable, laminate then cut, and use a dry-erase marker for tracing and writing.

k: kite, kick, kettle.   q: quail, question mark, queen   v: vacuum, vase, van.   x: x-ray, bo**x**, X block k

q

v

x

Lesson 6.15
continued

kqvxyz
☐ sensory tray
☐ laminating sheet + marker OR pencil
☐ stapler, scissors

y

z

y: yarn, yak, yam

z: zipper, zero, zebra

231

y

z

Lesson 6.17

kqvxyz

☐ pencil OR counters
OR
☐ laminating sheet + 4 clothes pins

Directions:
Invite your child to circle or place a counter on top of the correct picture to match each beginning letter sound.

Re-Usable Shelf Work:
Laminate sheet. Cut individual cards. Place clothespins in a basket next to the cards and invite your child to clip the clothespin on the correct picture to match each beginning sound.
Show your child how to check his work by flipping over the card as a control of error.

KEY: kangaroo, quarter, vase, x-ray, yo-yo, zebra

233

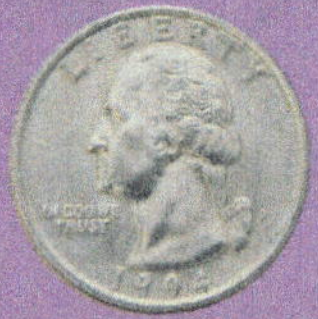
LIBERTY

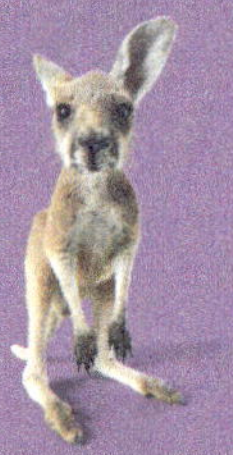

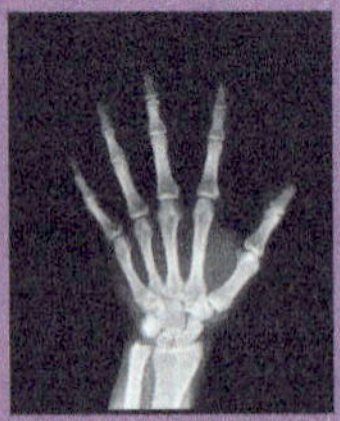

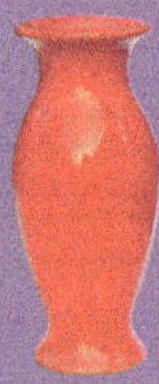

Lesson 6.17
continued

kqvxyz

☐ pencil OR counters
OR
☐ laminating sheet + 4 clothes pins

Directions:
Invite your child to circle or place a counter on top of the correct picture to match each beginning letter sound.

Re-Usable Shelf Work:
Laminate sheet. Cut individual cards. Place clothespins in a basket next to the cards and invite your child to clip the clothespin on the correct picture to match each beginning sound.
Show your child how to check his work by flipping over the card as a control of error.

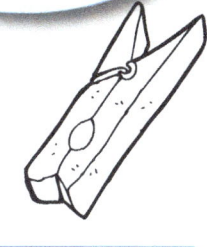

KEY: quarter, vase, yo-yo, zebra, x-ray

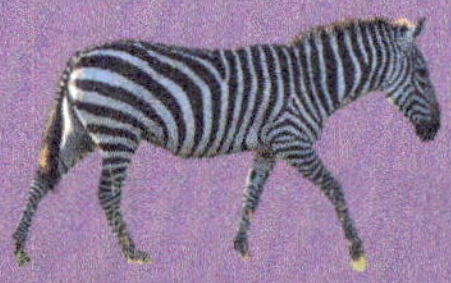

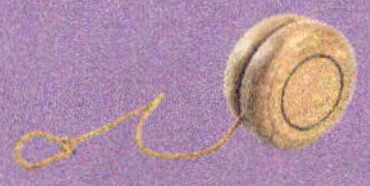

Lesson 6.18

kqvxyz
☐ movable alphabet organizer

Directions:
1. Laminate (optional, but recommended), cut, and add the alphabet tiles to your organizer. (There are two pages of tiles.)
2. Read each new letter sound. Keep the punctuation marks and introduce only if your child shows interest. These will be used in later work with the movable alphabet.
3. Build the word, "set" together on the first Pink Series Word Building Card for this unit.
4. Invite our child to build as many of the words as he shows interest on the Pink Series Word Cards pages.

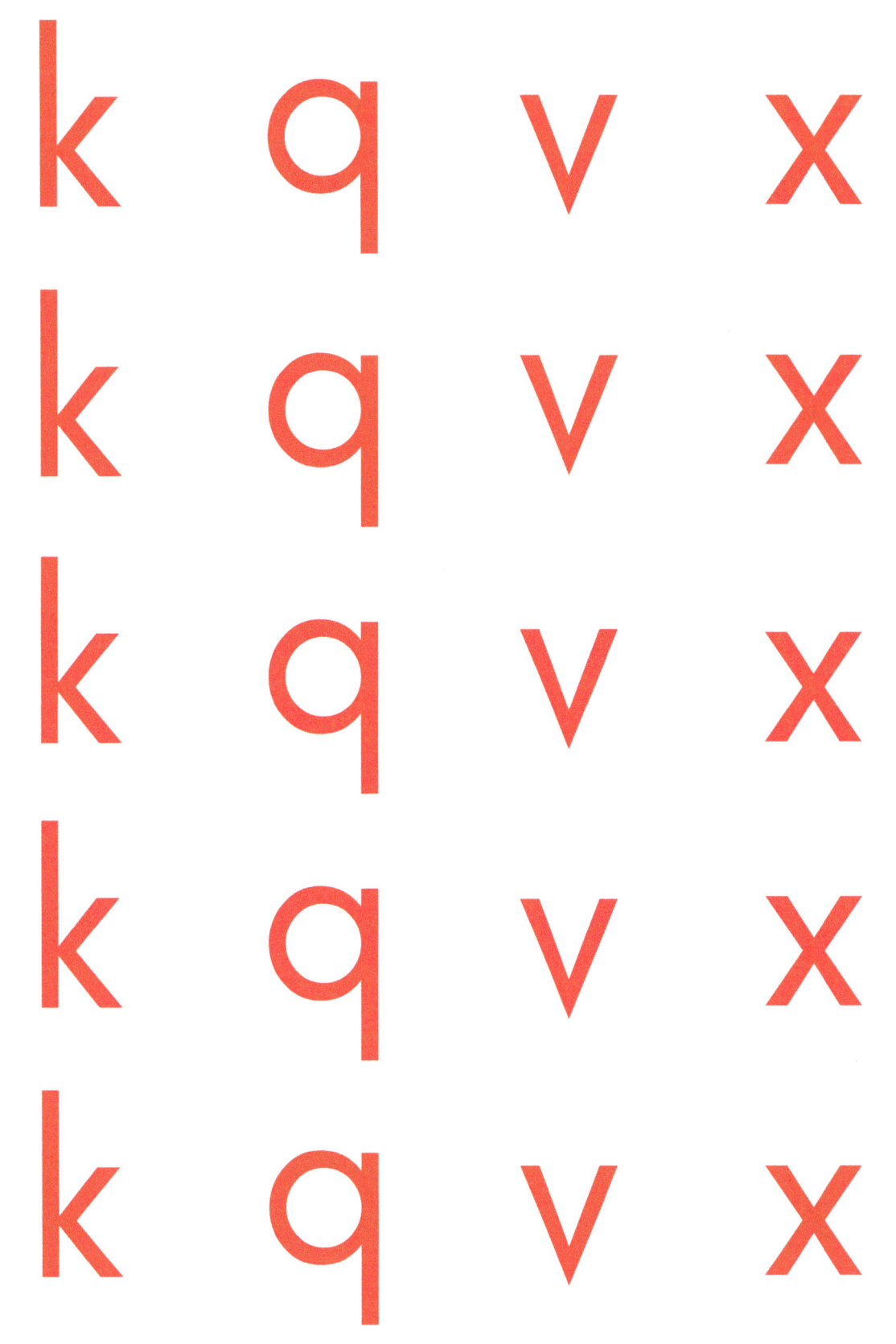

k	q	v	x
k	q	v	x
k	q	v	x
k	q	v	x
k	q	v	x

Lesson 6.18
continued

kqvxyz
☐ movable alphabet organizer

y	z	.	.
		!	!
y	z	!	!
y	z	?	?
y	z	,	,
y	z	.	.

239

Lesson 6.18
continued

kqvxyz
☐ movable alphabet

Directions:
1. Build the first card together, segmenting each sound slowly.
2. Invite your child to build as many words as he shows interest and/or as time permits.
3. See **Appendix C** for visual step-by-step instructions and a KEY.

Note:
There are many CVC words your child will now be able to sound out. You may want to set a goal for your child to write *3 words* in one sitting, allowing your child to pick which words she writes. You may also want to invite your child to spell words at non-school times if she shows interest. You can also start each Reading Games lesson by inviting your child to write one or two words with the movable alphabet.

Please do not feel that you need to have your child write every single one of these words!

84

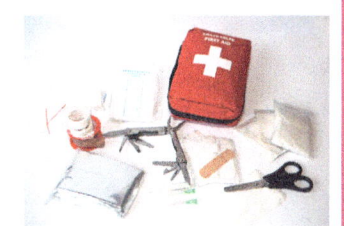

85

86

87

88

89

86

91

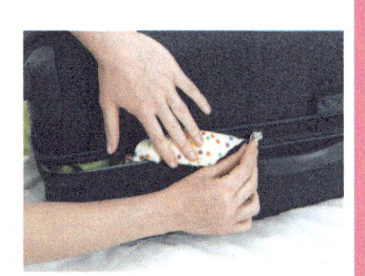

92

93

94

243

95

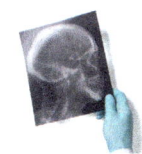

Unit 6 Assessment

kqvxyz
- ☐ sandpaper letters
- ☐ sensory tray (optional)
- ☐ movable alphabet

Directions:
1. Using the sandpaper letters you made for this unit (k, q, v, x, y, and z), invite your child to identify each sound as you hold up one letter at a time.

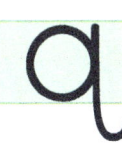

☐ k ☐ q ☐ v ☐ x ☐ y ☐ z

2. Using your sensory tray or the writing lines below, invite your child to write one of each letter.

k q v x y z

3. Draw a line from the letter to the object that has its beginning sound.

k

q

v

x

y

z

245

Unit 6 Assessment

kqvxyz
☐ movable alphabet

4. Build the following words with the movable alphabet by segmenting the words into their individual sounds.

Assessment Results and Next Steps:

Depending on how your child performed on this assessment, you may want to review letter sounds and letter formation before moving on. Rest assured that your child will continue to review the letter sounds, letter formation, and word building in the next step to reading fluency.

For further review if needed, see **Appendix A** for a list of games you can play with your child using the materials in the workbook!

If your child is ready to read words instead of just writing words, you should move onto the **Montessori Pink Series Reading Workbook**. If your child is not quite ready to read words, but has done well with this workbook, you can jump to the **Montessori Reading Games: Level 2** where your child will be introduced to the most common digraphs and sound blends but won't be required yet to *read* words.

Next Steps

Congratulations! You have finished the *Montessori Reading Games Workbook - Level 1!*

You have two options for your next steps!

If your child is doing well with the sound games and building words, you may want to move on to the *Montessori Reading Games Workbook - Level 2*. Your child will learn 16 of the most common digraphs to make writing even more accessible!

If your child is itching to *read* words instead of just write words, he or she is probably ready for the *Montessori Pink Reading Workbook!* You can tackle the *Montessori Pink Reading Workbook* on its own or alongside the *Montessori Reading Games Workbook - Level 2*. It's up to you!

Option #1 - Not Quite Ready to Read

1. *Montessori Reading Games Workbook - Level 1*
2. *Montessori Reading Games Workbook - Level 2*
3. *Montessori Pink Reading Workbook*
4. *Montessori Blue Reading Workbook*
5. *Montessori Green Reading Workbook*
6. *Montessori Grammar Workbook*

Option #2 - Ready to Read!

1. *Montessori Reading Games Workbook - Level 1*
2. *Montessori Pink Reading Workbook*
3. *Montessori Reading Games Workbook - Level 2*
4. *Montessori Blue Reading Workbook*
5. *Montessori Green Reading Workbook*
6. *Montessori Grammar Workbook*

Go to MontessoriforHomeschoolers.com to find out more about these options!

montessoriforhomeschoolers.com/pages/reading

Appendix A
Games for Letter - Picture Cards

Games for Letter - Picture Cards

Letter-Picture Card Sorting

Directions:
1. Use a work rug or towel to define your work space. Lay the letter cards across the top of your work surface.
2. Make a single pile of picture cards. Choose one at a time. Say the name of the picture, enunciating the first sound clearly. Place the picture under the corresponding letter card.
3. Inivte your child to finish the work.

Note: After showing this to your child for the first unit, she may or may not need you to demonstrate this setup for the subsequent units.

Letter-Picture Card Sorting Games

On the following pages, you will find directions for how to play six games using the Letter-Picture Cards. These games can be played using any of the cards for any of the units. One game is suggested for each unit, but feel free to choose any of the games or play more than just the one suggested.

Game Options: (See following pages for specific instructions.)
1. Scavenger Hunt
2. Treasure Hunt
3. Roll, Spot, and Cover
4. Swat the Sound
5. Hopscotch
6. Four Corners

Games for Letter - Picture Cards:
Simple Scavenger Hunt

Appendix A
Games for Letter - Picture Cards

Note: There are two versions of the Scavenger Hunt. The first one is a "Simple Scavenger Hunt" which consists of finding hidden cards and checking them off on a list. The second one is an "Advanced Scavenger Hunt" which requires the child to follow clues you read to him to find the next card.

Goal: The goal of the scavenger hunt is to collect all of the cards. Use one picture per sound.

Materials:
- Scavenger Hunt Checklist
- One picture card per sound
- pencil, clipboard

Preparation:
1. Cut out the corresponding "scavenger hunt checklist" for the correct sound group. You can use more than one sound group if you want, and you can even make your own combination using a blank card. (They are on the following page.)
2. Place the checklist on a clipboard.
3. Tape up or hide the picture cards (*one* for each sound) around a designated area (entire house, one room, even outside) at or below your child's level.

Play:
1. Using the scavenger hunt sheet and a small clip board, invite your child to check off the boxes when she finds a picture corresponding to each letter sound.
2. If your child is the only one doing the hunt, she may collect the cards as she finds them.
3. She will know she has found all of the cards when all of the boxes have been checked.

Appendix A
Games for Letter - Picture Cards

Games for Letter - Picture Cards:
Advanced Scavenger Hunt

The goal of the scavenger hunt is to collect all of the cards. You may want to put an extra "surprise" at the end, too! You can use five or more cards.

Materials:
- letter-picture cards (5 or more)
- paperclips

Preparation:
1. Cut out the clues and attach each one via a paperclip to a picture *or* letter card. Use five or more cards. The more cards you use, the more time you will need for the game. (Note: You can choose any cards in any order. The only *order* that will matter is the order you hide them.)
2. Hide all but the first card. The easiest way to do this is to make a stack of cards, keep the top one in your hand, read the clue on the top card, and hide the second card in the stack using the top card as your clue.
3. To hide the third card, you will want to use the clue on the second card, and so on.

Play:
1. Hand your child the starter card (i.e. the "top card" from the Preparation directions.) Read the card to your child, helping him decipher the location as needed.
2. Once a card is found, invite your child to say the sound of the letter or the beginning sound of the picture before reading the next clue!
3. Play alongside your child, aiding in reading and figuring out the clues as you go along!

This says ___, but the sound isn't the clue. Your next card will be **inside your shoe**.	You are so smart! Find the next picture where you **create art**.	That was a breeze. Go to the **tissues** you use when you sneeze.	The scavenger hunt is fun! Your next clue is on a **chair in the sun**.
For the next card, you may need a stool. Where you will find it is **very, very cool**.	Here is a clue that might take you far... you need to go to the **nearest car**.	Hurry now, but stay in your lane.. the next card is in a **window pane**.	For this one you may need to open a door... the next clue is inside a **cabinet touching the floor!**
You are doing so well saying each sound! Search in the **living room** all over the **ground**!	This next task can be done in a wink. Check **under the kitchen sink!**	Are you ready for one more? Try opening the **refrigerator** door!	The next clue is hidden by an object of joy. Go and find your **favorite toy!**
Where do you like to eat? Go and check **under your seat!**	This game is fun, but it may be time to rest your head. How about you check **under the pillow on your bed!**	The next clue is tricky. It is by the thing that **cleans your teeth** when you eat something sticky.	The last clue you will find if only you look inside the pages of your **favorite book!**

251

Sound Scavenger Hunt

s ☐ ☐ ☐
m ☐ ☐ ☐
a ☐ ☐ ☐
t ☐ ☐ ☐

Sound Scavenger Hunt

c ☐ ☐ ☐
d ☐ ☐ ☐
o ☐ ☐ ☐
h ☐ ☐ ☐

Sound Scavenger Hunt

g ☐ ☐ ☐
r ☐ ☐ ☐
i ☐ ☐ ☐
b ☐ ☐ ☐

Sound Scavenger Hunt

p ☐ ☐ ☐
n ☐ ☐ ☐
u ☐ ☐ ☐
w ☐ ☐ ☐

Sound Scavenger Hunt

c ☐ ☐ ☐
d ☐ ☐ ☐
o ☐ ☐ ☐
h ☐ ☐ ☐

Sound Scavenger Hunt

s ☐ ☐ ☐
m ☐ ☐ ☐
a ☐ ☐ ☐
t ☐ ☐ ☐

Sound Scavenger Hunt

p ☐ ☐ ☐
n ☐ ☐ ☐
u ☐ ☐ ☐
w ☐ ☐ ☐

Sound Scavenger Hunt

g ☐ ☐ ☐
r ☐ ☐ ☐
i ☐ ☐ ☐
b ☐ ☐ ☐

Sound Scavenger Hunt

j
f
e
l

Sound Scavenger Hunt

k
q
v
x
y
z

Sound Scavenger Hunt

Sound Scavenger Hunt

Sound Scavenger Hunt

k
q
v
x
y
z

Sound Scavenger Hunt

j
f
e
l

Sound Scavenger Hunt

Sound Scavenger Hunt

Games for Letter - Picture Cards:
Treasure Hunt

Appendix A
Games for Letter - Picture Cards

Treasure Hunt Directions

The goal of the Treasure Hunt is to find the picture cards in a sensory bin and tape them to a vertical surface underneath the correct beginning letter sound.

Materials:
- tape
- vertical surface
- sensory bin (any filling will work: rocks, popcorn kernels, rice, cereal, beans, water beads, etc.)
  - NOTE: If you are using a wet sensory bin, make sure to laminate over the edges of the letter and picture cards or reinforce the edges with clear tape.
- Optional: tweezers, tongs, scoops, or spoons to retrieve the hidden cards

Preparation:
1. Laminate the letter and picture cards.
2. Tape the letter cards on a vertical surface at your child's height.
3. Place rounded tape (sticky edge facing out of the circle) in three spots below each letter card.
4. Hide the picture cards in random order in a sensory bin.

Play:
1. Invite your child to go on a "Treasure Hunt" for the picture cards. Once your child finds a card, invite her to place it underneath the proper letter sound.
2. Play is complete when all "tape spots" are filled with pictures. (This acts as a control of error, as there are only 3 spots under each letter sound.)

Extensions:
- Use tongs, scoops, tweezers, or spoons to retrieve the hidden cards.
- Make a *themed* sensory bin, playing off of one of the letter sounds (like a *dinosaur* bin for "d" filled with sand, dinosaur figures, and excavating tools, or a *rainbow* bin for "r," a cars bin for "c," etc.)

Appendix A
Games for Letter - Picture Cards

Games for Letter - Picture Cards:
Roll, Spot, and Cover

Roll, Spot, and Cover Directions

The goal of the game is for each player to cover all of her pictures.

Materials:
- letter and picture sound cards
- dice (with labels for letters) OR the dice provided in the workbook.
- counters

Preparation:
1. You will need to make a dice for each set of sounds. I have included a printable version for each sound group that you can print, cut, fold, and tape or glue into die.
2. Set out four picture cards face up in front of each player, one for each sound in the current sound group.
3. Give each player 4 counters.

Play:
1. One player will roll and read the sound, then put a counter on top of the matching sound.
2. The dice is passed to the next player, and so on.
3. The first player to cover all of her pictures "wins.." (Note: You can play this as a non-competitive game by allowing your child to play by herself with you watching.)
4. The play ends when all players have covered all their sounds.

Extensions:
- Put out two sound groups at once, using 2 die instead of one.

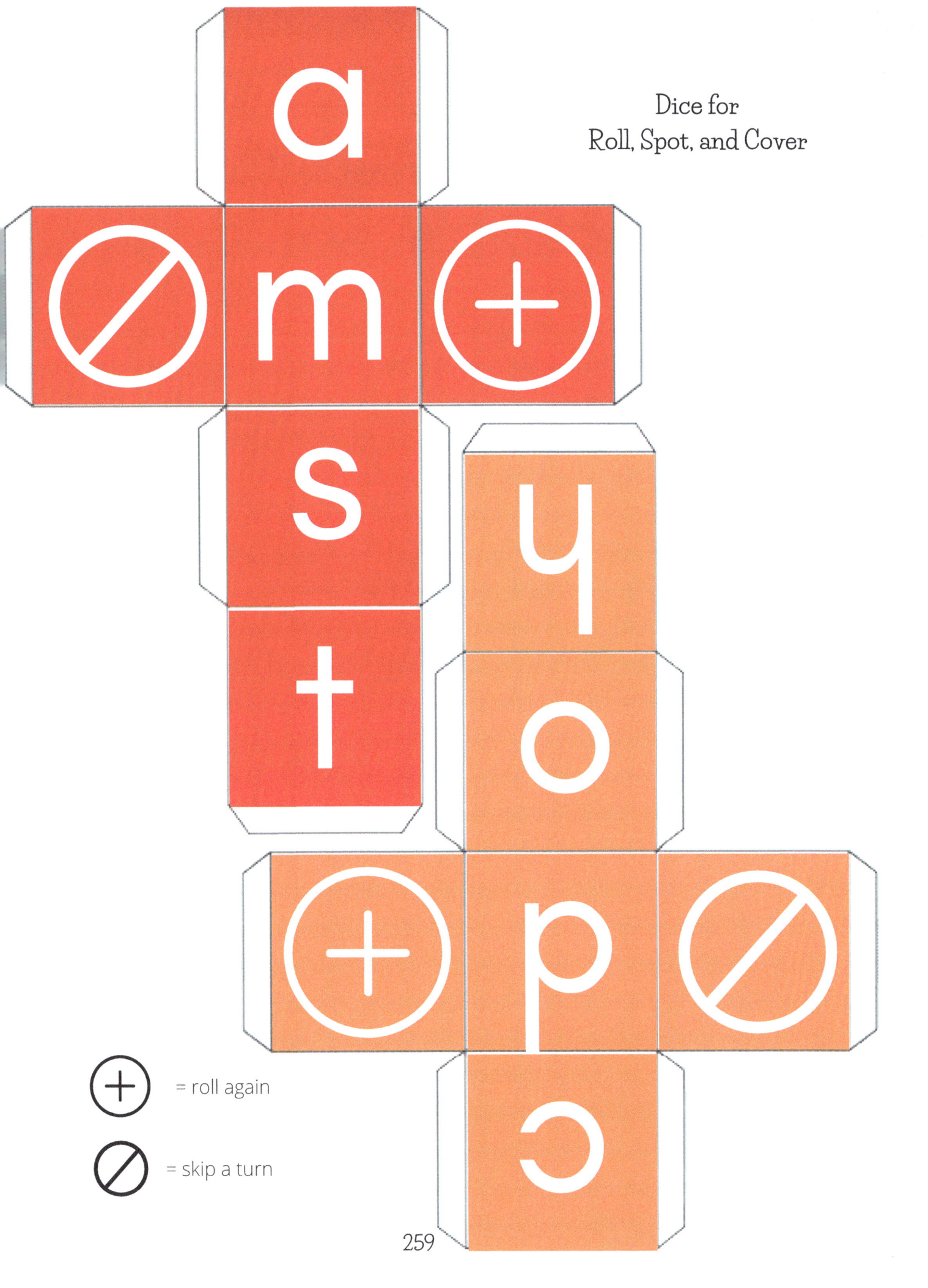

Dice for
Roll, Spot, and Cover

⊕ = roll again

⊘ = skip a turn

259

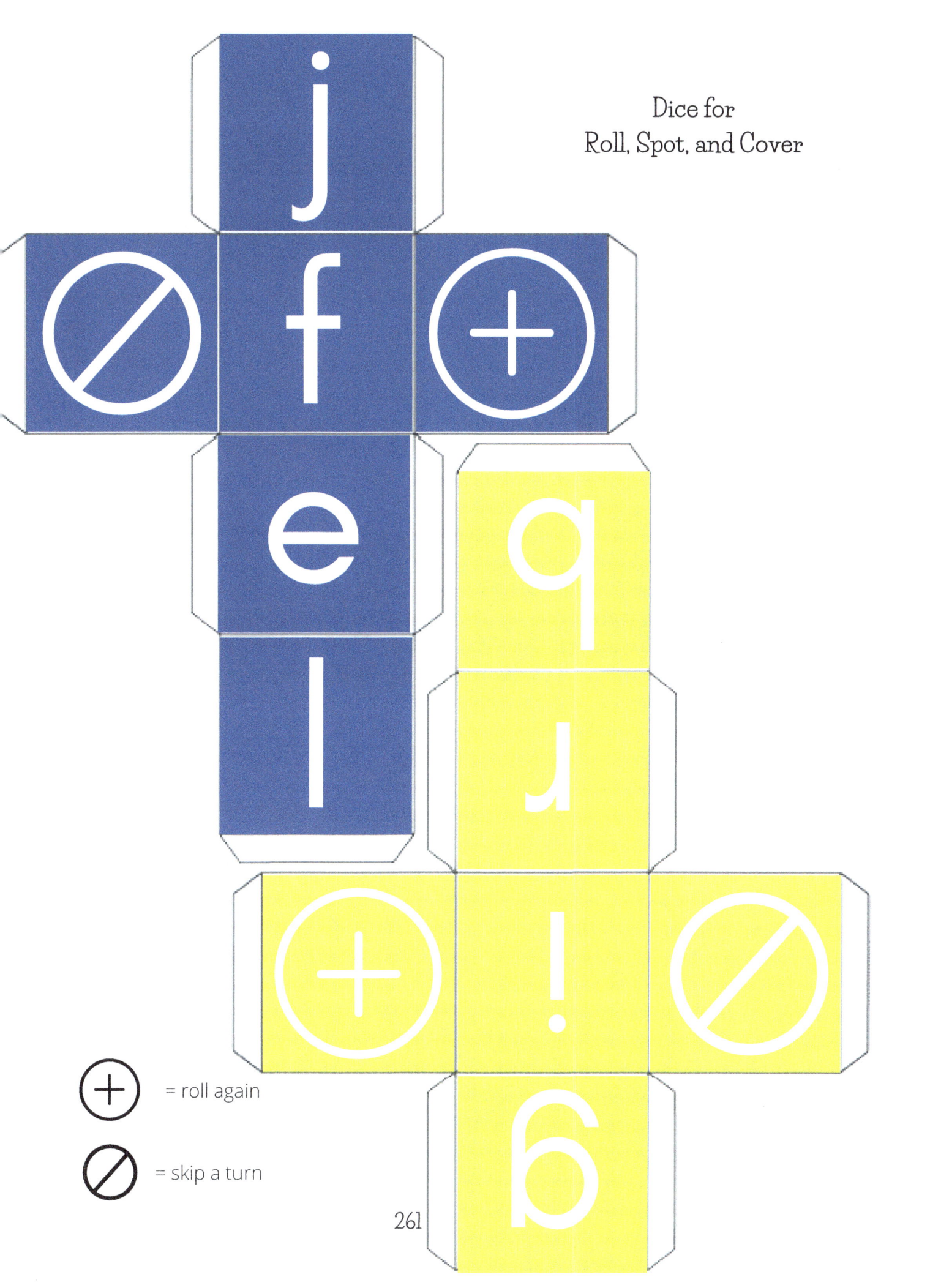

Dice for
Roll, Spot, and Cover

⊕ = roll again

⊘ = skip a turn

261

Dice for
Roll, Spot, and Cover

k
y q z
v
x

⊕ = roll again

⊘ = skip a turn

Appendix A
Games for Letter - Picture Cards

Games for Letter - Picture Cards:
Swat the Sound

Swat the Sound Directions

The goal of Swat the Sound is to increase fluency and speed in letter sound recognition.
The child will use a fly swatter to "swat" the letter or picture card of a sound that you call out.

Materials:
- tape
- vertical surface
- fly swatter
- letter and picture cards
- basket or bag

Preparation:
1. Laminate the letter and picture cards.
2. Tape the picture cards in random order on a vertical surface at your child's height. (A door, sliding glass door, or blank wall works well for this activity.)
3. Place the letter cards in a bag or basket.

Play:
1. Hand your child the fly swatter. Explain, "I want you to swat all of the pictures that match the sound of the card I pull out of this basket as fast as you can!"
2. Pull out a random letter card. If you pull out "g;," your child should proceed to swat all the pictures beginning with /g/.
3. Take down any correctly swatted pictures. Leave up any pictures that were not swatted or were swatted incorrectly.
4. Place the letter card back in the basket ONLY if a picture was left not swatted with that sound. This gives your child an opportunity to get it the next time that card is chosen.
5. Continue with the remaining letter sounds until all pictures are off the wall. (You may need to give a hint or two!)

Extensions:
- Use multiple sound groups, adding in sounds that need more practice!
- Use a timer! See if your child can get ALL of the pictures swatted correctly in under a set amount of time!

Games for Letter - Picture Cards:
Four Corners

Four Corners Directions

The goal of Four Corners is to collect the most (or a certain number of) the picture cards by being in the same corner as the first sound of the picture called.

Materials:
- tape
- a room with four "corners" - can be designated areas like a table, chair, or bookcase
- letter and picture cards

Preparation:
1. Laminate the letter and picture cards.
2. Tape one letter up in each corner of a room.
3. Place all picture cards, shuffled, in a pile face down in the middle of the room or next to you.

Play:
1. Say, "Go!" and your child should run as fast as he can to one corner of the room.
2. Randomly pick a picture card from the pile.
3. Show your child the card and say the name of the picture. Ask, "Are you in the corner with the /?/ sound?" If he/she says yes and is correct, he gets to "collect" that picture card.
4. The game ends when one of the following happens: all picture cards are collected; a certain # of picture cards are collected; the time to play runs out. (Make sure you are clear with your goals when you start playing so your child knows what to expect!)

Extensions:
- Use to review any 4 sounds that need more practice!

Appendix A
Games for Letter - Picture Cards

Games for Letter - Picture Cards:
Hopscotch

Goal: The goal of Hopscotch is to jump through the game grid without falling as you hop on one foot or the other, pick up your game piece, and hop back to the start. In our version, the child will say letter sounds as she plays!

Materials:
- sidewalk chalk (or masking tape for indoor version)
- something to toss: coin, rock, shell, beanbag, etc.
- picture cards

Preparation:
1. Draw or tape a grid of 8 squares on the ground in any arrangement that includes one or two squares. (See diagrams for ideas.)
2. Write the 4 new sounds for the week in 4 of the squares. Fill the remaining squares with sounds from past sound groups. (Note: Since your child will be jumping back and forth, you may want to draw a "baseline" under each letter, as shown.)

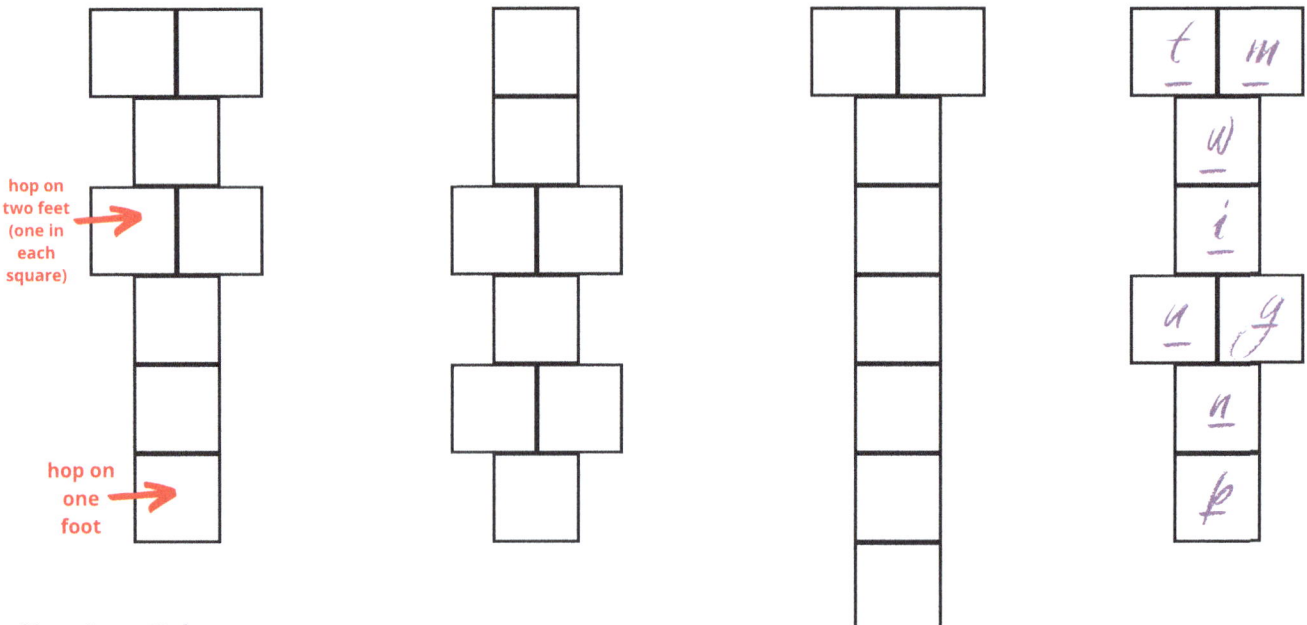

hop on two feet (one in each square)

hop on one foot

Play - Game Style:
1. Toss an object onto one of the squares. Name the sound. (Alternative: Name the sound *closest* to the object **or** place the object on a square if tossing is too hard.)
2. Hop (with only one foot in a square). Try to hop *over* the square containing your object.
3. When you get to the end, turn around and hop back, picking up the object on your way back to the start.

Play - Just the Sounds:
1. Encourage your child to hop with only one foot in each square, saying out loud the sound of each letter as he is in each square.

Play with the Picture Cards:
1. Invite your child to sort the picture cards to their proper squares on the hopscotch grid before playing.
2. Next, call out a letter sound. For example, "s," and say, "I want you to collect all of the "s" sounds!
3. Your child will throw a rock (or other small object), trying to get it on one of the "s" squares.
4. Your child will hop the length of the hopscotch grid, then hop back. On her way back, she will bend down and pick up the card closest to the spot where her rock landed.
5. When she picks up the card, she needs to pause, say the name of the picture, the sound it begins with, and draw the letter in the air with her finger.
6. When she has collected all the cards of whichever letter you called, she wins! (Note: she may have other cards, too, depending on where her rock landed. She "wins" when she has all of the called letter sound.)
7. Play as long as she shows interest.

Extensions:
- After you have played several rounds of "Game Style," switch to "Just the Sounds" for a couple of rounds, then the "Picture Cards."

Appendix B

My Letter Sound Adventure

This board game can be played by children who are ready to match letter sounds to letter symbols **and** by children who are still in the "I Spy" phase of learning letter sounds!

The game moves in progression of our letter sound groups 1-6. The game cards are numbered and categorized by the identifying shape for each group.

- **Group 1**: Cards 1-24
- **Group 2**: Cards 25-48
- **Group 3**: Cards 49-72
- **Group 4**: Cards 73-96
- **Group 5**: Cards 97-120
- **Group 6**: Cards 121-156

Preparation:
1. Remove and laminate game board. Optional: Tape or glue game board to a piece of foam board or poster board.
2. Cut out cards for the current sound group. You can laminate them for durability, but that is optional. You will have a growing pile of cards you can use, depending on which letters you have introduced to your child!
3. Print and laminate spinner page. Cut out spinners, and attach a spinner arrow or a paper clip held in place by a push pin, brass fastener, or pencil.
4. Gather one pawn for each player - anything you have on hand will do! (I love to use miniature objects corresponding to the current sound group!)

Directions:
1. Choose a player to go first. (Option: youngest goes first.) Place game counters (any will work) on the rainbow at the starting spot.
2. Pull a card from the shuffled pile of game cards.
3. Say the name of the picture on the card. For example, "cat." *There is Key included in the game, on the last page of the printables that you should keep with the game.
4. Then, identify the proper sound (**beginning**, **middle**, or **ending** sound), as indicated by the Key on the top of the card.
5. If your child is identifying letter symbols, invite your child to point to the letter sound she was asked to identify on the game board or in a pile of movable alphabet letters that you can optionally set out with the game.
6. If your child is *not identifying letter symbols yet*, ask your child to *say* the sound indicated by the key at the top of the card (beginning, middle, or end.) "What do you hear in the middle of the word 'cat'?"
7. After properly identifying the requested sound, your child will move to the next spot that matches the color square on the card. (*Note: Give your child plenty of time and chances to be *correct*, and give help as needed. With more practice with the sounds, your child will need less help.)
8. **Star Spots**: If a player lands on a star spot, he or she is invited to spin the spinner. If you've introduced most of the letter sounds, choose the spinner with "Build the Word." If your child has only been introduced to a few sounds or is not ready for the movable alphabet work, choose the spinner with "Sing ABC's." (You can choose to sing the ABC's in the traditional way *or* sing the sounds. If you choose **"Build the Word,"** invite your child to build the word on the card using the movable alphabet. There is a printable version in this pack or you can purchase the small Montessori Movable Alphabet on Amazon.
9. **Winning**: The first player to reach the ending rainbow spot wins!

Notes:
- Add cards to your pile as you learn new sound groups, making sure to place the NEW cards on top!
- Use the spinner most appropriate for your child. Different children can use different spinners.
- Older children can use a notebook and write the words for each card drawn (this can be done while the other children are taking their turns).

My Letter Sound Adventure

YOU MADE IT!

START HERE

draw again

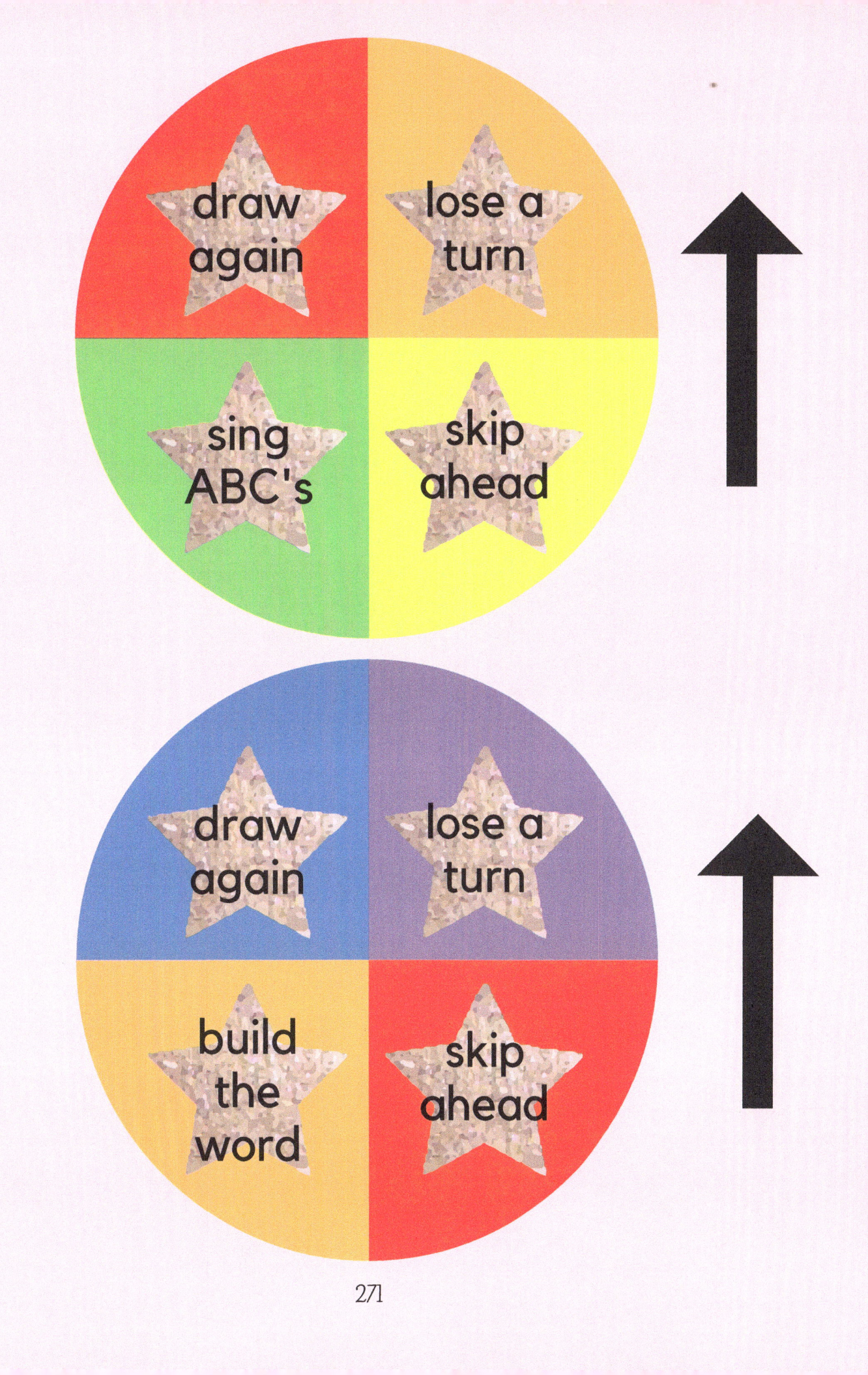

lose a turn

sing ABC's

skip ahead

draw again

lose a turn

build the word

skip ahead

a b c d

h g f e

l k j i

m n o p q

Appendix C

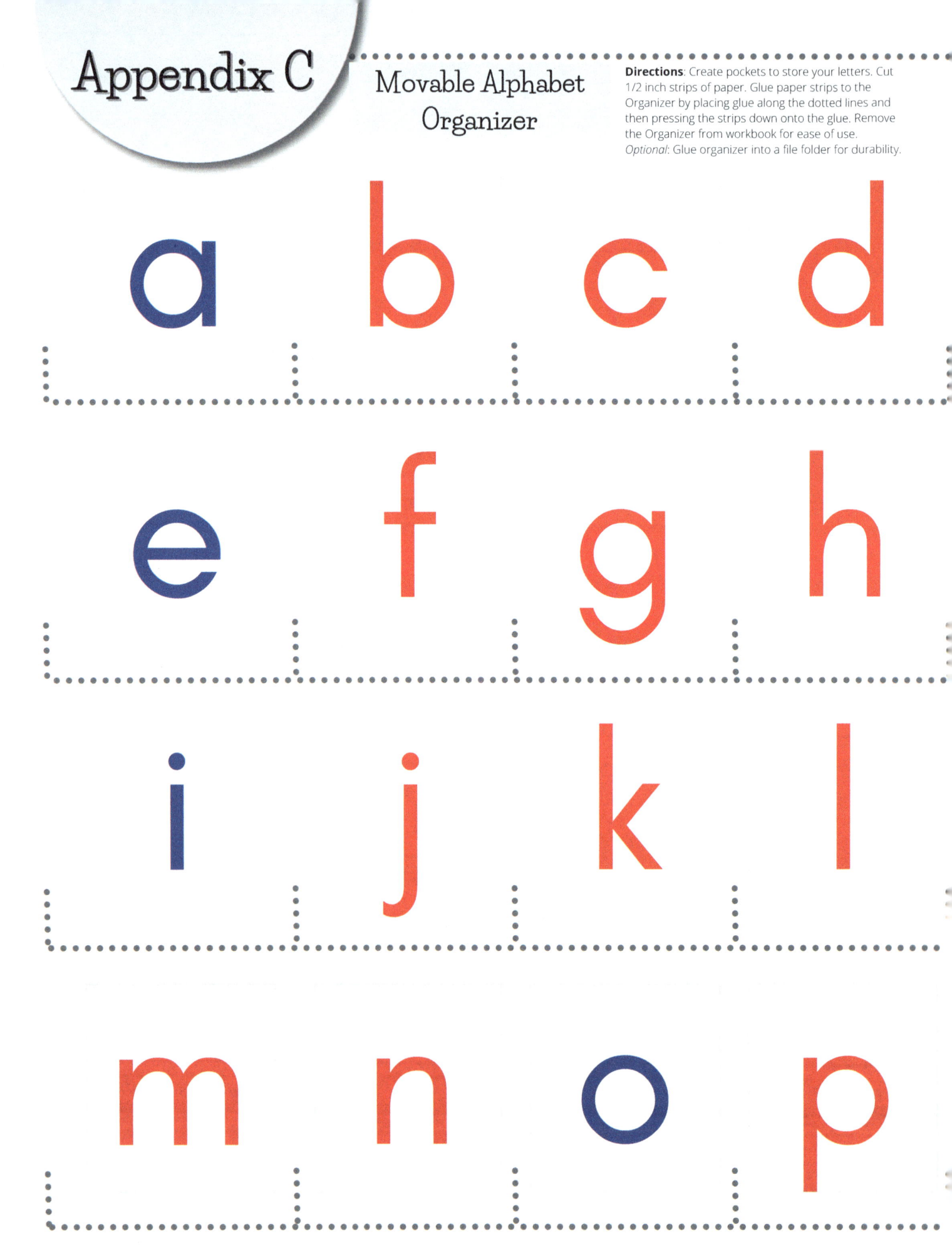

Movable Alphabet Organizer

Directions: Create pockets to store your letters. Cut 1/2 inch strips of paper. Glue paper strips to the Organizer by placing glue along the dotted lines and then pressing the strips down onto the glue. Remove the Organizer from workbook for ease of use.
Optional: Glue organizer into a file folder for durability.

a b c d

e f g h

i j k l

m n o p

Movable Alphabet Organizer

Appendix C

q r s t

u v w x

y y z .

' ? ! '

Appendix C

Pink Word Building Cards - Directions

When should I use these? Use these cards when your child is ready for "writing" words with the movable alphabet. Your child may not be ready until she is 4 or older, but you can introduce them whenever she shows interest or ability.

What about proper spelling? In true Montessori fashion, children are encouraged to build words without any hindrance of having to be corrected. Just let them sound them out and build away!

Self-Correcting for older children: I have included the correcting work for those who want it, but it may be best to leave it out of your instruction! You have free choice - it is *your homeschool!* All of the words are three-letter words (with the exception of "ax"), most of which have the pattern *consonant - vowel - consonant* (CVC). For older students working on spelling, you can cut out the Key Card (below) and show your child how to match up the number on the card to the number on the Key for a self-correcting work.

Corresponding Sound Groups: Here is a guide of when you can introduce the word cards, so you can make sure you are only using cards that contain sounds you have already reviewed with your child. These are segmented in each unit according to the guide below.

- **Group #1 (s, m, a, t):** through card #2
- **Group #2 (c, d, o, h):** through card #13
- **Group #3 (g, r, i, b):** through card #32
- **Group #4 (p, n, u, w):** through card #62
- **Group #5 (j, f, e, l):** through card #83
- **Group #6 (k, q, v, x, y, z):** through card #95

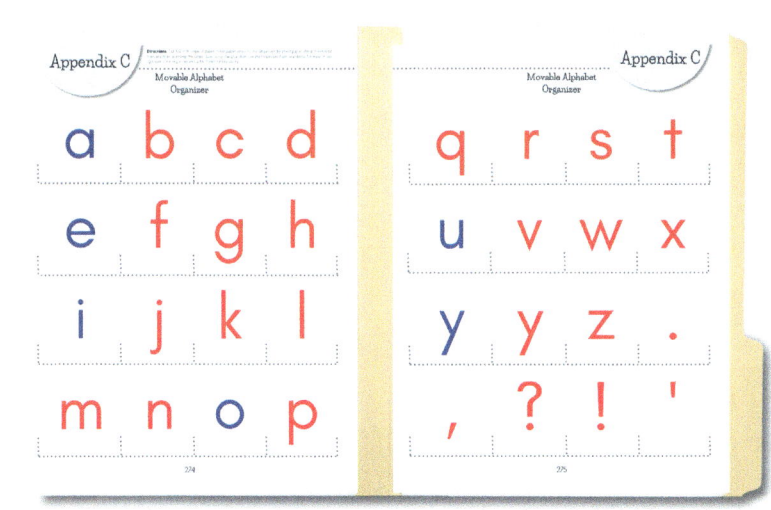

Directions:
1. Point to the picture.
2. Say the name of the picture (or invite your child to say it,)
3. Slowly enunciate the first letter sounds and find the letter. Place it on the card, starting at the left side of the card.
4. Say the next letter *sound* and find it. Place it on the card to the right of the first letter.
5. Say the word again and then each letter sound, finding the last letter and placing it on the card.
6. Invite your child to build as many words as he shows interest *or* a certain number of words (set a goal ahead of time) *or* work for a minimum number of minutes.

Example: :Choose 3 words to build." OR "Work on building words for 5 minutes."

Pink CVC Word Building Cards Key

1 sat	11 dam	21 sob	31 fin	41 nog	51 pin	61 pop	71 fan	81 pin	91 box
2 mat	12 sod	22 cob	32 tag	42 wig	52 pan	62 run	72 lip	82 ten	92 zip
3 cat	13 cod	23 rod	33 pot	43 wag	53 sap	63 set	73 lap	83 lid	93 zap
4 hat	14 rat	24 rag	34 pat	44 gun	54 nap	64 jet	74 lot	84 kit	94 yak
5 sad	15 sit	25 ram	35 rug	45 gum	55 bun	65 net	75 lug	85 kid	95 vet
6 mad	16 bat	26 gas	36 bug	46 gap	56 top	66 dip	76 log	86 van	
7 dot	17 rim	27 hog	37 mug	47 can	57 hop	67 fog	77 den	87 ax	
8 hot	18 dog	28 bot	38 tug	48 cap	58 win	68 jam	78 bed	88 fox	
9 ham	19 bog	29 rat	39 cup	49 cop	59 pug	69 hen	79 men	89 yes	
10 cot	20 rob	30 bit	40 pig	50 pot	60 mop	70 leg	80 pen	90 sax	

Appendix D

Household Items for Sound Games

Directions: When possible, use real, tangible objects for "I Spy" and sorting by beginning sound. Many people collect miniature objects, but you can also use items you already have laying around your house! This list is not exhaustive, but it will give you plenty of ideas to get you started! (Note: See Appendix F for cut-and-paste picture cards you can use instead of the household objects.)

a:
- apple
- avocado
- apricot
- aspirin
- aluminum foil
- almonds
- apple sauce

b:
- banana
- battery
- basket
- bobby pin
- blanket
- bonnet
- baseball
- baseball cap
- balloon
- box
- bucket

c:
- cat (toy)
- can
- carrot
- camera
- corn
- cap
- conditioner
- coin

d:
- dog (toy)
- domino
- dress
- dime
- drapes
- drum

e:
- egg
- eggplant
- eczema cream
- empty cup
- elephant (toy)
- exit
- entrance

f:
- frame
- feta
- fettuccine
- felt
- fork
- flap

g:
- game
- grapes
- gold
- gum
- goldfish
- guitar

h:
- house (play)
- hamper
- hot cake
- helicopter (toy)
- ham
- hummus
- hat

i:
- iguana (toy)
- isthmus (make with clay)
- igloo (toy or build with clay)
- internet
- incense
- inch
- itch cream
- inside (of something)

j:
- juice
- jam/jelly
- jingle bell
- jump rope
- joker (card)
- jacks

k:
- kite
- kitten (toy)
- kickball
- kit (First Aid, sewing)
- kitchen item (scissors, towel, etc)
- Kit Kat (candy)
- Kiss (candy)
- kindling (for a fire)

l:
- lightbulb
- lamp
- lemon
- list
- ladle
- leash
- lip balm
- lotion

m:
- medicine
- mail
- map
- mop
- music
- microphone
- measuring tape
- measuring cup

n:
- nightgown
- night light
- newspaper
- napkin
- net
- nickel

o:
- onion
- on/off (switch, bug spray brand "Off")
- onion powder
- ox (animal figure)
- octopus (toy/animal figure)
- octagon
- operation (game)
- oven

p:
- present
- peanuts
- pickle
- peanut butter
- pistachios
- pumpkin
- pan
- pancake mix
- pop
- popcorn
- plate
- paper
- pot
- pencil
- pen

q:
- quill
- quilt
- quick bake mix
- question (can clip from magazine)
- queen's crown
- quote (clip from magazine)
- quack (duck that makes noise)

r:
- rack
- take
- rod
- rainbow
- rice
- rim
- rake
- readers
- ream (of paper)
- rug
- ruler

s:
- socks
- sack
- sandal
- stick
- soap
- strawberry
- sucker

t:
- top
- ticket
- tank
- turtle (toy)
- tiger (toy)
- temperature gauge (thermometer)
- train
- toy
- tin

u:
- umbrella
- underwear
- udder (on toy cow)
- up (arrow)

v:
- vase
- vent (air vent)
- van (toy or even a picture of yours if you have one)
- vacuum
- Vaseline
- volume
- violin

w:
- water
- waste
- window
- wax
- warmer
- workbook
- wallet
- wig

x: (use as ending sound)
- tax (on printed receipt - highlight it)
- wax
- sax
- lox (salmon)
- fox (toy)
- fax
- axe

y:
- yarn
- yo-yo
- yams

z:
- zipper
- zebra (toy)
- zero
- zig zag

Appendix E

How to Play BINGO and Go-Fish

How to Play BINGO

Materials:
There are four BINGO cards for each group of letter sounds. There is also a set of "call cards" with the letter and a photo of the beginning sound. You can laminate them for durability or use them as-is.

Directions:
You can have your child be the "caller," and you can each place a counter on the corresponding letter sound she calls. Alternatively, you can take turns picking a card and only placing a counter on your own mat for each turn.

BINGO is when a player covers the full board OR when a player gets 3 in a row in any direction - you choose!

Have fun, and make sure you *play alongside your child*, taking turns! It's no fun to play alone.

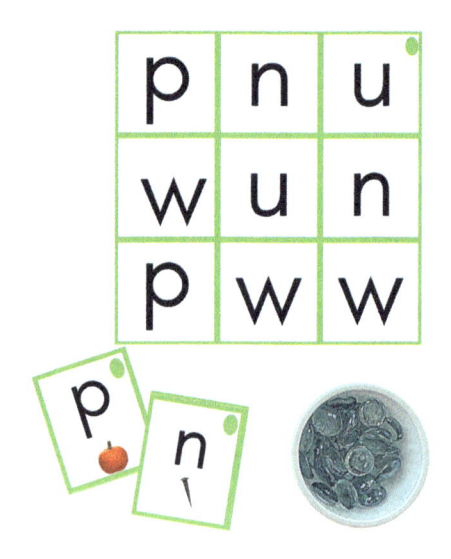

How to Play "Go Fish"

Materials:
- BINGO call cards for one more more sound groups

Directions:
1. Pass out two cards to each player, using the current sound group. (See notes below for multiple sound groups.)
   a. For more than 3 players, use at least 2 sound groups.
   b. Add 1 more card for each sound group added.
      i. 1 sound group = 2 cards each.
      ii. 2 sound groups = 3 cards each.
      iii. 3 sound groups = 4 cards each.
      iv. 4 sound groups = 5 cards each.
      v. 5 sound groups = 6 cards each.
      vi. 6 sound groups = 7 cards each.
2. Place the remaining cards face-down in the center "draw" pile.
3. The player to the left of the dealer goes first.
4. The first player chooses any player to ask if he/she has a particular sound. *Do you have any aaaaa's?*
5. If the player asked has the asked-for sound card, he hands it to the player who requested it. If not, he says, "Go Fish!" and the player who asked gets to draw a card from the center pile.
6. A "book" is **three matching sound cards** (all a's, for example.) When a player gets a "book" or matching set of three cards, he discards them face-up in front of him in a pile.
7. The player with the most "books" at the end of the game wins.

Appendix F

Optional Sound Sorting Cards

Use with the sorting lessons in place of (or in addition to) small objects!

Directions: Remove the corresponding group of pictures from the workbook. Pre-cut according to your child's ability. While scissor practice is wonderful fine motor work, the focus here should be on recognizing sounds.
Hardest: Cut out the group along the outside lines only. **Easier**: Cut into strips. **No Cutting**: Cut out all pictures before the lesson.

Sound Group 1: a, t

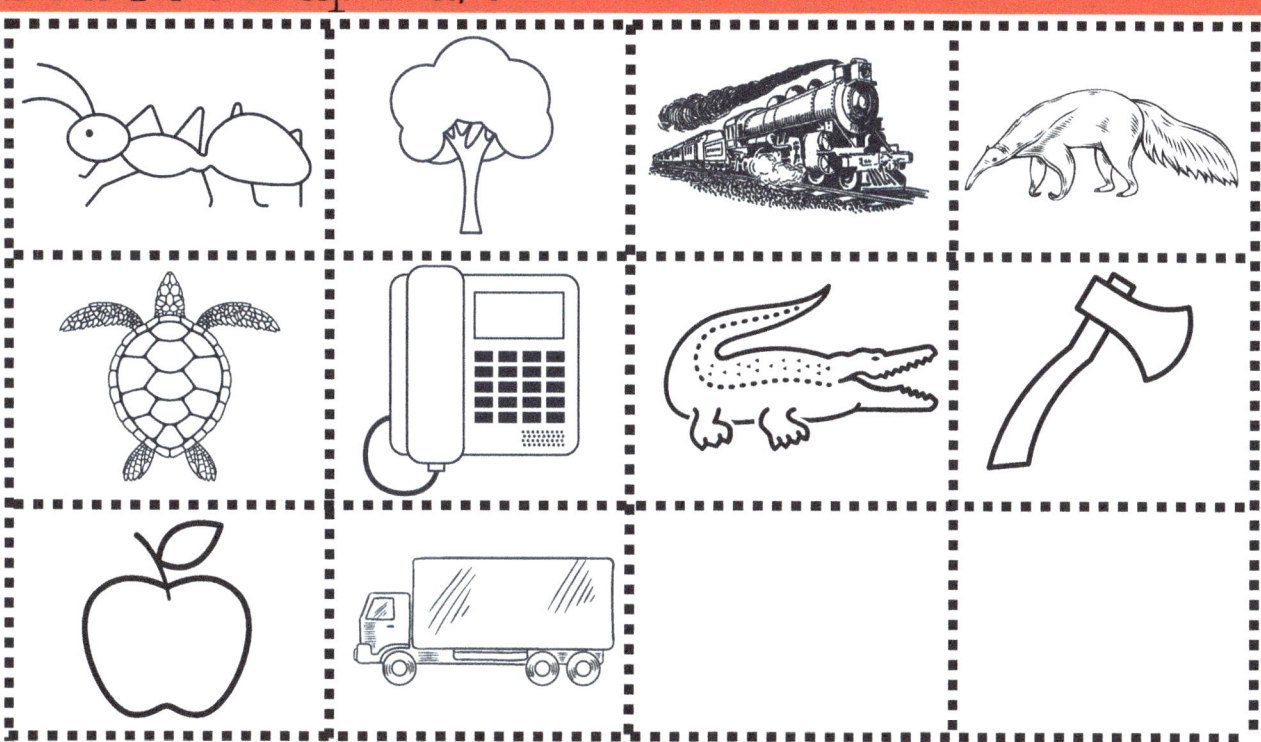

Sound Group 1: s, m

281

Use with the sorting lessons in place of (or in addition to) small objects

Optional Sound Sorting Cards

Appendix F

Directions: Remove the corresponding group of pictures from the workbook. Pre-cut according to your child's ability. While scissor practice is wonderful fine motor work, the focus here should be on recognizing sounds.
Hardest: Cut out the group along the outside lines only. **Easier**: Cut into strips. **No Cutting**: Cut out all pictures before the lesson.

Sound Group 2: o, h

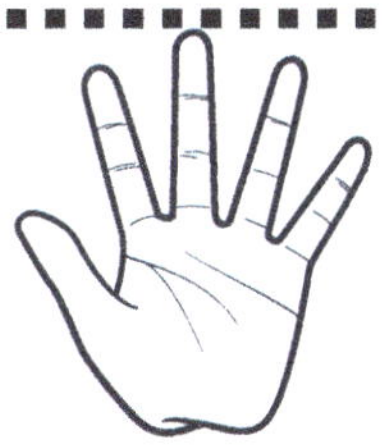

Sound Group 2: c, d

283

Appendix F

Optional Sound Sorting Cards

Use with the sorting lessons in place of (or in addition to) small objects

Directions: Remove the corresponding group of pictures from the workbook. Pre-cut according to your child's ability. While scissor practice is wonderful fine motor work, the focus here should be on recognizing sounds.
Hardest: Cut out the group along the outside lines only. **Easier**: Cut into strips. **No Cutting**: Cut out all pictures before the lesson.

Sound Group 3: i, g

Sound Group 3: b, r

285

Appendix F

Optional Sound Sorting Cards

Use with the sorting lessons in place of (or in addition to) small objects

Directions: Remove the corresponding group of pictures from the workbook. Pre-cut according to your child's ability. While scissor practice is wonderful fine motor work, the focus here should be on recognizing sounds.
Hardest: Cut out the group along the outside lines only. **Easier**: Cut into strips. **No Cutting**: Cut out all pictures before the lesson.

Sound Group 4: u, w

Sound Group 4: p, n

287

Use with the sorting lessons in place of (or in addition to) small objects

Optional Sound Sorting Cards

Appendix F

Directions: Remove the corresponding group of pictures from the workbook. Pre-cut according to your child's ability. While scissor practice is wonderful fine motor work, the focus here should be on recognizing sounds.
Hardest: Cut out the group along the outside lines only. **Easier**: Cut into strips. **No Cutting**: Cut out all pictures before the lesson.

Sound Group 5: e, l

Sound Group 5: j, f

289

Use with the sorting lessons in place of (or in addition to) small objects

Optional Sound Sorting Cards

Appendix F

Directions: Remove the corresponding group of pictures from the workbook. Pre-cut according to your child's ability. While scissor practice is wonderful fine motor work, the focus here should be on recognizing sounds.
Hardest: Cut out the group along the outside lines only. **Easier**: Cut into strips. **No Cutting**: Cut out all pictures before the lesson.

Sound Group 6: v, x

Sound Group 6: k, q

291

Use with the sorting lessons in place of (or in addition to) small objects

Optional Sound Sorting Cards

Appendix F

Sound Group 6: y, z

Appendix G

Handwriting Guide

Directions: Start at the dot. Don't pick up your pencil unless the "2" is in red! See each unit introduction page for more specific instructions for each stroke.

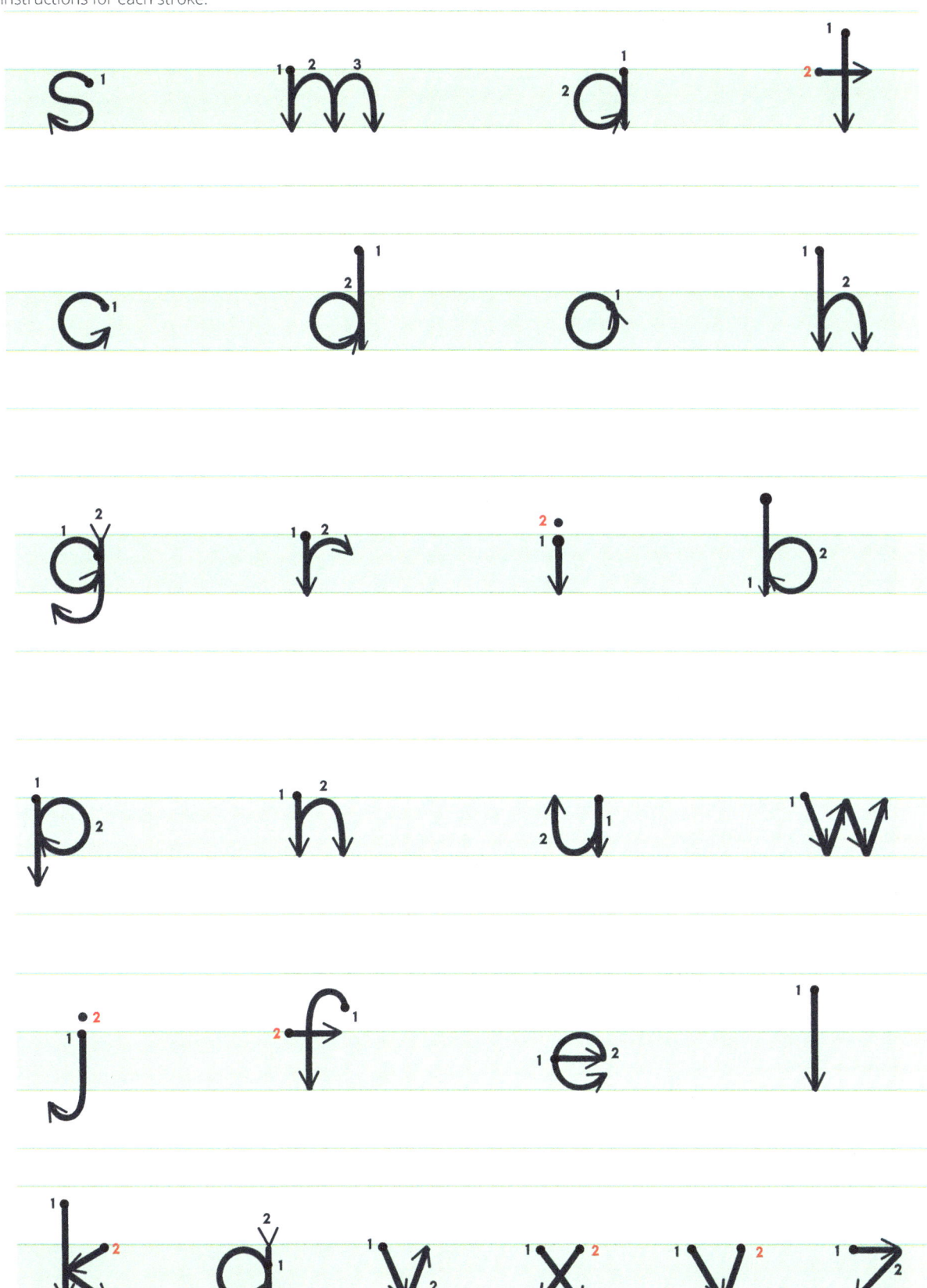

295

Made in the USA
Coppell, TX
01 February 2024

28461953R00168